Isabelle Graw

High Price

Art Between the Market and Celebrity Culture

Isabelle Graw

High Price

Art Between the Market and Celebrity Culture

Sternberg Press

Table of Contents

Chapter Two
Beyond the Dualistic Art/Market Model

Chapter Three
Art World and Artwork in the Age of Market Conformity

Chapter Four
Market-Reflexive Gestures in Celebrity Culture

Foreword

This book examines the relationship between art and the market. Its central theme is that there is no strict separation between the two, as is often assumed, but that art and the market are mutually dependent while also retaining some degree of autonomy. As far as its method is concerned, it combines critical theory with social analysis, presenting empirical data as the starting point for theoretical reflection. The following chapters show that art and the market are deeply entangled while constantly pulling away from each other. Their relationship can thus be characterized more precisely as a dialectical unity of opposites, an opposition whose poles effectively form a single unit. Many examples are cited to illustrate this dynamic, including the ways in which market requirements actually do influence artistic practice (at the level of format or production costs, for instance) without totally determining it; to the same degree as artworks obey external laws, they also possess their own logic. The idea that numerous market players have of themselves is also examined, as in the case of gallerists, artists, and also critics, who tend to banish the market to an imaginary outside with which they themselves do not identify. And yet, such rhetorical rejection of the market is often a precondition for the successful marketing of artworks.

Instead of conceiving of "the market" as evil Other, I work from the premise that we are all, in different ways, bound up in specific market conditions. Consequently, the market is not understood as a reality detached from society. Rather, after sociologist Lars Gertenbach, it is conceived of as a net that encloses the entirety of social conditions. But every net has its holes, holes that can be made wider, which in theory can cause the entire net to rupture. Being constrained by market conditions does not imply that we cannot reject them. On the contrary, this book advocates questioning market values precisely in the light of one's own involvement. It is possible to reflect on market conditions at the same time as striving for conditions other than those seemingly imposed by consumer capitalism.

It is one of the central assumptions of this book that art is a commodity unlike any other. This special character of art-as-commodity is considered to be at the root of the art market's inner contradictions. Compared to other commodities, the artwork-commodity is conceived of here as being split into a symbolic value and a market value. The specific quality of its symbolic value lies in the fact that it expresses an intellectual surplus value generally attributed to art, an epistemological gain that cannot be smoothly translated into economic categories. What is at stake here can indeed not be reduced to a price, but artworks nevertheless have a price, at least when circulating on the art market. If this price is based solely on an assumption of huge symbolic significance—a condition embodied by pricelessness—then it is all the more understandable when some players in this market (especially art dealers) insist that art is ideally priceless, that no price can be too high for art. The meaning ascribed to artworks goes beyond its equivalent in monetary terms, and this is why astronomical amounts can be asked for them at times. Here, as elsewhere, negation of the market and an insistence on an idealistic approach to art proves to be good for business. Consequently, the balancing act performed by the artwork as commodity between price and pricelessness is considered the matrix for the double game played by those who banish the market to an imaginary outside while at the same time constantly feeding it.

But what distinguishes the specific art-commodity from commodities in general, which are increasingly presented as branded goods, placing the emphasis on their symbolic value in a manner comparable to artworks? In my view, artworks are both a specific kind of commodity and a prototypical commodity that paved the way for the transformation of commodities into branded goods. But this does not alter the crucial observation that an artwork is unlike any other commodity. For instance, there is a certain structural affinity between luxury goods and artworks. In spite of such similarities, it is significant that all attempts to imbue luxury goods with the symbolic relevance of artworks have been in vain. A current example of this is the switch from "must-have" to "must-keep." Whereas in the past, consumers of fashion were exhorted to avail themselves of the latest must-haves (each season's "it" bag), in times of crisis they are now advised to acquire a "must-keep"—something durable that possesses lasting value. Traditionally, it was art that defined itself in such terms, as a lasting asset. Now, luxury objects are making a similar claim of long-term value, although this cannot protect the "must-keep" from going out of style.

Concerning the terminology used in the book, it should be noted that the art market is understood here, by analogy with financial markets, as a networking market; meaning that the market is wherever its participants interact with one another. In geographical terms, this market's sphere of influence has steadily expanded. Whereas after 1945 the art market was associated with Western financial centers such as Paris, New York, and London, such centers have since multiplied (Hong Kong, Beijing, Moscow) in the process of globalization. Although the global reach of the art market's sphere of influence is a fact, this book does not share the usual emphatic view on globalization. Instead, it concurs with French sociologist Alain Quemin, who points out that in many respects, the notion of a truly global art market is an illusion. Any artist aiming at commercial success in the premium segment is well advised to begin by settling in a city like New York, London, or, more recently, Berlin.

Nonetheless, this study assumes the art market to be highly differentiated and multi-dimensional, comprising a range of segments. Besides the commercial art market and its division into primary and secondary markets, the art market also includes what I call the "market of knowledge," consisting of art institutions, large-scale exhibitions, symposia, magazines, art academies, and publications like this one. The relationship between these two markets is characterized by a mix of attraction and opposition. Although there is a noticeable increase in the overlap between the commercial art market and the knowledge market, each possesses its own distinctive value system, criteria, language games, and set of rules. In other words, it makes a great difference whether an artist works for free for a community-based project within the knowledge market, from which symbolic capital is derived, or whether he hands his objects over to a major gallery to sell at an art fair.[1] To engage in a collective project implies a different set of expectations, especially in terms of financial prospects.

Without ignoring such crucial differences between the various segments of the art market, this study also shows that the commercial art market increasingly focuses its attention on the (seemingly) non-commercial activities of the knowledge market. One of many symptoms of this development is the blurring between "art fair" and "curated exhibition," as recently illustrated by an exhibition of works for sale initiated by Berlin gallerists under the title "ABC-art berlin contemporary" (2008), in which the art fair and exhibition format merged.

The term "art business" emphasizes the retail nature of this social system; as a business, it is organized on a retail model. Here, however, I assume that a structural shift has taken place. What was once called the art business transformed itself into an "industry engaged in the production of visuality and meaning." This theory of industrialization is exemplified by the observation that the art world, like the fashion and film industries, is now governed by corporate mergers and the celebrity principle. Aside from discussing such industry analogies, the book also notes that in large sections of the art world, archaic traits have survived. Both tendencies—the trend toward corporate culture and the survival of customs recalling a gift economy—are viewed as two sides of the same coin.

In a similar way, this study also claims that the term "art" itself has an economic charge: as a value-laden concept, it is inherently evaluative. Even when considering the invention of the modern concept of art in the eighteenth century, the idea that "Art" would be an economy-free zone cannot be maintained. I argue for a view that considers art's liberation from the constraints of utility by aesthetics as having created the ideal conditions for its marketing. The concept of "Art" has always been associated with the notion of a higher principle and an intellectual claim—convictions whose ongoing impact can still be discerned in the symbolic charge and popularity of contemporary art today. But this special status originally accorded to art by aesthetics is also viewed here as justified, since it is based on concrete characteristics and achievements of artistic practice. At the same time, the idea that art deserves special status is seen as exaggerated: It is just as much the product of misplaced idealization as it is the adequate expression of privilege granted to art by aesthetics as the result of a historical struggle.

Does this mean it is possible to argue simultaneously from an anti-idealistic and an idealizing position? This is the paradoxical premise on which I operate. While openly refusing to believe in "Art" as a mythical unity, I do credit some artistic practices with a high degree of epistemological potential.

When "art" is mentioned in this book, it always refers to the special case of the fine arts. Such usage tends to be guilty of the kind of dubious substantialization rightly criticized by art historian Helmut Draxler in *Gefährliche Substanzen* (Dangerous substances) (2007). But the term is used here more in the sense of a theoretical abstraction, which, for the clarification of certain issues, proves just as indispensable as occasional references to "the market"—despite the fact that "art" and "the market" do not exist as such.

While working on this project, I had to fight on two fronts. I wanted to break with the idealistic styling of art as Other to the market that is widespread among art-market players, while at the same time distancing myself from the market euphoria that became socially acceptable in the media, but also among insiders, during the art boom at the start of the new millennium. "Art boom" refers here to an economic phase in which artworks change hands on the commercial market for high prices. Such a boom in the art trade is generally

1 Where the masculine singular pronoun is used here in place of "the artist," it is intended as a theoretical abstraction that naturally also includes women artists.

linked to a flourishing of the economy in general. The last art boom, which came to a sudden end with the collapse of Lehman Brothers investment bank in the fall of 2008, conferred undreamt-of authority on the market and its value judgments. Never before had the market held such pronounced defining power, even on artistic matters. This diagnosis of the market's rise to the status of ultimate tribunal is complicated by another observation, namely, that money and commercial success are not all that matter in the "art world" as a social universe. While many insiders were cowed into submission by commercially successful artists during boom time, this milieu also must be regarded as the prototype for the now omnipresent knowledge-based economies in which "knowledge" and "criticism" occupy important positions. This calls into question the role of market success as a decisive criterion.

According to sociologist Ulrich Bröckling, "market imperialism" means that the commercial imperative encroaches on every aspect of life. While I wouldn't subscribe to this rather totalizing view, I nevertheless consider this economization of even the most private and intimate spheres to be the consequence of a biopolitical and bio-imperative turn that subtly influences the way people live their lives. If "life" is declared a privileged object of human activity, then art, for which life has always represented a productive force, takes on a prominent position. I therefore view artists as becoming purveyors of life and specialists in "injecting life into things." I also suggest that celebrity culture is the form of society best suited to the bioeconomical imperative that asks us to optimize all areas of our lives. After all, it is a system in which individuals are rewarded for successfully marketing their lives or what the media take for their lives. There is no life as such; life is always highly mediated. I also note that celebrity culture tends toward a personalization of everything and everyone—a personalization currently manifesting itself on the art market in the form of artworks mutating into subjects. Furthermore, the figure of the legendary artist can be seen as the original model on which the celebrity is based—with one key difference:

unlike the celebrity, the fine artist has a product that circulates independently of his person. This is the decisive advantage of the fine arts in terms of production. Precisely because product and person are not identical (although they rub up against each other metonymically), artists have the possibility of shaping the relationship between person and product in ways that reflect on these conditions, or even reject them.

I am not interested in deploring the developments described above—market euphoria, personalization of art, commercialization of life as a whole—or making alarmist forecasts about the end of art and the artist. Far be it from me to spread cultural pessimism. Instead, I aim to designate potential spaces for action under conditions of increasing economic pressure to succeed in view of the compulsive wholesale exploitation of life in celebrity culture.

As a result, it seems only logical that Andy Warhol should occupy a central position within this study, in which he is viewed as a theorist and practitioner of celebrity culture. His work is shown to revolve around the fraught relationship between product and person, as well as being stretched between the poles of market conformity and resistance to the market. When Warhol, Courbet, and numerous other examples of artistic treatment of market conditions are cited here—from Marcel Duchamp to Yves Klein to Robert Morris—there is no claim to draw a complete picture. They represent a subjective selection of exemplary cases of market reflexivity, to which further examples could be added. They should also not be misunderstood as strategies worth imitating—I do not offer a set of formulas for today's cultural producers. On the contrary, the image of "the artist as market strategist" often repeated in market-related art-historical monographs is subjected to a thorough revision.

This book was written during a period when auction records were constantly being broken and commercial success was celebrated. In the face of the worldwide economic crisis, talk of "triumphant progress of the market" may seem strange. But when times are declared to be tough, the rule of the economic imperative is all the more relentless. Artists who suddenly find their sales evaporating cannot rely on the support of their dealers, as they too must readjust to the new conditions. Similarly, the polarity between "art" and "the market," viewed here as fundamental to the functioning of the art market, is also more pronounced. One example of the way crises breed such dualism is the litany recited across the art world in the face of an allegedly 80 percent drop in turnover after the collapse of the global economy in 2008: the crisis is good for art; at last we will see a return to "content," "seriousness," and "true art." The real and the serious are evoked here as if postmodernism never happened. Quite apart from the questionable nature of such essentialisms, "art" and "the market" are once again presented as irreconcilable opposites—one "good," the other "bad." This dichotomy is something to which art-market players fiercely cling during phases of both bust and boom. It is the ideological cement that keeps the market working. Critic Holland Cotter went so far as to welcome the prospect of artists forced to return to "day jobs" by a lack of sales as an "energy source" for art.[2] The old reactionary tale of the starving artist, driven to creative heights by his hunger, is being resurrected once again.

My remarks are made from the viewpoint of the participating observer. As someone who publishes an art magazine that sells advertising space and editions, I am involved in the art market's activities. Despite this fact, I presume the right to denounce hegemonic value judgments, especially those of the commercial art market. This right is the right of criticism. Criticism is both associated with market conditions and capable of defying them. Consequently, pointing to the links between "market" and "criticism" does not mean we stop insisting on their differences. In their foreword to *Was ist Kritik?*, philosophers Rahel Jaeggi and Tilo Wesche describe the modus operandi of criticism, which oscillates between association and dissociation: "It distinguishes, separates, and distances itself, and it connects, relates, and makes links."[3] In such a scenario, criticism has a double role—as both partner *and* opponent of the market. In his essay "What Is Critique?" Michel Foucault further explains how criticism is condemned "by its function [...] to dispersion, dependency and pure heteronomy."[4] One could take his argument further still and say that precisely because criticism is held in check by external constraints, it is capable of resisting them. According to Foucault, criticism is "the art of not being governed or, better, the art of not being governed like that and at that cost."[5] The "not like that" is significant here—a certain degree of being governed is taken as given.

This book, too, argues for a critique of the market that is aware of its association with prevailing conditions, but denounces the assumptions taken for granted by the belief system called "art." Pierre Bourdieu's name for such a belief system was "illusio," by which he meant the collective belief in the game and the sacred value of what is at stake in that game. "Each field produces its specific form of the illusio," he writes, "in the sense of an investment in the game which pulls agents out of their indifference" and motivates them to play.[6] Insofar as Bourdieu's "illusio" is both a precondition *and* an effect of this game, there is no possibility to sidestep it completely. Especially as a critic, one takes part in the game from the moment one declares certain artworks to be worth discussing. Although I would like this book to demonstrate that it is worthwhile to speak in favor of particular artistic practices, at the same time I constantly question the market's normative power. That art's belief system is perfectly capable of absorbing heretical voices is a problem to which this study certainly will not be immune.

2 See Holland Cotter, "The Boom is Over. Long Live the Art!" *The New York Times*, February 15, 2009.
3 Rahel Jaeggi and Tilo Wesche (eds.), *Was ist Kritik* (Frankfurt: Suhrkamp, 2009), 8.
4 Michel Foucault, "What Is Critique?"in *The Politics of Truth*, eds. Sylvère Lotringer and Lysa Hochroth (New York: Semiotext(e), 1997), 24.
5 Ibid., 29.
6 Pierre Bourdieu, "The Illusio and the Work of Art as Fetish," in *The Rules of Art: Genesis and Structure of the Literary Field* (Stanford: Stanford University Press, 1996), 227.

Chapter One

The Triumphant Progress of Market Success

"For the past two hours Lucien had been hearing every problem reduced to terms of money. Neither in the theater nor in publishing, neither in bookselling nor in journalism, had there been any mention of art, or of glory. The beat of that great pendulum, money, struck like a hammer blow after blow on his mind and heart."
–Honoré de Balzac, *Lost Illusions*

"The capitalist order today is an immense cosmos into which the individual is born and which presents itself to him at least, as an individual, as an inalterable order of things in which he must live. It forces the individual insofar as he is involved in the system of market relationships, to conform to capitalistic rules of action."
–Max Weber, *The Protestant Ethic and the Spirit of Capitalism*

"What separates us from yesterday is not an abyss, but the altered situation."
–Alexander Kluge, *Yesterday Girl*

The Market as Arbiter of Art?

There was a time, as recently as the 1960s and 70s, when artists who succeeded commercially had to reckon with a loss of artistic credibility. But during the "boom" of the new millennium, if not before, market success shed this negative image. Artists on whom the art market conferred success were no longer eyed with suspicion. On the contrary, attention was lavished on them from all sides. When Andreas Gursky's large-format, digitally manipulated photographs fetched record prices at auction, for example, it was regularly equated in the German press with major artistic importance. In other words, economic data were confused with artistic achievement.[1]

1 See Olav Veltuis, "Accounting for Taste," *Artforum* (April 2008): 306: "We have moved into a situation where wealth is the only agreed upon arbiter of value."

On the occasion of the Gursky retrospective at Munich's Haus der Kunst (2007), the majority of Germany's art journalists bowed down before the monumental size of his pictures and their accessible iconography saturated with easily understood codes taken from the worlds of pop, fashion, and sports.[2] People literally fell to their knees before the work's capacity for creating monetary value. What is more interesting about Gursky's production, however, is the way it demonstratively reflects the structural changes that the art business, formerly organized around a "retail" model, has undergone since the 1990s: from a model on a manageable scale shaped by local scenes, it evolved into a globally networked *industry* engaged in the production of visuality and meaning. In the course of this transformation, the retail structure within the art business has been replaced by a tendency to establish large-scale enterprises (including multiple outlets) and gallery conglomerates. Parallel to developments in the music and film industries, the art industry now obeys the logic of celebrity, and its dominant competitive positions are occupied by corporate gallery agglomerations à la Gagosian.[3] Corresponding to this development, a shift has occurred in Gursky's work on the level of subject matter. Motifs from the Rhine and the Ruhr Valley have been replaced by metaphors for a globalized consumer and pop culture and the power of the financial system: the stock exchange in Tokyo or Kuwait, Formula One racing, Prada boutiques, the Tour de France, a Madonna concert. These artworks memorialize both the global triumph of pop culture and the general increased fascination with celebrity, fashion, and commercial success, while at the same time succumbing to their allure.

In an interview with German news magazine *Der Spiegel*, however, Gursky himself attempted to reinforce the art-historical references in his project, thus (inadvertently) triggering a kind of interpretational chain reaction.[4] In passing, he mentions a visit to a Caravaggio exhibition, during which he realized that in his new "pit-stop" pictures he had unconsciously used "a similar kind of lighting" to no lesser an artist than Caravaggio. This comparison, which blends artistic hubris and art-historical cliché, immediately became standard fare in articles on Gursky. As if by reflex action, everyone joined the chorus of delight: And his use of light, just like Caravaggio![5] The mere mention of this name, it seems, is today akin to art-historical ennoblement.

What this tells us is that even in an art world increasingly governed by economic imperatives, in which the global art market is often permitted to play the role of final arbiter on artistic matters, art history is still required as an insurance policy. Gursky's casually introduced art-historical reference manages to ensure the work is also significant on the symbolic level. For just as market success is now able to generate cultural relevance, in the long term this cultural relevance also depends on the kind of symbolic meaning for which art history and criticism are still decisively responsible.

This book provides numerous examples to support its principal claim that there was massive growth during the last art boom in the defining role played by the market and its players, who also increasingly had a say when it came to establishing artistic value. There is indeed much to suggest that in recent years, whether or not an artwork was considered artistically relevant depended to a greater extent on its market value. But this market value still needs the assumption of a "symbolic value" for ultimate legitimacy. Without the assumption of such a symbolic value, there is no market value—this is the book's second claim, also based on empirical observation (evaluation of media reports) and historical analysis (case studies).

2 See Christian Mayer, "Die Faszination des Großformats. Der Fotograf Andreas Gursky schätzt das Haus der Kunst als Heimat für seine Bilder – und geht im P1 tanzen," *Süddeutsche Zeitung*, February 16, 2007; or, Gabi Czöppan, "Seismograph der globalen Welt. Mit gigantischen Fotografien dokumentiert Andreas Gursky die Gegenwart – jetzt zeigt das Münchner Haus der Kunst sein Werk," *Focus*, 08/2007 (February17, 2007).

3 See Raymonde Moulin, *Le marché d'art: Mondialisation et nouvelles technologies* (Paris: Flammarion, 2003).

4 See "Fotos dürfen lügen," *Der Spiegel*, 4/2007: 152–154.

5 See Ira Mazzoni, "Das totale Bild," *FAZ*, February 21, 2007; and Niklas Maak, "In den Labyrinthen des Sehens. Vor der großen Münchner Ausstellung: Ein Gang in Andreas Gurskys Atelier und ein erster Blick aufs neue Werk," *FAZ*, February 12, 2007.

For if it is true that society has been changing since the 1970s from industrial capitalism into what Antonio Negri has called "cognitive capitalism," a form of capitalism in which the value of knowledge and information has risen, then under such conditions—which have always prevailed in the art world—increased importance would once more be accorded to the symbolic meaning bestowed upon an artwork, its *symbolic value*. The art world is by definition a knowledge society, even if the spell of commercial success long held sway over it. It is a social universe that is interested chiefly in knowledge and symbolic production (i.e., the production of pictorial and linguistic signs).

Sociologist Pierre Bourdieu uses the term "symbolic value" to describe value that goes beyond what can be measured in economic terms. One example he uses is that of a plot of land accorded a symbolic value in excess of its economic qualities.[6] Against an economism that recognizes only the interests of capital, he highlights practices that escape the logic of calculated interest while nevertheless developing an economy of their own. By analogy with "symbolic capital," which he equates with the accumulation of "prestige" or "authority," Bourdieu views symbolic value as the manifestation of a distinction that is hard to quantify or measure in material terms.

When examining the relationship between art and market, the concept of symbolic value is especially appropriate for the way it unites two concepts: "symbol" evokes cultural theory, while "value" refers to political economy. The symbol refers to a surplus of meaning that lies outside of itself. The value of a thing, too, is not founded in itself. According to Marx, it appears in the social relation between individual commodities.[7] To explain the fact that the value of an object is something fundamentally separate from its body, he used the example of a length of linen, whose value is related to that of another commodity (in this case a coat) as its equivalent.[8] The value of the linen is always to be found elsewhere—for instance in the coat that expresses it.

In this light, symbolic value may be defined as a dual social charge, a charge that is conveyed by specific symbol-bearers but cannot be apprehended in terms of these bearers themselves. It thus stands for a surplus and an assumption of meaning and worth that goes beyond the concrete object used to refer to it.

In the field of art history, it is usually art historians, critics, and curators who contribute to the generating of this symbolic value, although recently this role has also been increasingly performed by lifestyle and fashion magazines.

The waning power of criticism observed in times of thrall to the market, then, contrasts with the observation that critics are more powerful than ever in a knowledge-based economy. In their function as producers of knowledge, they ensure the creation of a symbolic value, which even forms the basis of auction culture—in spite of its near invisibility in this field. Apart from research into provenance, intellectual concerns with the meaning and artistic worth of an artwork are not what matters most in the auction world. But here, too, critics and art historians have performed preliminary work that is indispensable for the smooth functioning of the commercial art market, and which, moreover, actually represents what everyone in a post-Fordist economy most covets. In this light, perhaps critics are actually not the losers of a "market imperialism," where their opinion has long been claimed to be irrelevant. Instead, they may in fact be winners, especially since their skills in a knowledge-based economy are in extraordinarily high demand.[9] This question of the status of and range of possibilities for criticism runs through this book as a leitmotif. But answering this question calls for a differentiated

6 Pierre Bourdieu, "Structures, Habitus, Power: Basis for a Theory of Symbolic Power," in *Outline Of A Theory Of Practice* (New York / Cambridge: Cambridge University Press, 1977), 182.

7 Karl Marx, "Commodities and Money," in *Capital: Vol. 1: A Critique of Political Economy* (London: Penguin, 1976), 139.

8 Ibid., 143.

9 See Merlin Carpenter, "The Tail that Wags the Dog: A Lecture for Art Center in Pasadena, Not Delivered," in *Canvases and Careers Today: Criticism and Its Markets*, eds. Daniel Birnbaum and Isabelle Graw (Berlin / New York: Sternberg Press, 2008), 75–88.

approach, distinguishing not only between various sectors of the market, but more importantly still, between various manifestations of criticism. Depending on the market sector, the situation, and the type of criticism, a critic's scope of action varies widely.

Art as a Special Kind of Commodity

When artworks circulate on the art market, they inevitably assume the character of commodities. In itself, there is nothing condemnable about this. Even Adorno, usually far from partial to the market, did not consider the sale of artworks as an abuse, but simply as the consequence of their participation in the conditions of production: The fact that they belong to the capitalist system determines that they will be taken to market, and thus become commodities.[10] For Adorno, this commodity character becomes a problem when artworks are treated as consumer goods by what he terms "vested interests."[11] They are goods, but they should not simply be consumed. Although Adorno firmly rejects such "selling off" of art, his thinking about its commodity character is marked by a high degree of ambivalence. He wavers constantly between insistence upon awareness of market realities and defense of artistic autonomy. Although he approved of artworks registering an awareness of market realities, his final position was that these market realities should ideally benefit the artistic autonomy of the works in question. An artwork could surrender to its "opponent," completely exposing itself to the commercial character of society,[12] but only in order to raise an *objection* to this society by means of its own autonomous formal language.

What is assumed here is the existence of a clearly defined divide between art, which supposedly obeys its own rules, and the market, which is seen to remain external to it. Adorno praises Baudelaire's poetry, for example, for its ability to "surmount the heteronomous market" by "immersing its autonomy in society's *imagerie*."[13] In this view, the market amounts to an external constraint that is ultimately unable to touch an art that follows its own logic.

Unlike Adorno, I work with the premise that the dividing line between art and market conditions must be considered as fundamentally unstable. One can assume neither a market that is external to art, nor an art with its own immanent rules that draws on market realities only in order to finally triumph over them. But I concur with Adorno's basic intuition concerning art as commodity to the extent that I also underline the *special status of art as commodity*. Artworks can most certainly be viewed as commodities—without being a commodity like any other. But what is it that makes them a special kind of commodity?

Firstly, artworks must be distinguished from other products insofar as they are usually one of a kind. This singularity adds significantly to their special symbolic charge, as well as putting the artist in the privileged position of a monopolist—he owns the sole rights to their manufacture. What he has to offer is available nowhere else. Artists today might operate with a division of labor, employing a large number of assistants and technical staff in their studio, or company, to whom the lion's share of work is delegated. But this work will still bear the mark of *the artist's own* studio / factory / enterprise. The artist's signature remains intact, and this is the place where the promise of originality essential for art is upheld.

Even under conditions of mechanical reproducibility, artworks are able to preserve this aura of the unique—contrary to Walter Benjamin's prediction that mechanical reproduction causes aura to wither.[14] In fact, the impression of a "here and now" to which, according to Benjamin, this aura is attached has even been successfully heightened in works such as the digitally manipulated large-format photographs

10 See Theodor W. Adorno, *Aesthetic Theory* (London: Continuum, 2004), 309.
11 Ibid., 22.
12 Ibid., 27.
13 Ibid., 28.
14 Walter Benjamin, "The Work Of Art in the Age of Mechanical Reproduction," in *Illuminations* (New York: Harcourt, Brace & World, 1968), 217.

of the Becher school. Artists working with media that are by nature reproducible, such as photography or screen printing, take care to ensure that the resulting pictures only circulate in small numbers and, of course, always with a signature. Multiples, too, due to their limited numbers, suggest the specter of uniqueness, offering the owner a feeling of having secured some scarce commodity. A crucial difference between an artwork and a product capable of unlimited mass manufacture is that the artwork promises a closer connection to its "master," allowing the owner to imagine that an intimate relationship exists between himself and the artist.

Another factor contributing to the special status or art is its promise of durability. Its value is not used up like that of a consumer product, and it does not diminish over time. On the contrary, the possibility exists that it may later develop an unsuspected topicality. Every artwork is a wager on the future. And it seems no price is too high for a belated importance, which cannot yet be gauged from today's point of view. What the buyer pays for, finally, is the *potential* for future significance and value creation.

Unlike consumer products subject to depreciation, such as designer clothing, the values associated with works of art are lasting. Whereas a fashionable garment declines in value during the course of the current season, artworks are associated with a notion of duration. This belief in their longevity draws on their material presence. Works of art are things that actually exist in concrete form and are potentially capable of outliving us. As such, art—and in this it resembles gold—evokes substance by virtue of materiality.[15] This explains why in times of crisis, as in the recent global economic downturn, money seeks refuge in universally recognized "masterworks" of classical modernism (Matisse, Picasso) and in gold.[16] Unlike the immaterial assets traded on the financial markets, "masterworks" and gold bars nourish the deceptive feeling of holding something in one's hand, of having got something for one's money.

Traditional Conceptual art tried to cancel out the commodity character of art by means of dematerialization.[17] By vanishing in material terms, it sought to avoid becoming reified and commodified. As attempts to outsmart commodification, however, these efforts failed. Even the most immaterial artworks have a material dimension. One need only think of handwritten instructions on scraps of paper or the still widespread practice of issuing certificates—both perfectly marketable formats.[18]

Symbolic Value, or: The Price of the Priceless

As soon as they are exchanged, works of art assume the character of commodities. This means that they inevitably take on properties of the "very strange thing" that gave Marx such a headache.[19] He attributed the theoretical difficulties posed by the commodity to its *dual nature* as an "object of utility" and a "bearer of value."[20] This principle has long since been applied to artworks, for example by Pierre Bourdieu: by classifying works of art as "symbolic goods,"[21] he literally put their dual nature into words, as a symbolic good is a cultural asset and a commodity in one. One step further, however, would be to say that artworks are *split* into a symbolic value and a market value. This results in an exceptional degree of inner tension.

15 On art's promise of substance, see also Helmut Draxler, *Gefährliche Substanzen. Zum Verhältnis von Kritik und Kunst* (Berlin: Reihe polypen, 2007).
16 See Benedikt Fehr and Stefan Ruhkamp, "Die nächste Welle der Finanzkrise," *FAZ*, March 14, 2008.
17 See Lucy Lippard, *Six Years: The Dematerialization of the Art Object* (London: studio vista, 1973).
18 One important difference that remains, however, is that works of Conceptual art traditionally sell for less than a painted picture. This reflects both the mythical status of painting as an institution and the advantages of the painted canvas. According to Vasari, as Martin Warnke has shown, the canvas panel picture as an innovation in painting came about above all for reasons of transportation—because it could easily be moved from place to place in any size. On this, see Martin Warnke, *Hofkünstler. Zur Vorgeschichte des modernen Künstlers* (Cologne: DuMont, 1985), 266.
19 Karl Marx, "The Fetishism of the Commodity and its Secret," in *Capital Vol. 1* (op. cit.), 163.
20 Ibid., 138.
21 Pierre Bourdieu, "The Market for Symbolic Goods," in *The Rules Of Art: Genesis and Structure of the Literary Field* (op. cit.), 141 175.

But what constitutes this symbolic value? It is the expression of an elusive charge derived from a range of factors: singularity, arthistorical verdict, artist's reputation, promise of originality, prospect of duration, claim to autonomy, intellectual acumen. It follows that this symbolic value also encompasses the increased expectations on art that were already being formulated in the eighteenth century, for example by Kant, Schiller, and Winckelmann. The kind of views it draws upon hold that art should be a selfless pleasure, or that it should be kept free from any specific function. In this light, symbolic value is the result of those historical strivings for idealization, which to this day credit fine art with superiority and uniqueness. In symbolic value, art's historically hard-won special status has come into its own.

It is thus also the culmination of a belief system established in the eighteenth century, which French philosopher Jacques Rancière has termed the "aesthetic regime of art."[22] This aesthetic regime, he writes, "asserts the absolute singularity of art and, at the same time, destroys any pragmatic criterion for isolating this singularity."[23] To the same degree that art was declared to be something special, aesthetic experience was conceived of as something that should be accessible to all, as a matter of principle. If one follows Rancière, then specialization and de-specialization, autonomy and heteronomy are two sides of the same coin.

It is clearly not enough to merely dismiss the belief system established by idealist aesthetics—its claim to autonomy, for example—as a "theology of art" (Walter Benjamin). The boosting of art's value pursued by Kant, Schiller, or Karl-Philipp Moritz is more than a doctrine that keeps a tight hold on its believers—not least because of its basis in a concrete artistic practice that was becoming more strongly aware of its own value and autonomy.[24] The insistence on art's radical specificity, then, rather than being pure invention, had a basis in artistic praxis. For symbolic value, this means a similar overlap of claim and reality: it is both the consequence of the idealization and hopeless overburdening of art, and an expression of its *perfectly justified* special status.

The peculiarity of symbolic value is that it cannot be measured in terms of money, that it won't translate smoothly into economic categories. What critics and art historians put forward as the aesthetic achievement of an artwork cannot be measured in terms of economic value, and certainly not converted into a price. At the same time, works of art undoubtedly have their price while circulating on the market—a fact dutifully glossed over by idealistic views of art as simply priceless. But this notion of symbolic value as something that cannot be measured in gold, something absolutely irreducible, also contains a grain of truth, and this is what makes the matter so complicated. In terms of its symbolic value, the artwork is priceless but has a price nonetheless. In other words, its symbolic value is not identical to its market value, and this in spite of the fact that it has a named asking price. This price, conversely, is justified with reference to a symbolic value that cannot be accounted for in financial terms. One might say, then, that the work's price is based on the assumption that it is priceless. And this is also what makes the artwork a special kind of commodity: the fact that its market value is justified *purely* by its symbolic value, which in turn is an expression of the manner in which it is loaded with idealistic concepts.

Admittedly, other commodities, especially branded goods, are increasingly defined by symbolic value. But a designer item like a pair of Dior sunglasses would not be expected to produce "truth" or "epistemological insight" as does a work of art. The artwork, on the other hand, is expected to achieve great things in intellectual terms: it offers insights for which no price can ever really be high enough. What necessarily follows from this founding of price in pricelessness

22 See Jacques Rancière, *The Politics of Aesthetics: The Distribution of the Sensible* (London: Continuum, 2004).

23 Ibid., 23.

24 See Petra ten–Doesschate Chu, *The Most Arrogant Man in France: Gustave Courbet and the Nineteenth–Century Media Culture* (Princeton / Oxford: Princeton University Press, 2007), 29: "As Neil McWilliams has shown … artists, during the 1830s and 1840s claimed for themselves an authority and distinction that set them apart from their fellow human beings."

is that the price of art must be viewed as something arbitrary insofar as it refers to a symbolic value that cannot be measured in objective terms. This is also the reason for the "maximum uncertainty" observed in the contemporary art market by sociologist Raymonde Moulin.[25] The price is so precarious because it represents only the form behind which the problem of value is concealed. Marx pointed out the possibility that "the price may diverge from the magnitude of value, [...] a thing can, formally speaking, have a price without having a value."[26] As examples of this, he named such non-commodities as "conscience" and "honor," which are suddenly priced at a certain level, thus taking on the form of a commodity. Like the work of art, "honor" and "conscience" are also characterized by a symbolic value, whose desirability is expressed in its price. However in such cases, says Marx, the expression of a price is "imaginary." It is attached to the valueless thing as a way of obscuring its actual lack of value. Such fantasy prices are encountered in the art market, too, where they are asked for objects of no artistic merit. Except that nowadays, these prices are often equated with value, or mistaken for it. In reality, there is a void that opens up not only behind the price of these artworks, but also behind their value, as the latter is always subject to negotiation and can always be called into doubt. No expression of price will be adequate, since the peculiarity of symbolic value lies in the impossibility of measuring it.

There are, however, ways and means to avoid this "maximum uncertainty" on the issue of value. Dealers especially are extremely inventive when it comes to rendering the price *plausible*. One popular method is to refer to the production costs, making the price appear justified in objective terms. For modern painting, a "coefficient" has been invented for this purpose, taking age, size, artist's reputation, and other factors into account in order to calculate the price in such a way as to avoid the question of value. Such measures serve to lift the price out of the zone of the arbitrary and give it the appearance of something with an actual, material basis.

We have seen that art's symbolic value comprises a wide range of elements. Beside the intellectual acumen traditionally ascribed to artworks, it draws on the historically hard-won special status of art, on its singularity, its greater closeness to the artist, and its promise of uniqueness. If one considers the historical over-determination of this symbolic value, then "exorbitant" prices hardly come as a surprise, appearing instead as its adequate expression. After all, when it comes to putting a price on the priceless, the sky's the limit. Viewed in this way, current auction records reflect all the sometimes hopelessly exaggerated, sometimes not entirely unjustified hopes and expectations that have been and continue to be associated with fine art.

Market Value and Symbolic Value

Compared to the diffuse character of symbolic value, which recalls the aesthetic topos of *je ne sais quoi,* market value is easier to define. It is calculated on the basis of the price, fittingly defined by Marx as the "expression in money of the magnitude of value."[27]
The price is thus an index of the market value, a magnitude of value that should not, however, be confused with the value of the artwork. After all, high prices can be obtained for worthless artworks. Thus two realities coincide in the artwork—pricelessness (via symbolic value) and price (via market value). Bourdieu had this paradox in mind when he defined the trade in art as a "commerce in things that are not commercial."[28]

One must add, however, that the art trade makes a virtue out of this necessity by using its wares' lack of price as an argument in their

25 See Raymonde Moulin, *Le marché de l'art: Mondialisation et nouvelles technologies* (op. cit.).
26 Karl Marx, "Money, or The Circulation of Commodities," Chapter 3 of *Capital: Vol. 1* (op. cit.), 196–197.
27 Ibid., 196.
28 Pierre Bourdieu, *The Rules Of Art* (op. cit.), 148.

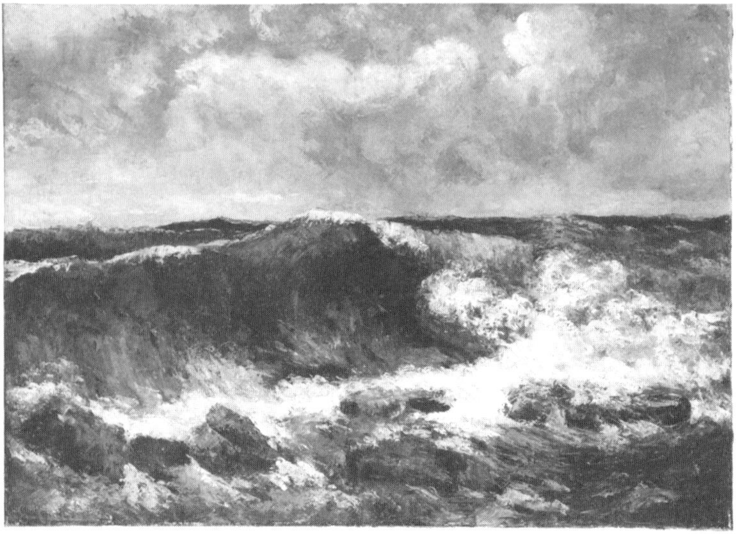

Gustave Courbet, The Wave, *circa 1870*

favor. The elevated price of an artwork is justified by its extraordinary symbolic importance, for which no price is too high.

But what is the relationship between symbolic and market value? Simply put, they make life hard for each other while ultimately depending on each other to survive. Contrary to Bourdieu's claim of relative independence, the relationship between market value and symbolic value is in fact one of attraction and repulsion. Bourdieu describes the artistic field as an "economic world turned upside down,"[29] in which the norm of economic success does not apply. Under these conditions, he claims, artists constitute a market of their own, with the result that symbolic value and market value are "relatively independent of each other." This position reflects his fundamental, heuristic assumption of the artistic field as a "relatively autonomous universe."[30]

Were this so, then a sudden rise in the market value of a given artwork would leave the symbolic value attributed to it relatively unaffected. Is this the case? Has symbolic value ever—for example, in the period examined by Bourdieu, the literary milieu of nineteenth-century France—proved insensitive to market value? Using the letters of the painter Gustave Courbet as my example, I will try to show that in the nineteenth century, commercial success was already quite capable of generating symbolic value—although only in the eyes of the broader public, and not (unlike in today's situation) in the eyes of a specialist audience.

Freedom Leads to Fame: Gustave Courbet

At first glance, the painter Gustave Courbet seems to fit the cliché of an artist initially spurned by the Salon but appreciated by critics like Champfleury, Baudelaire, and Castagnary. This would confirm Bourdieu's assumption of a profound divide between symbolic and market value, especially since the lack of institutional recognition did nothing to harm Courbet's reputation. Precisely because the works he submitted to the Salons were at first regularly rejected (i.e., declared worthless by government officials), his symbolic credibility grew. At second glance, however, Courbet proves to have been a master of self-marketing who, rather than limiting his activities to the symbolic-artistic sphere, personally took pains to increase his market value.

From his correspondence, it is abundantly clear that Courbet took the interrelatedness of symbolic and market value into account. At the same time as underlining the necessity to earn money—"They pay me fifteen hundred francs a piece for these portraits."—this allowed him to insist equally on his right to paint with no thought as to the price of the resulting work: "Art emerges spontaneously and is inspired without taking money into account."[31] He proves to be a market realist *and* a defender of the notion of autonomy, the perfect embodiment of Adorno's ideal. When reporting the completion of a

29 Ibid., 21.
30 Ibid., 141.
31 Petra ten-Doesschate Chu (ed.), *Letters of Gustave Courbet* (Chicago / London: University of Chicago Press, 1992), 267, 599.

picture, for example, he never failed to name the amount it could be expected to fetch.[32] Depending on the situation, he was capable of defending the symbolic sphere against the presumptions of the market, or of realistically assessing the intrusion of market realities into the everyday routine of his artistic production. He regularly asked for more time and for delivery deadlines to be extended on the grounds of artistic demands, which dictate their own economy of time. At the same time, he perceptively noted that his work involved more and more administrative tasks, thus demonstrating his market realism: "You oblige me to do a lawyer's work, for which I am not trained, and you don't want me to do that of a painter, which is mine."[33]

Courbet must be counted among the artists who refuse to leave the fate of their exhibitions to chance, attempting instead to take matters into their own hands. It does not seem exaggerated to call him the master of the genre of the self-organized exhibition. Coinciding with the official government exhibitions of 1855 and 1867, he organized shows of his own works at nearby venues, both hoping for a *succès de scandale* and speculating openly on high entrance prices: "The site that I have just rented is within the site of the government exhibition. People will think that I am a monster, but I'll earn a hundred thousand francs by all estimates."[34] What this initiative stands for above all, however, is his attempt to square the circle: On the one hand, he insisted on his artistic independence by taking things into his own hands and distancing himself from the Salon. And on the other, this exhibition represented his aspiration to live by his art: "I hope to live by my art all my life without ever having departed an inch from my principles, without having betrayed my conscience for a single moment, without having made a painting even the size of a hand to please anyone or to be sold."[35] Courbet was clearly not an artist to be satisfied with mere reputation. In his pioneering study of Courbet, T. J. Clark points out that, throughout his life, the artist was always on the lookout for customers—especially because he sold almost nothing during his first ten years in Paris.[36] It is an indication of Courbet's intuitive grasp on the importance of symbolic capital that this situation did not discourage him in the slightest, as detailed in his correspondence. At regular intervals, we read in letters to his family that breakthrough is imminent: "I am about to make it any time now, for I am surrounded by people who are very influential in the newspapers and in the arts, and who are very excited about my painting."[37] Here, he equates the fact that the influential believe in him with a credit, recalling Bourdieu's description of symbolic capital as a credit that can only be granted by the peer group's belief.[38] Courbet rightly assumed that this credit would soon pay off. Prophesies of this kind must of course also be read as attempts to mollify his family, who were supporting him financially. This notwithstanding, Courbet possessed a heightened sense of the potential for converting symbolic into economic capital. He quite obviously speculated on the fact that in good time, the support of these "influential people" would pay off in terms of wealth and fame. Bourdieu, too, refers explicitly to this fundamental convertibility of symbolic into economic capital.[39] But if symbolic value can be converted into market value, then it should conversely be true that it does not possess immunity with regard to fluctuations in the latter. Instead of being conceived of as relatively independent, then, as they are in Bourdieu's model, symbolic and market value must be imagined as variables that impact strongly on one another.

32 Ibid., 116.
33 Ibid., 291.
34 Letter of 1855 to Courbet's patron Bruyas. Ibid., 149.
35 Ibid., 122.
36 See T. J. Clark, *Image of the People: Gustave Courbet and the 1848 Revolution* (London: Thames & Hudson, 1973).
37 Petra ten-Doesschate Chu, ed., *Letters of Gustave Courbet* (op. cit.), 264.
38 See Pierre Bourdieu, "Critique of Theoretical Reason," in *The Logic Of Practice* (Palo Alto: Stanford University Press, 1990), 120.
39 Ibid., 119.

Courbet, or: The Authority of Market Value

Courbet proves especially prophetic when he refers openly to the market value of scandal. Early on, he pointed out that rejection by the Salon amounted to a prize: "It becomes an honor to be refused."[40] But it was not just rejection and scandal whose potential for value-creation he clearly identified. He noted that political resistance, too, can pay off. Although his involvement with the Commune de Paris caused him considerable trouble, including time spent in prison, these political activities had a noticeably positive effect on the prices paid for his pictures: "If the Commune caused me some difficulties, it also increased my sales and my prices by one half," and: "The action that I took during this revolution has caused the prices of my paintings to triple."[41] Courbet was evidently aware that political resistance is capable of positively influencing market value. The fact that his political engagement in the Commune was an existential risk is another matter entirely. One should not forget the price Courbet paid for his perceived role in the destruction of the Place Vendôme column: debt, life in exile, and the loss of the majority of his pictures. This proves once again that the artist himself does not necessarily profit from the higher prices of his work.

The converse ability of prices to generate symbolic importance was also becoming clear at this time. In a letter to Alfred Bruyas written in 1867, Courbet pointed out that the pictures purchased by his patron had risen considerably in value: "Last year, either I or those who held my paintings sold twenty-five thousand francs worth of my paintings. Consequently yours are already worth more than a hundred thousand francs." Immediately adding, however: "Those figures mean nothing to me, but for collectors and the public they are the touchstone."[42] By adopting the rhetoric of the artist detached from the market, he displays an indifference that is strikingly refuted by the obsessive focus on prices throughout his correspondence. However, more important in this statement is the suggestion that these prices were based on his recognition among collectors and the general public. This statement of Courbet's can be taken as conclusive evidence that in the nineteenth century, high market value was already capable of consolidating an impression of artistic importance. In this light, it is impossible to speak of the kind of "relative independence" of symbolic value from market value postulated by Bourdieu for the late nineteenth century. But it is interesting that for Courbet, only collectors and the general public were impressed by money. What we have witnessed in the recent art boom might be seen as a gradual worsening of this situation, in which even the expert public, specialists, and insiders allow their own value judgments to be dictated by high prices. Increased market value is now even capable of redefining personal preferences. One need only think of the posthumous rise in market value of the work of an artist like Martin Kippenberger, who had been quite controversial when alive and rather unpopular in large sections of the art world. Even the most incorrigible Kippenberger haters of yore now seem to cite him as a favorite artist. But the history of the reception of his work also shows that there can be no market value without symbolic value. Finally, it is the symbolic value attributed to his oeuvre, the art-historical importance now (quite justifiably) accorded to it, that is used to prop up its market value.

Damien Hirst and the Return of Material Value

In the early years of the new millennium, until the art market stopped booming in the second half of 2008, we were confronted by a situation in which the market value of an artwork *alone* was capable of helping it achieve symbolic meaning. Damien Hirst's much-discussed *For The Love Of God* (2007) is a good example of this—a

40 Petra ten-Doesschate Chu (ed.), *Letters of Gustave Courbet* (op. cit.), 62.
41 Ibid., 462, 492.
42 Ibid., 312.

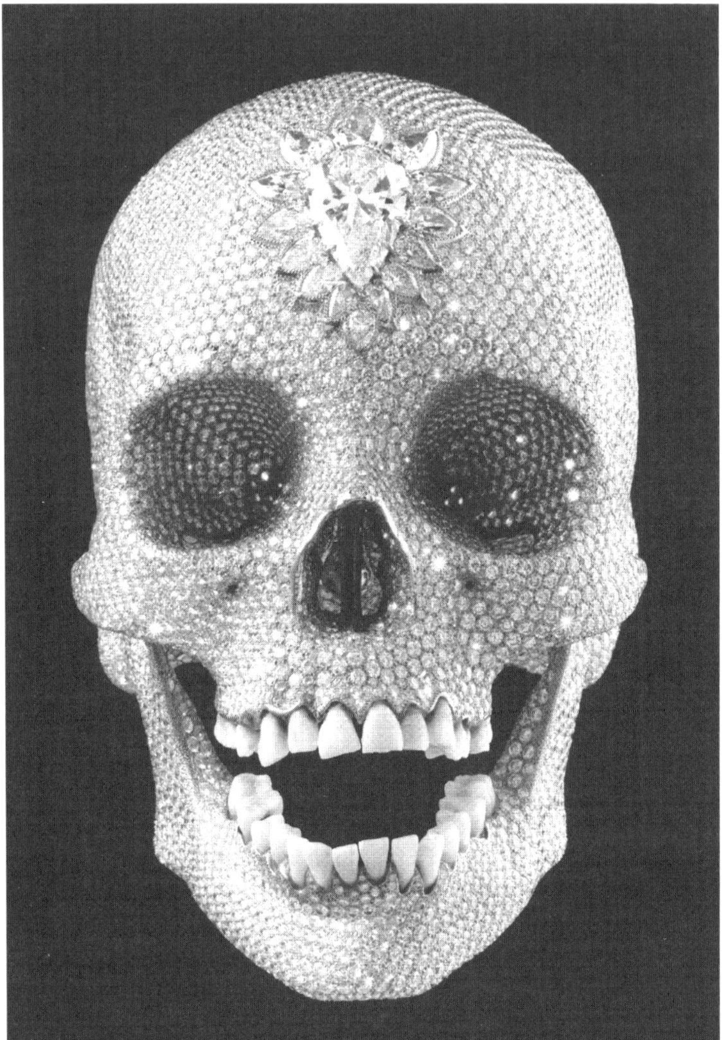

Damien Hirst, For the Love of God*, 2007*

skull covered with an alleged 8,601 diamonds whose claim to cultural significance is based primarily on its horrendous price (100 million dollars), which press reports never fail to mention.[43] It is as if this skull fuses with its market value, which is in itself enough to secure the artistic significance of the work. Hirst himself tried to justify the astronomical price by pointing to the enormous amount of money it cost to make (30 million dollars). Diamonds alone are so expensive, he claimed, that the profit margin is actually modest when compared to its material value.[44] This attempt to legitimate the price by referring to materials recalls the strategies of Renaissance artists described by Michael Baxandall. They, too, used expensive gold leaf with a view to the resulting steep increase in the prices of their pictures.[45] Hirst's use of diamonds corresponds with these historical attempts to render the price of art plausible, thus counteracting the fundamentally arbitrary character of price formation. It is a kind of antidote.

Against the background of the theory of value, however, the high material value of Hirst's skull can also be interpreted as compensation for a symbolic value that falls short of the high expectations placed on it, coming up instead with platitudes. In other words, the material value is a consolation for the fact that on the symbolic level, the skull offers nothing but the crudest of *vanitas* metaphors. At best, the work can be taken as an opportunity to sound off about death and transitoriness, or about the fact that luxury alone will not lead to happiness, especially as death awaits us all. This diamond skull might also prompt us to muse over the return of the cult of relics in the form of worshiped luxury goods. But such thoughts, which barely go beyond postulating anthropological constants (from relic to luxury article), miss the actual point of this work, whose strength lies precisely in its lack of complexity—in the fact that it disappoints on the symbolic level and leaves something to be desired. By unrestrainedly evoking clichés about death, it refuses the kind of episte-

43 See Gerrit Gohlke, "Diamantstaub-Connection. Damien Hirst tritt als Käufer seines rekordteuren Schädels auf," www.artnet.de, September 7, 2007 (accessed June 19, 2008); see also Christian Schaernack, "Größter Blender aller Zeiten," *Art. Das Kunstmagazin* (November 2007): 125.

44 See "Damien Hirst, Lebendige Kunst," www.vanityfair.de, December 24, 2007 (accessed May 18, 2008).

45 See Michael Baxandall, "Conditions of Trade," in *Painting and Experience in Fifteenth-Century Italy* (Oxford University Press, 1972).

mological gain that has been expected of artworks since history painting, if not before, as a source of insight unavailable elsewhere. Hirst appears to refuse the intellectual claim traditionally made for art. But he took no real risk in doing so, as the market value of his skull was in no way threatened by this emptying on the symbolic level.[46] The "Hirst brand" was simply too established, essentially guaranteeing symbolic relevance.

The creation of the Hirst brand, however, must be credited less to critics in the art press than to lifestyle publications, popular media, and the auction trade. At this stage in the process of institutional recognition, the critic is clearly no longer required. This means that *on this level* of marketing and auctioneering, those responsible for the production of meaning are dispensable, if not actually superfluous—and thus obsolete. It is highly improbable that a big collector like the French entrepreneur François Pinault would consult a critical treatise on a particular work by Hirst before acquiring it at auction. But while criticism plays little part in this so-called "secondary market" (the selling-on by dealers and auction houses), there is much to suggest that in a knowledge-based economy it is an increasingly coveted good. Even art fairs like the Frieze Art Fair or Art Basel Miami Beach try to involve critical discussion via symposia integrated into their program.[47] Here, critics serve as purveyors of credibility, which is good for business because they produce the kind of significance that underpins market value. Another indication of the increased importance of knowledge is the fact that more and more galleries are beginning to employ in-house art historians to endow their wares with art-historical noblesse. Throughout the art boom, while many such theorists were hired, others were invited to appear at symposia or write catalog essays. Even if they take no part in auction culture, demand for them as producers of significance has risen massively. They profited from a mood akin to gold fever, which compelled private gallerists to offer adequate pay for such texts. Just as the secondary market can do without them, they are roped in elsewhere via lucrative commissions.

That Was Years Ago

For a long time, until well into the 1990s, commercial success was disreputable. Especially among cultural producers, it was viewed as a rather conflicting and certainly dubious affair. Bourdieu has pointed out that this was already the case in the literary milieu of late nineteenth-century France. Whereas under normal economic conditions success equates with a guarantee of quality, in the "economic world turned upside down" of "pure art" there was something suspect about it: "The artist can triumph on the symbolic terrain only to the extent that he loses on the economic one."[48] This pattern of valuation dominated the art milieu for a long time, until well into the second half of the twentieth century. In one anecdote about Blinky Palermo, for example, the artist was sharply criticized in the early 1970s for the popularity of his textile paintings by friends who accused him of producing them solely for the market—striking a blow to his artistic credibility and damaging his aura as an incorruptible artist-subject[49] Apparently, the respect and favor shown to him by fellow artists outweighed the applause from the wrong side (the market). Since then, much has changed. Today, rather than posing a threat to artistic repute, success in the market and in the media is actually capable of generating such prestige.

46 See interview with Damien Hirst by Sean O'Hagan, in which the artist himself remarks that he produces pure kitsch, but that he "can get away with that stuff" because he is considered a "high art" artist. Damien Hirst, *New Religion* (London: Paul Stolper and Other Criteria, 2005), 7.

47 At Art Basel Miami Beach, the "Art Basel Conversations" function as a forum "that encourages the exchange of ideas through a series of platform discussions." www.artbaselmiamibeach.com/go/id/hbv (accessed June 20, 2008). The official website of the Frieze Art Fair announces the following: "The fair also includes specially commissioned artists' projects, a prestigious talks programme and an artist-led education schedule." www.friezeartfair.com/visitors (accessed June 19, 2008).

48 Pierre Bourdieu, "An Economic World Turned Upside Down," in *The Rules Of Art: Genesis and Structure of the Literary Field* (op. cit.), 83.

49 See "Palermo's Cloth Pictures: Modernism by the Yard: A Conversation Between Yve-Alain Bois, Christine Mehring, and Ann Temkin, annotated by Christine Mehring," in *Palermo*, ed. Susanne Kruger (Cologne: DuMont, 2007), 55.

Even insiders who should really know better cannot help discovering artistic merit in the work of commercially successful artists. This willingness to "elevate the stock market value of the modern artist to a sign of quality,"[50] as sociologist Pierre-Michel Menger has aptly put it, is now quite widespread even in the specialist press. Well-founded objections or justified misgivings concerning the artistic relevance of a commercially successful artist are rarely to be found, at least until recently.[51] In the traditionally market-critical arts and culture pages of German broadsheet newspapers, the output of commercially successful artists like Neo Rauch and Daniel Richter suddenly met with a reverence reminiscent of the Catholic Church's worship of saints. In the *Frankfurter Allgemeine Zeitung,* for example, various critics were asked to engage with a picture by Neo Rauch.[52] The result could not have been more assiduous, recalling the narrative style of high school art students asked to describe a painting. And Daniel Richter was recently permitted to pose as a fake street artist sitting in front of the Centre Pompidou, where he committed quick portraits to paper for passing tourists.[53] With a mix of bewilderment and enthusiasm, we were informed of the market value of these works on paper, a value their clueless owners were shown to have been completely unaware of. Apart from the populist impetus of this test setup, which sends the famous artist into the lowly realms of street art purely to remind us all of his great potential for value creation, this experiment was also significant insofar as the question of the aesthetic quality of the resulting portraits—which, incidentally, looked alarmingly dull and feeble—was never raised. It was as if the name of their creator, who vouches for a certain market value, was enough to guarantee their artistic relevance.

The Omnipresence of Ranking

The journalistic field as a whole has also seen the rise of ranking, by which I mean the widespread use of top-ten or best-of lists. In the

1980s, such personal hit-lists were used in intellectually ambitious music magazines like *Spex* as a way to break with the kind of anti-hierarchical consensus attributed to hippies and old-guard leftists. In contrast to the normative ritual of discussing a topic to death for hours, this format claimed the right to presumptuous positions and personal likes or dislikes, which were unjust by nature and which also no longer required lengthy justification. The result could be as instructive and entertaining as it could be tiring and trivial.

This kind of ranking has long since conquered "high-brow" arts journalism in German papers including *Die Zeit*, *FAZ*, and *Süddeutsche Zeitung*.[54] Top-ten charts and questionnaires seem to be the formats of the hour. American art magazine *Artforum* has been filling an entire end-of-year issue with top-ten lists by its writers, who use this as a way to name their favorite exhibitions.[55] These rankings satisfy the desire for clearly defined hierarchies in a global art world that is perceived as increasingly confusing, just as they stand for the current tendency toward the personalization of all aesthetic phenomena. What counts here is not what the notables in question say they like, but how they position themselves by means of their selection. If one reads these lists as a cartography of aesthetic preferences and consensus figures in the current art world, then they do have the potential to offer certain insights, articulating a particular "space of the possible" (Bourdieu).

The hit-list is now also long established as a conversational format in the culture industry, corresponding as it does to the social require-

50 See Pierre-Michel Menger, *Portrait de l'artiste en travailleur. Métamorphoses du capitalisme* (Paris: Seuil, 2002).

51 Doubts over commercially successful artists like Olafur Eliasson have recently been voiced in the daily press, which is in principle a very welcome development. See Julia Voss/Niklas Maak, "Die Technik und die Leere," *FAZ*, June 25, 2008.

52 See "Was macht einen Rauch aus?" *FAZ*, November 11, 2006, Z3. Responses requested from Peter Geimer, Cord Riechelmann, Peter Richter, Niklas Maak and Werner Spies.

53 See Niklas Maak, "Das Daniel-Richter-Experiment," *FAZ*, August 18, 2007.

54 One example is the short questionnaire in the weekly newspaper *Die Zeit* titled "What do you lack Mr./Ms. … ?" For instance: "What do you lack, Ms. Graw?," in *Die Zeit*, 48/2006.

55 For example: "Best of 2005: 11 Critics and Curators Look at the Year in Art," *Artforum* (December 2005).

ments of the milieu. Especially at major events like the Venice Biennale, one can observe art-world figures literally scrutinizing each other's aesthetic preferences, and doing so in telegram style. At every corner, one is asked, "What did you like?" meaning, "What do you rate?" Due to a lack of time and as part of a general sense of being in a rush, people just call names to each other in passing. This "idle talk," as described by Italian philosopher Paolo Virno (in a tone of Heideggerian cultural pessimism), is both infectious and fast-spreading: the information received is processed and immediately passed on.[56] When Virno observes that in the "post-Fordist situation," idle talk and curiosity are no longer excluded from the domain of work, then the art world represents a model of this development. Here, communication equals work. And the widespread use of rankings may be seen as an attempt to convert this work into a standardized form.

As a historic precursor to this omnipresent use of rankings, one might mention the "Kunstkompass" founded in 1970 by Willi Bongard.[57] Unlike the forms common today, however, this "compass" was still at pains to apply criteria, taking major exhibitions and mentions in publications into account when ascertaining an artist's prestige. Today's lists, such as the notorious rankings that fill entire issues of German lifestyle-art magazine *Monopol*, for example, make no mention of criteria whatsoever.[58] They constantly claim to have identified the "most important" figures in the art world, without ever giving details to support these assertions. Judging by the frequency with which such lists have appeared, demand for them must be enormous. And though they present themselves as normative, the impression they make is both arbitrary and rash. Few members of the art world take them seriously, although this does not mean they are ignored.[59] A significant feature in this context is the absence of critics from the lists published in *Monopol*, as if they didn't qualify as the "best" or the "most important." This is all the more astonishing as it implies that the magazine's editors are cutting the ground from beneath their own feet. For if criticism doesn't exist, who exactly puts together these lists? If criticism is without significance, then such lists have no claim to authority either.

Don't get me wrong: I'm not saying that ranking is a problem in and of itself. Instead, it is typical of the collective tendency, in the face of growing uncertainty, to set increased store by a brand of gossip that seems to provide security via unambiguous hierarchies. In some cases, top-ten lists may contain trenchant value judgments while also being quite entertaining. But the proliferation of rankings across the entire field of journalism is symptomatic of a market logic that also constantly establishes orders of precedence.

The widespread use of rankings only becomes a genuine problem when it hinders reflection and contributes to a naturalization of this market logic. Even an established critic like Roberta Smith of *The New York Times* is not immune to losing sight of obvious market connections out of sheer enthusiasm for what she has elevated to number-one status. As her favorite exhibition of 2006, she named a Donald Judd solo show curated by Christie's at the Rockefeller Center.[60] But she failed to reflect any further on the fact that the works were being presented in this "breathtaking" setting as the prelude to an auction. Smith went into raptures about the event as if it was an academically prepared museum exhibition without the slightest commercial ambition. And this time, the mimetic endeavors of the auction house, which uses specialists and provenance research in an attempt to lend itself the credibility of a museum, certainly paid off. From the auctioneer's point of view, it really would have been damaging to business if Smith had stated the obvious: that the works on display were soon to go under the hammer. But the more Smith praised the "pristine display" of the installation, the more positive the impact

56 See Paolo Virno, "Idle Talk and Curiosity," in *A Grammar Of The Multitude* (New York / Los Angeles: Semiotext(e), 2004), 88–94.

57 See Linde Rohr-Bongard (ed.), *Kunst = Kapital. Der Capital Kunstkompass von 1970 bis heute* (Cologne, 2001).

58 For example, "Top 100 – die Monopol-Liste 2006," *Monopol* (March 2006): 22–43.

59 See interview with Olafur Eliasson in *Der Spiegel*, 17 / 2008: 182–184. Asked to comment on his placing in *Capital* magazine's "art compass," he answers: "You must be joking. No one I know takes such rankings seriously."

60 See Roberta Smith, "The Met Got Up-to-Date, Graffiti Said Goodbye," *The New York Times*, "The Year in Review," December 24, 2006.

became on the market value of Judd's works, which grows larger the less one is explicitly reminded of it.

For this reason, auction houses have recently begun to organize receptions in honor of artists—like Cindy Sherman—whose works are on offer.[61] The advantage of such luxurious events is that the actual reason for them, the auction, recedes effectively into the background. Suddenly, it seems to be all about the artist, with no effort spared in her honor. Smith, too, blurs the distinction between "art as cultural asset" and "art as commodity," as if it were no longer worth mentioning. In view of the lengths gone to by auction houses to obscure the commodity character of artworks by means of receptions or museum-like presentations, precisely these efforts should have been dealt with in more depth—even within the ranking format. But due to the profound connection between hit-list and market logic, the market is a presumed given in the former. Finally, hitlists are an expression of market-dictated ratings, to whose autonomous existence they contribute. In this context, it is barely conceivable that someone might step back and ask themselves what it means when an auction house preview is named best exhibition of the year.

Of course, a cry of indignation over auction houses posing as museums is not what is called for here. I don't envisage a hit-list entry that casts this steady blurring of the "commercial" and "institutional" spheres as a sign of the impending decline of the Western world. More appropriate would be to highlight this bid for symbolic legitimacy on the part of the auction house, instead of taking it as given, as Smith does, thus helping to render it "natural." As a second step, it then makes sense to consider this development as a symptom of the general tendency toward "market imperialism."[62]

The Market in the Mind

The degree of authority accorded to the market in bullish times, even on artistic matters, is evident in a comment made by Tobias

Meyer, director of the Contemporary Art Department at Sotheby's, styled a "star auctioneer" by much of the German media. Interviewed on the art boom in news weekly *Der Spiegel*, he brazenly claimed that the most expensive works were the best.[63] He quite openly equated high prices with aesthetic significance, lending the market the infallible authority of an artistic tribunal. What is important here is less Meyer's demonstration of his own belief in the market, which could be excused as a *déformation professionelle* and is hardly surprising. Of interest is the absence of critical questions on the part of the *Spiegel* staff writers who conducted the interview, from whom Meyer's elevation of the market to the status of absolute yardstick for artistic achievement did not elicit even the slightest protest.

It's as if the two sides agreed in advance to subscribe to the credo of neoclassical economy, which states that the market is always right because it sets a "fair price" on the basis of a supposedly intrinsic free interplay of supply and demand. On closer inspection, however, the art market is far removed from this ideal of a "fair price." As on the financial markets, manipulation and insider trading are the order of the day. Collusion between bidders at auctions, for instance, assures in advance that prices are either driven up or not allowed to fall in the first place. One institutionalized example of such interference in the free play of market forces is the auction house practice of offering guarantees to gain access to good merchandise. If the supplier has a potentially valuable artwork, then he is lured with a high guaranteed price. The worse the times, the greater the insecurity, the less generous the guarantees offered by the auction houses. The decisive issue, however, is that this practice violates the idea of a

61 When Sotheby's was due to auction Cindy Sherman's *Untitled (A, B, C, D, E)* (1975), Lisa Dennison organized an artist dinner similar to one previously held in honor of Ellsworth Kelly. Cf. Linda Yablonsky, "Sin and Redemption," www.artforum.com, May 13, 2008 (accessed June 20, 2008).

62 Ulrich Bröckling, *Das unternehmerische Selbst. Soziologie einer Subjektivierungsform* (Frankfurt am Main: Suhrkamp, 2007), 85.

63 See *Der Spiegel*, 2/2006: 127.

freely functioning market. Auction houses vouch for a selling price that will not be below a certain minimum; they are able to risk such a guarantee because they have already found a collector willing to pay this price. The auction is thus a far from perfect setting for the free interplay of supply and demand. Instead, it is a highly choreographed event, which, while unable to entirely prevent unwelcome market developments, is certainly able to contain them.[64]

In the eyes of a market-believer like Tobias Meyer, however, the market is transfigured, becoming the sole, ultimate, and seemingly neutral arbiter. During an interview with *Vanity Fair* magazine, he lauded the "truth" about artistic quality revealed by auctions—for Meyer, economic and artistic criteria coincide rather than forming irreconcilable opposites as they do in the market-phobic worldview.[65] I use the term "market phobia" here to refer to the tendency, especially common among commercially successful figures, to (often quasi-obsessively) deny the role of the market in their own activities. Whereas market phobia denies the role played by market conditions in artistic practice, market euphoria tends to elevate the market to the measure of all things.

The blind spot of any belief in the market, however, lies in the market's obvious errors of judgment. The art market in particular offers ample proof that its value judgments are occasionally mistaken. Every decade, be it the 1960s, 70s, or 80s, has a large number of artists who enjoyed short-term commercial success but whose work has since been largely forgotten. Their falling by the wayside of current consensus is not necessarily justified, however, either in the long term or on the basis of artistic criteria. And rediscovery can always be expected when their artistic approaches prove to be of topical interest. The key point here remains, however, that market value alone is no guarantee for long-term symbolic importance. Admittedly, Meyer makes a certain effort to artistically legitimate artists like Lisa Yuskavage and John Currin, whose paintings have fetched sensational prices at his auctions, by attempting to discuss them on the same level as Richard Prince, whose work also enjoyed massive market success during the boom.[66] They are all "smart," he says, and have no problem with the bourgeoisie. This attempt to establish similarities between dissimilar projects does express the unfortunate sociological truth that many commercially successful artists today indeed aspire solely to an elevated bourgeois lifestyle, which couldn't be further removed from the self-image of the nineteenth-century *artiste maudit*. Although Prince and Currin may be comparable in terms of social aspirations, Prince's work offers far more on the symbolic level.

Too Early, Too Late: Market Success Versus Symbolic Relevance

One reason Richard Prince's work from the late 1970s in particular is worth considering today is that it deals with the specific conditions of consumer capitalism, already crystallizing at the time, which awakened needs for security and attempted to satisfy them with luxury goods. His re-photographed advertisements, begun in 1977, of watches, pens, necklaces, or living rooms further heighten the intended appeal of these items by means of an aesthetic procedure that intensifies the glow of the original image.[67] There is also the way his identifiably fetishizing approach violates the orthodox view on appropriation in the early 1980s. With the best will in the world, the then-common understanding of "appropriation as critique" could not be projected onto his work, where the voyeuristic gaze and fetishization of the object in question were too clearly inscribed.

64 On the subject of manipulation in auctions, see Isabelle Graw on Amy Cappellazzo, "co-head" of the Department of Postwar and Contemporary Art at Christie's, *Artforum* (April 2006): 292–303.

65 Meyer says the following: "For me there's truth to the auction process – that's what is actually quite beautiful. It is: Who has the greatest artistic quality?" See "Money On The Wall," group discussion in *Vanity Fair* "The Art Issue," (December 2006): 199.

66 Ibid., 292.

67 See Isabelle Graw, "Reconsidering Prince," *Texte zur Kunst*, issue 68 (December 2007): 163–166.

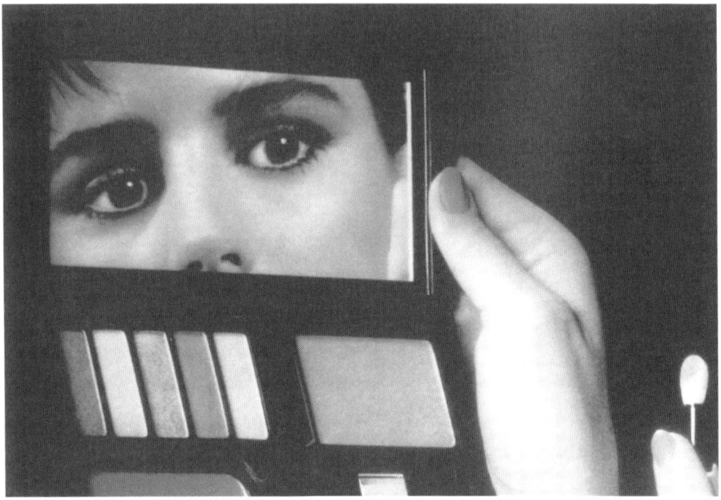

Richard Prince, Untitled (Woman with Compact), *1983*

The pictures of Currin or Yuskavage, on the other hand, cannot be linked to any such symbolic achievement. They neither demand the revision of a critically charged model of appropriation, nor do they engage with the specific problems inherent in consumer capitalism.

Currin in particular exemplifies the kind of artist whose pictures enjoyed huge success on the art market without having been discussed by prominent critics. Demonstratively borrowing from tradition (Cranach, Manet), they seem to satisfy the undying desire for "mastery," just as their superficially sexist provocations—women with oversize breasts literally bouncing against one another as they try on underwear (*The Bra Shop*, 1997)—give their future owner the frisson of having made a daring move. Instead of performing the grammar of sexism in a kind of "second order sexism," which would imply an examination of its semantic and visual makeup, Currin's early work simply presents variations on the eternal topos of the dumb blonde.[68] Currin's apologists regularly make allowances for such provocations, saying that he has merely offended against the deliberately invoked chimera of a supposedly overpowering political correctness. Art historian Robert Rosenblum praised Currin in all seriousness for challenging political correctness by giving such free reign to his heterosexism in his pictures.[69] Currin's pictures, it would seem, play to a decidedly under-complex concept of art, according to which the artwork is to be understood as an expression of an artistic inclination or personal obsession.

With the revival of this antiquated expressive paradigm, however, Currin's work has not been able to prompt sustained controversy, nor have younger artists or art students oriented themselves toward his old-masterly style, which attempts to create a link to the present by overdrawing sexist or pornographic clichés.

In the long run, a lack of symbolic import can become a problem. This view seems to be shared by the Gagosian Gallery empire, to which Currin switched (allegedly in return for a large transfer fee) following his spectacular departure from Andrea Rosen Gallery, a middle-league player.[70] For the monograph on which work immediately began as proof of Currin's importance, Gagosian tellingly hired renowned art historian Norman Bryson to write an essay transforming Currin into an *artiste maudit* and shoehorning his work's apparent sexism into art discourse by referencing feminist theorists like Laura Mulvey and Judith Butler.[71] Evidently, the time has come when elevated market value must be symbolically propped up by theorists with a reputation for being progressive.

Just as market value requires this kind of symbolic underwriting, symbolic importance attributed to an artist's early work can function as long-lasting credit. It covers the future, so to speak, allowing even works that have since lost some of their artistic relevance to shine in the light of a former significance. Starting with his joke pictures of the late 1990s, if not before, Richard Prince's artistic process became increasingly self-referential, and Jeff Koons, too, seems

68 On the subject of second-order sexism, which discusses and highlights sexism, see also Isabelle Graw, "Show Girls," *Texte zur Kunst*, issue 41 (March 2001): 99–105.

69 See Robert Rosenblum, "John Currin and the American Grotesque,"in *John Currin* (Chicago / London: Museum of Contemporary Art and Serpentine Gallery, 2003), 19.

70 See Dorothy Spears, "The First Gallerists' Club," *The New York Times*, June 18, 2006.

71 See Norman Bryson, "Maudit: John Currin and Morphology," in *Currin*, with essays by Norman Bryson, Alison M. Gingeras, and Dave Eggers (New York: Gagosian Gallery / Rizzoli Publications, 2006).

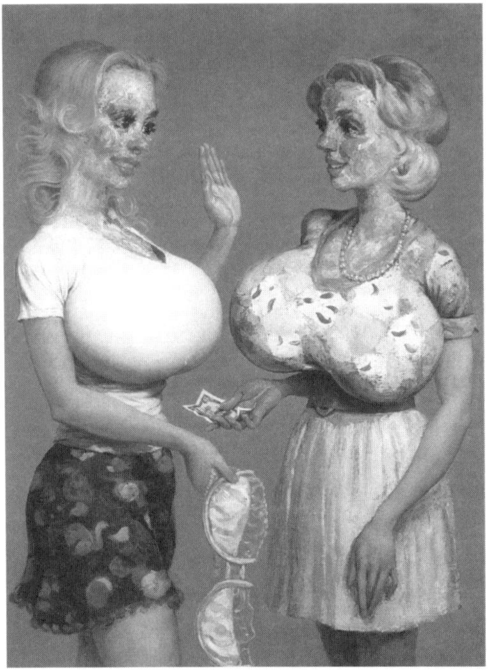

John Currin, Jaunty and Mame, *1997*

to have settled comfortably into the regressive universe of his "Celebration" series originally begun in 1994.

While Prince's new work tends to revolve around his own bibliophile interests, his love of automobiles and bare-breasted girls, his repertoire of jokes, and his unbroken ambition as a painter, Koons has begun to produce increasingly monumental and technically sophisticated versions of "Celebration" motifs.[72] For a long time, the lack of symbolic relevance in these works did nothing to harm their high market value. In Prince's case, it was his much-discussed "Nurse Paintings," with their unambiguous narration, that enjoyed huge popularity not only at auction but also among fashion designers like Marc Jacobs (who seems to harbor an inimitable love of figurative painting).[73] In Koons's case, another auction record was broken during the art boom with his monumental *Hanging Heart (Magenta/Gold)* (1994–2006), a work that symbolizes the gift of love in the form of a heart with ribbons. Although it lacks the trace of evilness that characterizes Koons's best objects, it is exemplary of the astronomical production values generated in his studio, embodied here in the immaculate surface of chrome-plated stainless steel.[74]

For both Prince and Koons, however, it was an earlier achievement on the symbolic level that formed the basis for the high market value of their later works. The symbolic achievements of the early Koons cannot be ignored. One need only think of his "Banality" series (1988) of grotesque figures carved in wood, which inflicted the final death blow on notions of high culture. Friendly-looking teddy bears evoked an idealist belief in the redemptive function of art, only to render it absurd once and for all. Unforgettable, too, was the dubious image of the artist projected by Koons with his advertising campaign simultaneously placed in different international art magazines (1988–89) for three parallel exhibitions. By posing in them as a slightly perverse-looking teacher, Koons undermined the expectations of salvation placed on the artist. And with this concerted action, he also proved to be an artist eminently aware of and engaged with market conditions. This advertising campaign could be said to have anticipated the forced mobility that, in a globalized art world, obliges the artist to constantly travel, or to be present in several cities at the same time. Koons seemed both to submit to and reflect on this self-marketing imperative, an imperative that has now become the norm. What in the late 1980s seemed prophetic has since lost its potential to disturb, as we now have an art world structured along corporate lines and governed by the celebrity principle. With his entrepreneurial self-

72 Several of Koons's more recent objects are truly inspiring, however, in the way they rule out any suggestion of meaning. These include his iconic *Balloon Dog* (1994–2006), which exudes an inimitable vacuity at the same time as being immediately memorable. Or the inscrutable object *Cat on A Clothesline* (1994–2006), a monumentalized version of a cat hanging in a sock on a clothesline. But most of his objects are no more than allegories of their own value (e.g., *Diamond* [1994–2005]).

73 See Christopher Bagley (with photos by Philip-Lorca DiCorcia), "Marc Jacobs. Long intimidated by the art world, Marc Jacobs didn't start collecting until five years ago – and now he just can't stop. Inside the designer's Paris apartment." *W* (November 2007).

74 See Lisa Zeitz, "Da knallt der Hammer," *Frankfurter Allgemeine Zeitung,* May 20, 2008; "Rothko für Quatar, Koons für die Ukraine," *FAZ*, May 17, 2008; and "Platz der Kunst das Herz?" *FAZ*, December 8, 2007.

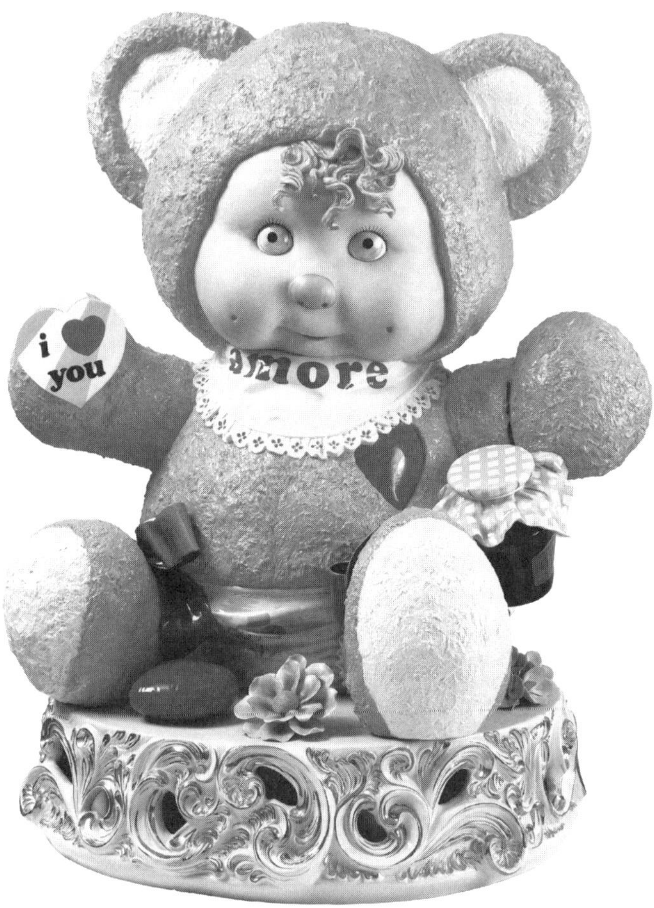

Jeff Koons, Amore, *1988*

image, his excessive fixation on Hollywood, and his self-transformation into an industry, Koons confronted an art world that then still considered itself marginal, but his continued willingness to cooperate with a now hegemonic celebrity culture seems stale. Instead of harnessing the huge media interest in his person to engineer a complex response to media conditions in the style of his earlier advertisement projects, he now merely grins a standard media grin into the lens of any camera pointed his way. The regressive, if not infantilizing vocabulary of his new sculptures, too, has largely lost its earlier disruptive potential. In fact, Koons's endless preaching of reconciliation and self-confidence actually started to fit the prevailing idealistic-populist mood in a booming art market.[75]

Each of these cases shows that the market value of an artwork can refer to a symbolic relevance attributed to an artist at some earlier moment just as, conversely, symbolic value once attributed extends to future works, amounting to a long-term credit. There are also artworks that circulate successfully on the secondary market without ever having been attributed symbolic significance by qualified parties (renowned critics or art historians)—witness Currin or Yuskavage. The case of Currin proves that high market values are capable of creating their own form of symbolic meaning. But in the long term, efforts will eventually be made to raise the kind of cultural capital aptly described by Bourdieu as "titles" (titles of nobility, deeds of possession, academic degrees, etc.).[76] The degree of power wielded by symbolic relevance, once attributed, can be gauged by the way it is projected onto the future, for instance, whether it continues to impact the market value of a Prince or a Koons today. At some point, however, the void lurking behind the value inevitably opens up and further symbolic bolstering becomes necessary.

The Rise of the Market as an End in Itself

During the art boom of the first years of the new millennium, market success became the measure of all things, while at the same time remaining curiously dependent on the consecrating authorities that vouch for symbolic importance (criticism, art history, the museum). But this development by no means came from nowhere. Rather, it

75 See Jeff Koons, interview by Peter Klaus Schuster, in Jeff Koons, *Celebration* (Ostfildern: Hatje Cantz, 2008), 16–31.

76 Pierre Bourdieu, "Structures, Habitus, Power: Basis for a Theory of Symbolic Power," in *Outline Of A Theory Of Practice* (New York / Cambridge: Cambridge University Press, 1977), 159–196: 184.

must be seen as the result of a gradual structural change within the art world that took place in cyclical movements, the pace of which sped up in the 1980s and 90s.

Whereas the market had previously been considered in purely functional terms, as a means of doing business, its status was gradually elevated to that of a normative authority. In the art world, too, the market transformed itself into what Ulrich Bröckling has called a "permanent economic tribunal," in front of which we have to prove ourselves again and again.[77] In such a situation, the moment to lean back and rest on one's laurels never actually comes. Not that it's desirable to live off of once-attained privileges for a lifetime, but it's surely no bed of roses either when, in the eyes of this tribunal, one has never done enough, never achieved enough. Ultimately, favor is only secured by those who keep moving and produce a continuous stream of unexpected performances that explode society's expectations.[78] Such are the excessive new requirements to which the advocates of market success turn a blind eye. In their eulogies to the ceaseless dynamism of the market, they are utterly rapt by the seductive power of a neoliberal doctrine, the mental and emotional costs of which they suppress. Younger writers for mainstream publications in particular, eager to break with blanket demonization of the market (a style usually denounced as "old-school leftist" and which was indeed often undifferentiated, resentment-ridden, and totalizing), sometimes go to the other extreme. Now, the market (alternately, the mainstream) is credited with the ability to filter out what is (apparently) of no artistic worth in favor of what is (allegedly) of artistic value. In recent years, the focus on an incriminated "spectacle culture" (rejected in a often totalizing, if not arrogant manner and with little understanding of pop-cultural phenomena), has been replaced by an equally dubious fixation on market success, which fascinated publications across the media spectrum from the weekly *Die Zeit* to the German edition of *Vanity Fair*—and the more hedonistically this success was celebrated, the harder they fell for it.

The focus was less on the art produced than on the commercially successful individual and his or her lifestyle, which were presented as compelling proof that commercial success was possible and very much worth striving for. But the market also enjoyed high esteem among those directly involved in artistic production. Gallerists, critics, and artists outdid each other in dismantling their former reservations about the market. In the 1970s and 80s, the market was viewed as a necessary means of making sadly inevitable financial transactions. But by the dawn of the twenty-first century, it had advanced in the collective unconscious to the status of an end in itself.

This transformation recalls the "growth of a means into an end" observed with respect to money by sociologist Georg Simmel in his treatise "On the Psychology of Money" (1889).[79] According to Simmel, money's purpose had become an end in its own right in the eyes of its human users, who clung to it "in psychological immediacy." In the case of the art market, we see a comparable phenomenon of something taking on a life of its own in people's heads, for here, too, there is a growing willingness to view the market as something given and self-justifying: It is no longer considered a mere tool for the purposes of exchange that alienates art from itself and degrades it to pure exchange value. Instead, its ability to merge means with end seems to have worked to its advantage. In any case, the willingness to view it as something natural, as a kind of higher authority, was very widespread in the early years of the new millennium. Following this naturalization, the true character of the market—something relative and conditional—was lost from sight, obscured by the conviction that it embodies what is actually at stake.

77 Ulrich Bröckling, *Das unternehmerische Selbst. Soziologie einer Subjektivierungsform* (op. cit.), 79.

78 In the case of artistic production, however, the surprise may also consist in it remaining static, continuing to operate according to the same pattern, as in the work of artists like Balthus, Katz, and many others.

79 Georg Simmel, "On The Psychology Of Money," in *Simmel On Culture: Selected Writings*, eds. David Frisby and Mike Featherstone (London: Sage, 1997), 235; see also Otthein Rammstedt with Christian Papilloud, "Georg Simmel: Zur Psychologie des Geldes (1889)," in *Georg Simmels Philosophie des Geldes. Aufsätze und Materialien* (Frankfurt am Main: Suhrkamp, 2003), 267–299.

This tendency to render the market absolute is well illustrated by the central position given to auction prices in reverential articles on the major Gursky retrospective in Munich.[80] Reviewers spelled out the recently established auction record like a piece of conclusive evidence, as if such inconceivably large sums were tantamount to some kind of art-critical index. In this way, they created an economic-aesthetic self-evidence that seemed immune to any kind of justified art-critical objection.

The Religion of Success

Why is success so highly valued in society? In an attempt to explain this, sociologist Sighard Neckel writes that in modern society, success is among the "fundamental categories of action,"[81] and being successful amounts to a "modern duty." In his view, one has no choice: Only success in the sense of "social achievement in competition" entitles one to experience one's own existence as meaningful. Neckel distinguishes between various indicators of success such as power, money, titles, or prestige, each of which stands for a different type of success. In the case of the commercially successful artist, these different types of success are clearly merged. But the popular fixation on the commercially successful artist is also linked to the fact that he illustrates the dominant view in such a radically individualized and success-oriented society, which holds that "life's what you make it" and "you can make it if only you try hard." What is obscured by such an individualizing and voluntarist view, however, are the social contingencies which deny one person what they may grant to another. But this structural problem is individualized, that is, it becomes each person's own burden. To crown it all, those who bend under the pressure to succeed are made to feel that this is *their* problem, possibly due to their own personal failings. This results in a new form of depression, fittingly described by Alain Ehrenberg as an "illness of responsibility."[82] The individual takes the blame for his own failure upon himself. He is driven by the fear of not doing justice to his own ideals and feels inadequate with regard to these internalized demands of society. What he experiences as personal failure is in fact a structural problem, since it counts among the structural truths of any society based on competition that only the few are lucky enough to win the jackpot, as noted already by Adorno and Horkheimer in their *Dialectic of Enlightenment*: "Only one can draw the winning lot, only one is prominent, and even though all have mathematically the same chance, it is so minimal for each individual that it is best to write it off at once and rejoice in the good fortune of someone else, who might just as well be oneself but never is."[83] In this view, the success of the few is founded on the large majority of the unsuccessful. According to Adorno and Horkheimer, those excluded from success at least have the possibility to "rejoice in the good fortune of others." It should be added, however, that such participation in the life of the rich and famous is always shot through with feelings of resentment or schadenfreude. Whereas in the past, it was primarily the tabloids and the film industry that channeled this identificatory desire, today, the whole of society appears to devote itself to the production of celebrity.

Expansion of the Market Zone

Alongside the increased authority of market success, a global broadening of the market's sphere of influence is also taking place. This process can be characterized as an "expansion of the market zone," a description that captures both the processual nature of this devel-

80 See "Wie Andreas Gursky zum weltweit teuersten Fotografen wurde," *Welt Online*, www.welt.de, January 31, 2007 (accessed June 20, 2008).

81 Sighard Neckel, "Success," in *Glossar der Gegenwart*, eds. Ulrich Bröckling, Susanne Krasmann, and Thomas Lemke (Frankfurt am Main: Suhrkamp, 2004), 63.

82 See Alain Ehrenberg, "Depression: Discontent in the Civilization or New Style of Sociality," *Texte zur Kunst*, issue 65 (March 2007):129–134.

83 Theodor Adorno and Max Horkheimer, "The Culture Industry As Mass Deception," in *Dialectic of Enlightenment* (Palo Alto: Stanford University Press, 2002), 116.

opment and its all-encompassing spatial dimension. But the progression of the development we are now witnessing has by no means been linear, marked instead by cycles and non-contemporaneity. Nonetheless, the first decade of the twenty-first century has seen an increase in the authority of market thinking. Especially in the art world, the market acquired a heightened defining power over artistic issues—although this process is a gradual intensification and expansion of conditions that should be viewed less as a radical break with the past and more as a specific increase in an already existing trend toward economization. But this trend also manifested itself in the general reign of a neoliberal doctrine, which can be defined as a political program that claims, as Lars Gertenbach has written, to establish "a link between state government praxis and individual freedom."[84] Contrary to the usual understanding of neoliberalism, which links it to a laissez-faire approach, Gertenbach assumes a specific neoliberal governmentality, which practices not laissez-faire but a constant pampering and "cultivation" of the market. In this light, efforts by the state to regulate the market in times of crisis do not represent a break with neoliberalism; even when trying to nationalize banks, the economy remains the "main focus of governing." Moreover, according to the principles of neoliberal economic policy, everything can be economized.

Consequently, there is no area where the market cannot go. Instead, as Gertenbach so fittingly puts it, the market is like a net that encloses *the entire level of the social.*[85] The specific social universe of art must also be viewed as being within this net, as illustrated by a remark from art collector Axel Haubrok describing artists, galleries, and himself as "business partners" who all live in a *single* economic sphere.[86] This puts everyone in the same boat; each in his own way is part of an all-encompassing market continuum. But this rather totalizing diagnosis fails to recognize that there are still many people, especially artists, who explicitly refuse the role of business partner. It is also not true that all artistic milieus have been incorporated into the sphere of the commercial art market. There are still individual art scenes and entire geographic zones that can only dream of belonging to this commercial market. The role played by this market may even be considered secondary by those not operating within it, who might not want to have anything to do with it. But even here, whether in the form of negative distancing or positive longing, some relationship is established with events taking place inside the commercial sphere.[87]

In the past, the geographical center of commercial market activity was located primarily in the United States and Britain, mainly between the global financial centers of New York and London, although other cities, such as Hong Kong, also aspired to this role. According to *Newsweek*, however, recent years have seen a geographical shift in the location of the largest fortunes. Before the current market crisis, a city like Moscow was allegedly home to more billionaires than New York.[88] While people with money don't necessarily spend it on art, new types of collectors can be seen to emerge wherever excessive wealth is accumulated. But the most spectacular deals and the most exorbitant prices for art were still more likely to occur at auctions in New York and London; this is where the players with the largest fortunes operated, circulating financial volumes not seen in other regions (with no access to this market). In view of this centralization, sociologist Alain Quemin has gone so far as to dismiss as an "illusion"[89] the currently widespread notion that the art world is global, since beyond the biennial circuit, non-Western countries still play a comparatively marginal role. He also points out that artists as-

84 Lars Gertenbach, *Die Kultivierung des Marktes. Foucault und die Gouvernementalität des Neoliberalismus* (Berlin: Parodos Verlag, 2008), 19.

85 Ibid., 98.

86 Quoted from Chris Dercon, "Indiana Jones und die Ruine des Privatmuseums," *Süddeutsche Zeitung*, July 4, 2008.

87 See Okwui Enwezor, interview by Joachim Bessing, "The Only Thing Modernity Teaches Us: There Are No Innocents," *032c*, issue 15 (summer 2008): 138–141.

88 See Stefan Theil, "Special Report," *Newsweek*, special issue on "Unsinkable Luxury," (May / June 2008): 48–52.

89 Alain Quemin, "The Hierarchies of Countries in the Contemporary Art World and Market: An Empirical Survey of the Globalization of the Visual Arts," in *Österreichische Zeitschrift für Geschichtswissenschaften*, vol. 17, issues 2 and 3, eds. Alexander Mejstrik, Peter Melicher et al. (Innsbruck: 2006), 55–56.

piring to market success on the highest level are still best advised to settle in New York.[90] To these justified doubts concerning the current emphasis on globalization, it should be added that parallel to the geographical concentration of market activity in cities like New York and London, it is in the nature of this market to break down borders and to continually expand: most recently, Russia, the Arab Emirates, and, above all, China have been discussed as sources of fresh supplies, not only providing the market with new merchandise (which, in China's case, fetches high prices), but also offering a whole host of extremely wealthy potential buyers interested in luxury goods. For a long time, this never-ending stream of new buyer groups was cited as proof of the art world's immunity to crisis. It was wrongly assumed that supply and demand would be guaranteed in the long term.[91] That a global crisis necessarily impacts everyone, and especially newcomers, seemed barely conceivable.

What Kind of Market Is the Art Market?

So far, we have spoken of the market in familiar terms. But what do I mean when I say "market"? The more ubiquitous it becomes, the less clear its actual meaning. This diffuse impression is due not least to the fact that the market has long become what Nico Stehr has named a "political icon" of our time.[92] Regardless of whether it is trusted with establishing a "fair price" or whether its "invisible hand" (Adam Smith) is met with nothing but mistrust and resentment, the market is always treated as a phantasm, a surface for the projection of various fears and hopes, but also referring—and this is the concept's great potential—to actually-existing market conditions. This link to actual market activity is what renders the concept of the market indispensable, in spite of its vagueness.

Literature dealing specifically with the art market can be divided roughly into three genres: First, the kind of guidebooks of which many have appeared in recent years, promising orientation for young collectors with funds to invest;[93] second, large numbers of anecdote-rich and sensation-hungry investigations and reports, which lack any trace of a theoretical approach to the commodity in question;[94] and third, accounts self-published by associations of gallerists containing portraits of or interviews with market insiders, which lack critical distance and always adopt an apologetic tone.[95] Piroschka Dossi's *Hype* represents a blend of these genres. On the descriptive level, the book has much to offer, but anyone looking for a treatment of the problem of value will be disappointed (Dossi does remark that the value of an artwork stands on clay feet, but then fails to pursue the issue further). [96]

There is one point upon which the guidebooks, art-world detective stories, and eye-witness accounts all agree: that the art market knows only unwritten laws and is rife with murky goings-on. The picture of a close-knit, secretive community reluctant to reveal its practices is regularly evoked. The fact that price lists are rarely displayed in galleries or that auction houses keep the names of bidders secret is read as a sure sign of a "lack of transparency." This outsider's impression naturally contrasts with the view of the insider, who has experienced first-hand that nothing at all, and certainly not string-pulling or dodgy transactions, can be kept secret in the art world. What to the insider is an open book appears to the outsider as a book with seven seals.

Both views contain a grain of truth: that this market is a perfect example of an *informal economy*, which thrives on personal agreements, unwritten laws, and casual conversations. It is one thing to

90 Ibid., 55.
91 Thomas Crow, "Historical Returns," *Artforum* (April 2008): 286.
92 Nico Stehr, *Moral Markets: How Knowledge and Affluence Change Consumers and Producers* (Boulder: Paradigm, 2007), 81.
93 For example: Claudia Herstatt, *Fit für den Kunstmarkt* (Ostfildern: Hatje Cantz, 2007).
94 For example: Peter Watson, *From Manet to Manhattan: The Rise of the Modern Art Market* (New York: Random House, 1992).
95 For example: *Sediment. Mitteilungen zur Geschichte des Kunsthandels*, issue 6, (Cologne: 2006).
96 See Isabelle Graw, "Das Kunstwerk in Zeiten der Marktlogik," *Die Zeit*, July 26, 2007.

examine the concrete functioning of this informal economy,[97] but it is quite another to retreat to the convenient position that what we are facing here are shadowy dealings and a mafia-like state of affairs that cannot be illuminated in any case. Those who argue in this way allow themselves to be guided by insinuation and resentment.

Instead of declaring the players in the art market suspect as a rule, it makes more sense to analyze their rituals and language games, as well as their social customs.

But how should we imagine this market functions, especially compared to other markets? After sociologist Karin Knorr-Cetina, I suggest we refer to the art market, by analogy to the financial markets, as a "networking market."[98] On the basis of their relations to each other, the participants in such a networking market themselves define where the market is to be found. Sociologist Nico Stehr has also advocated such a model of the market as "sociocultural practice." (*Gemeinschaftshandeln*).[99] Consequently, the market is wherever a few market players stand together and communicate among themselves. It is the diverse relationships between those involved in this market that define its essence. Once again, communication proves itself the "queen of productive forces" (Virno), creating value and inscribing itself into the value of a product. Not only has the communicative process become a commodity, but the exchange value of an artwork actually depends on its becoming the subject of communication. Collector Harald Falckenberg has pointed to this major role of communication in the art market. In his collected writings, he notes on the subject of art fairs that people meet here above all "to bitch and to praise."[100] Excessive forms of communication are indeed what give the art fair experience its peculiar character: People always talk too much and speak to too many people, and in the course of this communicative overdrive it is easy to work oneself up to exaggerated hymns of praise or hysterical tirades of hate.

During a boom, the art market presents itself as a seller's market, a market where demand exceeds supply. The prolonged abundance of buyers in recent times is referred to in a laconic remark by New York gallerist Stefania Bortolami, quoted in a *New York Times* report about Chelsea as a growing gallery neighborhood: “There are always buyers. The competition in Chelsea is for artists.”[101] Then, it was a question not of wooing collectors, but of poaching artists from one another. Many middle-league gallerists could only look on as their commercially successful artists were lured away by more powerful empires like Gagosian. So does this mean that under the conditions of a seller’s market, young fine artists are always in a strong position because gallerists will be fighting over them? Far from it. On closer inspection, only a very few of the often-mentioned MFA graduates from Columbia University received offers from multiple gallerists before completing their studies.[102] Most of them stand to end up without gallery representation. This notwithstanding, one can say that the chances of gaining gallery representation were better in recent years than ever before.

Art and Its Markets

In comparison to other markets, the art market is obviously special, being defined as it is by the sale of *specific* goods. The distinctive quality of this market is thus founded on the specificity of its product

97 Sociologist Olav Velthuis thankfully attempted this and came to the conclusion that gossip, hearsay, and access to information are the key to survival in this market. See Olav Velthuis, *Talking Prices: Symbolic Meanings of Prices on the Market for Contemporary Art* (Princeton / Oxford: Princeton University Press, 2005), 40.

98 Karin Knorr-Cetina, “The Market,” in *Theory, Culture & Society*, vol. 23 (London / Thousand Oaks / New Delhi: SAGE, 2006), 551.

99 Nico Stehr, *Moral Markets: How Knowledge and Affluence Change Consumers and Producers* (op. cit.), 79.

100 Harald Falckenberg, *Aus dem Maschinenraum der Kunst. Aufzeichnungen eines Sammlers* (Hamburg: Philo & Philo Fine Arts, 2007), 97.

101 Randy Kennedy, “Chelsea: The Art and Commerce of One Hot Block,” *The New York Times*, online edition, http://www.nytimes.com/2006/11/03/arts/design/03chel.html, November 2, 2006.

102 See Lauren A.E. Schuker, “Art of the Deal: Finding Great Works,” *The Wall Street Journal*, July 27, 2007.

("art"). In the compound concept "art market," "art" and "market" are directly related to one another in a way that pushes the aspect of art's marketability into the foreground.

Even in the concept of "art" itself, the border between "art" and "market" begins to crumble, as "art" is an evaluative term that thus possesses an economic dimension. As a collective singular noun, the term rose to prominence in the eighteenth century, used to denote a *higher principle* shared by the various arts. The concept of art thus bore a heavy symbolic charge from the outset, and it remains over-determined by normative and idealistic notions of value. The decisive fact for us here, however, is that the descriptive and evaluative levels of the term "art" inevitably mix. As soon as I say the word "art" or declare something to be art, I evoke a category loaded with value judgments, at the same time as bestowing a seal of quality. And valuation is an essential feature of the economic. As a concept, then, "art" is *not* an economy-free zone. Consequently, the notion of art and economy as a pair of polar opposites is untenable.

The composite concept "art market" also leaves no doubt that art here remains tied to a specific context—that of the market—and must therefore be thought of *in market terms*.

Whereas any theoretical approach to the relation between art and market seems to require the use of a quasi-totalizing definition of "market," thinking in terms of a single art market makes no sense in empirical terms. I would suggest a basic distinction—between *the* market as a theoretical abstraction to which thinking about the "art-market relationship" must necessarily resort, and the empirical reality of different market segments.

From an empirical point of view, the art market is indeed a multi-dimensional market, composed of different sectors: the commercial art market, which is split into a primary market of artists, galleries, and collectors, and a secondary market of dealers and auction houses; the knowledge market, including conferences, art academies, and publications like this one; the market of institutions, dominated by museums and art societies; and the market of major exhibitions such as the Biennales, Manifestas, and Documentas. Each of these segments develops its own criteria and has its own set of evaluative standards. What is in demand in one market, at the Manifesta or Biennale for example—let's say, an aesthetic of critical documentation—may prove hard to sell in another segment of the commercial art market, such as the Art Basel fair. From the viewpoint of artistic production, too, it makes a huge difference whether one is operating in the knowledge market or whether one is trying to sell paintings directly through a gallery. This difference should not be underestimated: If, for example, an artist tries to build a subculture and finances this project by working in a library, his financial situation will be far more precarious than that of an artist selling his product. This is because the artist selling his product can hope for a direct payback, whereas the cultural producer accumulating cultural capital cannot be quite so sure whether he will ever market himself successfully.

However independently these different markets may exist side by side, however different the risks they imply, they increasingly overlap.[103] An example of such a merging of the commercial art market with the market of institutions and the market of knowledge was the 2006 Berlin Biennale. During the opening days, a young, international, theoretically informed biennial audience mingled with well-known American dealers (Jeffrey Deitch, Barbara Gladstone, et al.) and art agents (Yvonne Force). This may have been due to one of the curators, artist Maurizio Cattelan, who is especially skilled at transforming symbolic capital accumulated in the world of biennials into economic capital. But there are also cases of artworks, like the paintings of Anselm Reyle, which for a time circulated extremely successfully in one field—on the commercial art market—only to remain almost entirely invisible in the other (the market of knowledge). We are dealing here with two parallel universes that are capable of existing separately, alongside one another, while at the

103 See Rose-Maria Gropp, "Die Art Basel kann die bessere Biennale sein," *FAZ*, June 12, 2007.

same time increasingly experiencing crossovers.[104] This points to a fundamental paradox of the art market: While marketability and critique of the market, closeness to the market and detachment from the market, are not necessarily mutually exclusive, and in fact shape one another, they may also diverge. One thing is certain however: The commercial art market regularly, and with astonishing purposefulness steers a course toward those segments of the market associated with "knowledge," "market critique," or even "resistance." These segments in turn tend to view themselves as detached from the market, a view that is partly at odds with reality.

Place and Time of the Market, or: Welcome to the Office

What applies to markets in general also applies to the art market in particular: it requires a place and a time that facilitate and regulate exchange. The idea of place is already inscribed in the word itself, which derives etymologically from the Latin *mercatus* (trade, marketplace). And where there's place, there's also time. Although marketplaces may take on a virtual character, as seen in online art trading or the model of the itinerant art dealer (art agent), shop or gallery spaces have traditionally been preferred as locations for bringing together supply and demand. Here, merchandise can be inspected directly in its specific materiality.

In recent years, however, the lion's share of profits has been made at the ever increasing number of art fairs. From Dubai to Majorca to St. Moritz, every enclave of luxury seemed to want to raise its cultural profile with an art fair all its own.[105]

But what does it mean if a gallerist's core business shifts to these fairs that take place several times a year? For gallerists who must spend a large portion of their life in the glare of a fair booth, it means that market conditions increasingly define the ways they think and act. And further, it means that market requirements encroach on artistic production from the moment a work is conceived. Whereas in the 1990s it was still primarily a matter of making a lasting impression with a solo show at a gallery once a year, artists today are increasingly faced with demands from gallerists to deliver new work several times a year for the growing number of art fairs. Work is now more likely to be seen by international collectors at art fairs than in local gallery shows. As a result, then, market requirements are exerting more and more influence on the rhythm and orientation of artistic production.

Jack Bankowsky has gone so far as to identify "art-fair art" specially produced for such events as a new genre, covering a wide variety of practices from Tino Seghal to the Wrong Gallery.[106] All these practices, he writes, have in common the acknowledgement that the art fair is an inevitable part of their reality. But Bankowsky does not distinguish between different understandings of site- and context-specificity—and it does make a difference whether, like Tino Sehgal, one hires "baby dealers" to transfer the legacy of Andrea Fraser's analytical gallery performances into more harmless territory, or whether one adjusts one's own installation to the special conditions of the art fair booth, something now taken for granted in the aesthetics of production. Whereas in the early 1990s site-specific "interventions" still aimed to achieve socio-critical insight—concerning the background of a gallery, for instance—engagement with location now has the largely meaningless status of an artistic reflex. The key factor here is not *that* an artist engages with the conditions of the art fair, but *how* this engagement plays out.

Even in spatial terms, exhibition value and market value coincide in the art fair booth, which makes no distinction between sales and

104 On the increasing overlap between the Venice Biennale and Art Basel, see commentary by Rose–Maria Gropp, *FAZ*, June 9, 2007.

105 These fairs are now multiplying exponentially. No less than twenty small auxiliary fairs took place in the wake of the recent Art Basel Miami Beach. For cities with cultural aspirations, art fairs have proven to be ideal factors for attracting new businesses, as they signal connectedness with the present, progressiveness, openness, and cultivation, while at the same time bringing growth in high-end tourism.

106 Jack Bankowsky, "On Art Fair Art," *Artforum* (October 2005): 228–232.

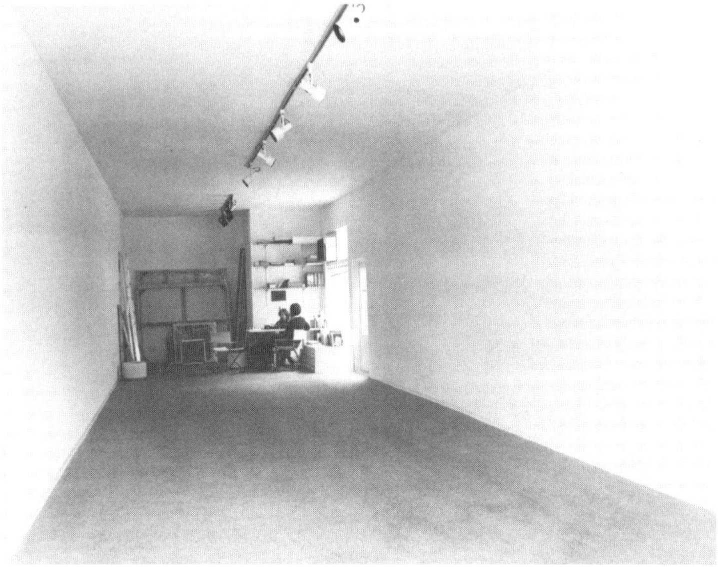

Michael Asher, installation view at Claire Copley Gallery, 1974

presentation space—unlike the classical gallery, which maintains a rigid spatial separation between the two, as Brian O'Doherty emphasizes in *Inside the White Cube*. The ideal gallery, he writes, "subtracts from the artwork all cues that interfere with the fact that it is 'art.'"[107]

Until well into the 1990s, architecture and interior design were used to create the impression that presentation was of primary importance, with sales as a secondary aspect banished to the back room. As well as the exhibition space, which has largely remained true to the aesthetic of the white cube, the average gallery also had separate office and conference rooms that were inaccessible to the public. In the 1970s, this demonstrative banishment of business from the exhibition space prompted Michael Asher and other practitioners of Institutional Critique to push this covert business dimension into the foreground. In his legendary exhibition at Claire Copley Gallery in 1974, Asher had the partition between office and exhibition space removed.[108] This opening literally laid bare the commercial activities that are normally hidden, but that here become the real content of the art.[109] On entering the gallery space, one immediately had a view of the commercial space. To the same extent as it works against the notion of "art in and of itself," however, it also elevates the location of economic distribution to the status of an artwork. From today's point of view, Asher's intervention is interesting insofar as it did not aim to symbolically abolish the gallery context. He viewed this context as an "essential" setting for the reception of his work.[110] In exemplary fashion, Asher's work highlights the economic structure in which it is embedded and the way this structure functions.

In the course of the 1990s, however, when the lessons of Institutional Critique were picked up and updated by many artists such as Fareed Armaly and Renée Green, galleries themselves began to take these lessons into account when designing their premises. In some cases, this went so far that Heimo Zobernig and Cosima von Bonin, both associated with "Context art," were commissioned to design the interiors of the galleries that represented them (Galerie Christian Nagel in Cologne and Berlin), giving their spaces a thoroughly programmatic quality. The reluctance to make communicative activities and business transactions public had given way to candid artistic interventions taking these working conditions as their theme—leading, incidentally, to an artistic ennoblement of these conditions. The best example of this is presented on the premises of the neugerriemschneider gallery in Berlin, whose interior features an almost seamless transition between exhibition and office spaces. Upon entering, one finds oneself in a generously proportioned office showcasing workplaces with their computers and staff members. A

107 Brian O'Doherty, *In The White Cube: The Ideology of the Gallery Space,* expanded edition (Berkeley: University of California Press, 1999), 14.
108 See Benjamin H.D. Buchloh (ed.), *Michael Asher: Writings 1973–1983 on Works 1969–1979*, (Halifax/Los Angeles: Press of the Nova Scotia College of Art and Design and the Museum of Contemporary Art Los Angeles, 1983), 95–100.
109 Ibid., 95: "The exhibition area walls seemed to vignette the office area and its activities and turn them into the content of the exhibition."
110 Ibid., 100: "I felt at the time and still feel that the gallery is one essential context for the cultural reception of my work."

large shared table is used to stage "transparency" and "teamwork," matching the latter's enhanced standing in society.

Offering visitors an insight into communicative processes is also a programmatic choice, however, insofar as artists associated with this gallery—including Rirkrit Tiravanija—tend to use communicative and interactive processes as artistic material. At times, this can give the impression that communication is a value in its own right, something to be approved of per se. This emphasis on communication for communication's sake corresponds to the increased importance of communication in the post-Fordist condition. Rather than being something exterior to the trade in commodities, communication has long since arrived at the center of production.

Other galleries, too, like Gagosian in New York and Contemporary Fine Arts in Berlin have recently made visible efforts to enhance their working conditions with expensive equipment and ever-greater numbers of staff, although the most important phone calls and the most crucial conversations are still conducted in separate rooms closed to the public. In spite of this, the era of the office separate from the white cube seems to have come to an end. Transparency is signaled with the welcome side-effect of breaking down the unapproachability of which galleries are often accused. Whereas in earlier years, gallery visitors felt intimidated or even repulsed by an atmosphere experienced as "stiff," "elitist," or "cold," visible desktops and a show of teamwork now suggest openness at the same time as confronting visitors with obvious signs of economic triumph.

The Anti-Commercial Pose

Although, as we have seen, the market is sometimes entrusted with the role of global art tribunal, the power of the market is not unbroken, as illustrated by the example of Anselm Reyle, whose works stopped selling when the crisis began. There comes a time when even the most commercially successful artist has to prop up his symbolic relevance, revealing a strangely tense relationship between "commercial success" and "symbolic relevance."

It comes as no surprise, then, that alongside the rhetoric of market apologists like Tobias Meyer, there has also been an increase in voices propagating detachment from the market. In one of many media appearances, the artistic director of Documenta 12, Roger M. Buergel, made a pathos-laden promise not to abandon "beauty" to "commerce."[111] In this way, as well as denying both the involvement in the market implied by his job and his personal membership in the market of institutions, he also wielded a fundamental concept of idealistic aesthetics ("beauty") against the market in such a way as to suggest that this concept (unlike the "evil" market) is totally above suspicion. Furthermore, declaring Documenta an event detached from the market is also a denial of its historical ties to the market. In retrospect, Documenta 2 (1959), for example, could be viewed as a trial run for the first "Kunstmarkt" fair in Cologne (1967). Hein Stünke, co-founder with Rudolf Zwirner of the "world's first fair for modern art," was permitted to operate a stand selling graphic art because there was no money left to pay his fee as a member of the Documenta committee.[112] It was here, Stünke claims, that he realized that art was a saleable commodity.[113] In other words, he recognized the huge commercial potential of contemporary art, which inspired the idea of an art fair. Documenta 2, then, saw the birth of the art fair format, meaning that historically, commercial interests were integrated into the prototype of the large-scale public exhibition from the outset. In spite of this, Documenta has managed to present itself as an authority with the right to make judgments largely independently of art-market hierarchies, and it has featured works by many artists of whom commercial market players are barely aware. But this does

111 See German *Vogue* (June 2007): 88.
112 See Claudia Herstatt, "Kommen, sehen, sofort kaufen," *Die Zeit* (May 19, 2005): 56.
113 See Günter Herzog, "Aus dem Himmel, auf den Markt. Die Entstehung der Kunstmesse und die 'Säkularisierung der modernen Kunst,'" in *Sediment. Mitteilungen zur Geschichte des Kunsthandels*, issue 6 (Cologne: 2003): 18.

not preclude participation at Documenta from being a green light for market success. After all, the event is among the most important consecrating authorities in the art world, capable of generating large amounts of symbolic capital. And this symbolic capital can (potentially, though not necessarily) transform itself into economic capital. Especially from a dealer's point of view, it acts as an engine of ennoblement, a provider of fresh supplies, and a promotion booth, even without making market success a foregone conclusion.

The relationship between Documenta as an institution and the commercial art market is clearly marked both by contradictions and discontinuities, and by a kind of inner bond ignored by the market-phobic position of its last artistic director.

Not only curators, but also commercially successful artists tend to banish the market to an imagined exterior. In the above-mentioned interview in *Der Spiegel*, for example, Andreas Gursky categorically refused to comment on the record prices fetched by his pictures at auction, politely asking the interviewer to understand that, "as an artist," he preferred to talk about "content." Privileging "content" in this way is nothing unusual and is widespread among art world players. With touching regularity, the call goes out for "more content," as if such content were a given and by definition positive, on account of its promise of "substance" and thus detachment from the market.[114] Apart from the questionable nature of such an essentialization of content, any privileging of content implies a dichotomy of form and content that goes against Adorno's dictum that aesthetic forms are sedimented content. Form and content cannot be played off against each other for the simple reason that they are interwoven.

In the course of the *Spiegel* interview, however, it becomes clear what Gursky means by "content," that is, his enthusiasm for the German Formula One race car driver and national celebrity Michael Schumacher. With a certain pride, he reveals that he now counts Schumacher among his friends and collectors.

Gursky's "no" to the market turns out to be a "yes" to a prominent place in celebrity culture, which is styled as the good "Other" to the bad art market. In truth, however, the laws of this new community (star principle, theatrical imperative, marketing of body and person, life as catwalk) have long since become part of the art world. Moreover, the traditional image of the artist—from da Vinci to Kippenberger—includes the notion, both mythical and biographically underpinned, that he gives his whole life to art. Art is his life. And like the inclination to legend-making in the art world, celebrity culture also tends to pick on individual subjects and style them as special beings.

As such, the widespread star cult can by no means be seen as a "better" alternative to an art world that is supposedly left behind by submerging oneself in the world of newspaper gossip columns and by developing an admiration, as many male artists do, for Kate Moss. Instead, celebrities present, in concentrated form, a set of requirements that previously applied specifically to artists, but that today all are expected to strive for: Everyone is meant to throw their body into the bargain, to take their entire life to market, to constantly work on their performance. With his fascination for Schumacher, Gursky has not escaped the market logic he would rather not discuss. On the contrary, the image of the Formula One driver captures the cliché of a tough contest in which there can only be one winner—an allegory for the sort of competitive environment also embodied by the art world.

This notwithstanding, Gursky's refusal to discuss his work purely in terms of price is also legitimate in the sense that, as he rightly insists, artistic and economic criteria are not identical. The only problem is that his justified rejection of the economic reductionism put forward by the *Spiegel* interviewers veers off, as so often, into a polarizing gesture that denies any link whatsoever between the "content" of art and events on the market, taking refuge in an imaginary alternative, in this case celebrity culture. While there is nothing fundamentally wrong with artists resisting the reduction of their

114 See Gerrit Gohlke, "Neuer Sendeplatz für eine alte Debatte?" www.artnet.com, May 29, 2008 (accessed May 20, 2008). He calls for the creation of the kinds of "content" that he considers worth fighting for.

work to market categories, this protest usually calls on a false art/market dualism: on the one hand the market, from which one should distance oneself as a matter of course, and on the other, its exact opposite, the "content" of art.

Polarization and Protest

An example of the tenacity of this polarizing approach to art and market is the open letter composed by Thomas Demand, Thomas Struth, Thomas Ruff, and Andreas Gursky in 2001 on the occasion of an auction of their works from the Grothe Collection.[115] In view of the fact that auctions now face no resistance at all, the mere existence of such a note of protest is enough to bring on a wave of nostalgia. Lamenting the growing power of auction houses may be considered good form among market players, but while complaining outwardly of their tightening grip on artists and galleries and their huge influence on prices, cooperation takes place behind the scenes. Most gallerists are also involved to some degree in selling works on, as dealers on the "secondary market." Such re-selling and deal-brokering is almost the only way to finance an exhibition program. Officially, the gallery sector is still skeptical of prices achieved at auction because they force galleries to correct prices upwards or downwards. Nevertheless, it is quite possible for a commercially successful artist today to be congratulated in the street by dealers or fellow artists on an outstanding auction result, as if he had just opened an exhibition to rave reviews in the press. The auction sphere has clearly lost its aura of enemy territory. Whereas in the 1990s, a dealer like Larry Gagosian was criticized for his aggressive market practices, today he is universally respected and admired.[116] Correspondingly, it is now inconceivable that artists might vehemently protest the sale of their work at auction.

The last time such a protest took place was the legendary 1973 Scull Collection auction of mainly Pop art in New York.[117] This auction prefigured speculative trading in contemporary art, clearly showing for the first time that this, too, was a field in which profits could be made. This set the ball rolling. Auction houses established separate departments for contemporary art, which accounted for the lion's share of their turnover. But the auction of the Scull Collection prompted artists' organizations like the Art Workers' Coalition to call for a protest, and many artists directly affected turned up for the demonstration.

The late Robert Rauschenberg is said to have carried a sign bearing the words "Scull's a pig."[118] In another version of the legend, he is supposed to have personally given Scull a beating.[119] Be that as it may, compared with this style of protest from the 1970s, which didn't stop at personal attack, the protest letter from Demand, Struth, and co. seems positively mild-mannered. The artists in question declared that they had only sold their works so cheaply to Hans Grothe because he promised not to sell them during his lifetime. A similar argument was used by the painter Sean Scully in 1989 against the auctioning of his pictures from the Saatchi Collection—he claimed to have given the works to Saatchi believing they would ultimately be bequeathed to the British nation.[120] Looking back, these artists appear to have been appealing to an ideal image of the collector motivated purely by philanthropy, a patron of the arts who of course never sells, trying instead to keep his collection together and eventually donate it to a museum. Even in the 1980s and 90s, this type of collector was rather uncommon. Today, it would be pure illusion to characterize the modern collector as free from speculative interest. And why shouldn't he be interested in converting parts of his collection back into money?

115 See Olav Velthuis, *Talking Prices* (op. cit.), 87–88.
116 On Gagosian as a figure subject to criticism, see ibid., 36–37.
117 See Bob Colacello, *Holy Terror: Andy Warhol Close Up* (New York: Harper Collins, 1990), 169.
118 Ibid.
119 Peter Watson, *From Manet to Manhattan* (op. cit.), 473.
120 Ibid., 492.

Even Reiner Speck, a German collector known for his love of art, recently parted with important works from his collection, handing them over to an auction house at an opportune moment. In the media, he presented this sale as a purifying act, thus playing down the fortune that this "restructuring" of his collection would bring him.[121] Even the most seemingly selfless donations and supposed permanent loans are now threatened by restrictive clauses, as shown by the case of Eli Broad, who converted large parts of his promised gift to the Los Angeles County Museum of Art (LACMA) into an independent foundation.[122] Another example is the donation of works to the Tate Gallery by former gallerist Anthony d'Offay, which on closer inspection turns out to be riddled with specific conditions.[123] The Tate Gallery must raise a certain sum of money and fulfill conditions concerning presentation—far from the selfless and unconditional gift it was described as in glowing media reports.

When, at the beginning of the new millennium, the signatories of the above-mentioned open letter evoked the ideal of the philanthropic collector who is reluctant to sell, they were ignoring a development that was already emerging at the time. It is true that collectors still become indignant when accused of commercial activities, preferring to emphasize their love of art.[124] But the motifs that underlie collecting must always be viewed as "hybrid" (Olav Velthuis). Alongside a love of art, which can hardly be denied, the collector is of course also interested in appreciation, prestige, belonging to a certain circle, sharing certain experiences promised by art as an "experience good," and so forth.

According to Nico Stehr, those who reduce the behavior of market agents to a desire for maximum profit are guilty of assuming that the players' motivations are static, an assumption typical of neoclassical economic theory. In reality, he points out, economic action is always accompanied by moral action—and moral considerations must indeed be involved when someone is ready to pay a price that cannot be justified in rational terms.

Was the open letter's insistence on the collector as patron perhaps a discursive stratagem? Were the signatories only referring to ideal conditions as a way of making the absence of such conditions all the more blindingly obvious? Where there is protest, there is also necessarily a certain degree of polarization and exaggeration. Thomas Demand then explained his fundamental aversion to auctions by saying that those present look at his work with "dollar signs in their eyes."[125] The problem he names here cannot be dismissed—at large auctions, artworks are subsumed under the names of their creators and immediately reduced to price. At this point, anything else that might be at stake in the work goes by the wayside. Naming the problem is one thing, but it is quite another to do so, once again, at the price of polarization between art and market. Demand indirectly declares his works as a zone actually detached from the market, which should be viewed on its own terms, that is, without "dollar signs in the eyes"—as if the relationship between art and market were a purely external one, as if the market had nothing to do with "true art."

121 See "Ein Gespräch mit dem Kölner Sammler Reiner Speck: Ich bin ein Regulator meiner Obsessionen," *FAZ,* April 4, 2008.
122 See Edward Wyatt, "An Art Donor Opts to Hold On to His Collection," *The New York Times*, August 1, 2008.
123 See Gina Thomas, "Ortstermin: Zum Tee bei dem Londoner Galeristen Anthony d'Offay, der Großbritannien seine Kunstsammlung überlässt. Jeglicher Besitz ist doch nur Leihgabe," *FAZ*, March 15, 2008.
124 For example, at the symposium "Private Goes Public. Privates Sammeln und Öffentlichkeit," at the Museum Moderner Kunst, Stiftung Ludwig, Vienna, October 8, 2005.
125 Olav Veltuis, *Talking Prices* (op. cit.), 88.

Chapter Two

Beyond the Dualistic Art / Market Model

When Commercial Success Isn't Everything: The Artist's Artist

The codependency between art and the market is matched in degree by a notorious need for distancing. The more outspokenly the market is condemned by its participants, the deeper the entanglement usually runs. Just as events on the market seem to constantly refute any talk of the freedom of art, it is precisely this "freedom" traditionally attributed to art by aesthetics that makes it so irresistible to market players. One might say that art and the market possess an intrinsic link that, at the same time, causes them to constantly pull away from one another. This chapter illustrates this dialectic interrelation and examines it in theoretical terms.

When the market is given increased authority in artistic matters, as in recent years, then this extreme situation has the advantage of bringing the art/market dialectic more clearly into view. After all, as Siegfried Kracauer observed, reality can only be revealed in extreme situations,[1] such as the art boom. Thus, it is particularly during boom times when one can observe how art and the market are fundamentally interrelated, but remain distinct from one another. It therefore makes sense to differentiate between them in some respects, while examining places of overlap. This means arguing on two fronts at the same time: against the false equation of commercial success with artistic relevance *and* against the idealistic belief in art as the market's Other.

Unlike most art history, which tends to be market-averse (commendable exceptions include books by Svetlana Alpers, Michael Baxandall, and Martin Warnke[2]), I do not view "art" and "market" as irreconcilable opposites. The line between the two has become highly permeable. We are dealing with a dynamic and conflict-rich

1 Siegfried Kracauer, *The Salaried Masses* (1930) (London: Verso, 1998), 25.

2 Martin Warnke, *Hofkünstler. Zur Vorgeschichte des modernen Künstlers* (Cologne: 1985); Svetlana Alpers, *Rembrandt als Unternehmer. Sein Atelier und der Markt* (Cologne: 1989); and Michael Baxandall, *Painting and Experience in Fifteenth-Century Italy* (op. cit.).

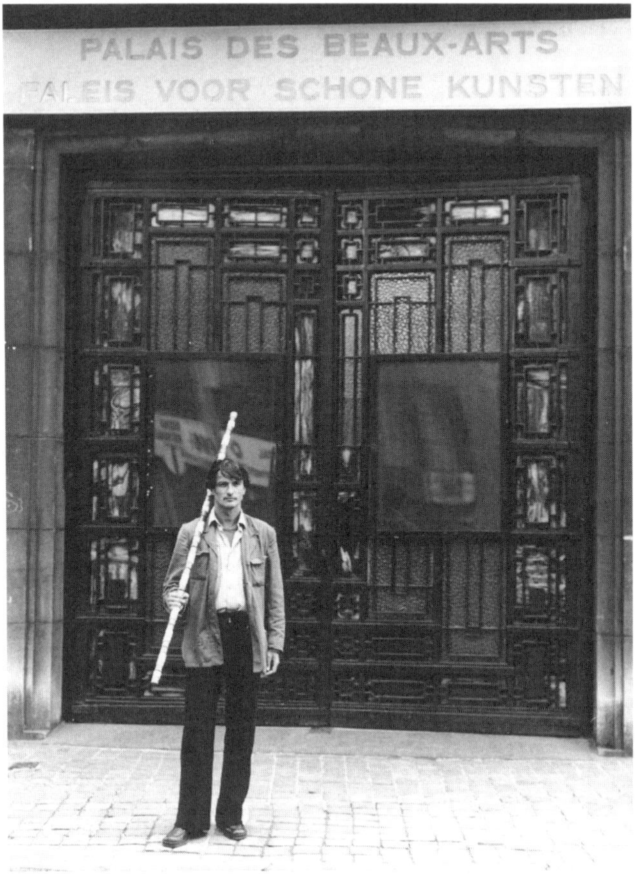

André Cadere in front of the Palais des Beaux-Arts, Brussels, September 1974

interrelation here that resembles a balance of power subject to constant renegotiation. Sometimes it is the market that dictates its conditions to art; at other times, artistic criteria win over those of the market.

The figure of the "artist's artist" stands as paradigmatic proof that commercial success is not everything. As the term suggests, the importance of such an artist derives solely from the recognition shown to him by his peer group. By definition, he sets no store in his artistic reputation paying off in his own lifetime. Any commercial success he enjoys will most likely be posthumous. This only inspires more admiration among younger artists and insiders, due not least to the fact that a dead artist's artist is a harmless competitor. This enthusiasm leads to an accumulation of the kind of symbolic capital so fittingly defined by Bourdieu as "credit and the capital of trust."[3] According to Bourdieu, this symbolic capital *can* be transformed into economic capital—but there is no guarantee that such a transformation will take place.

One reason typical artist's artists like André Cadere, Paul Thek, or Bas Jan Ader are so well suited to retrospective transfiguration is the emphasis in their work on the performative. Instead of making sure their products are marketable, they opt for a practice sustained by throwing themselves wholeheartedly into the work, which in turn charges their objects with performative energy. Cadere, for example, carried his wooden rods with him all the time, positively merging with them and taking every opportunity (often unauthorized) to deposit them in exhibitions.[4] His "legendary" presence has become retroactively inscribed in these objects so that they seem marked with existential risk. This privileging of a performative dimension is also found in the work of Ader and Thek. In all of these cases, the commodity character of the object is reduced in favor of the prospect of reification of the artist-subject.

For Cadere, the consequence was his cult status as a person coupled with the low market value of his rods. As we know from an interview, he knew perfectly well that these objects had little commercial potential.[5] It is this limited market value of the artist's artist's work—in spite of his great symbolic attractiveness—that makes his position, in the sense of the place he actually occupies within society, appear even more impractical today.

The groundwork for the current popularity of the artist's artist was laid during the late 1990s. Prompted by younger artists like Cosima

3 Pierre Bourdieu, "Symbolic Capital," in *Outline of a Theory of Practice* (op. cit.), 119.
4 See Isabelle Graw, "Marktforschung mit Hirtenstab," *taz*, February 12, 2008.
5 André Cadere, interview by Lynda Morris, March 1976, in *André Cadere: Peinture Sans Fin*, eds. Karola Grässlin, Astrid Ihle, and Fabrice Hergott (Cologne: Walther König, 2007), 18.

(quote): it was a congenial meeting & was only occasionally broken
by small farts - screw, the weekly sex review.

DIALOGUE PIECE (STARTED APRIL 21, 69)

CALL, WRITE OR SPEAK TO PEOPLE* YOU MIGHT NOT OTHERWISE SEE+ FOR THE SPECIFIC PURPOSE OF INVITING THEM TO YR LOFT FOR A DIALOGUE.°

IN PROCESS PERPETUALLY FROM DATE OF FIRST CALL (APRIL 21, 69). DATE OF FIRST INTEREST IN DIALOGUES - 1948. DATE OF DECISION TO PURSUE INVESTIGATION OF DIALOGUES - APRIL 8, 69.

NOTE: THE PURPOSE OF THIS PIECE IS TO HAVE DIALOGUES,»» NOT TO MAKE A PIECE. NO RECORDINGS OR NOTES ARE MADE DURING DIALOGUES, WHICH EXIST SOLELY FOR THEIR OWN SAKE AS JOYOUS SOCIAL OCCASIONS.°°

*the definition of "people" remains open. "perfect strangers," an animal, an infant will be included.
+due to general strike piece, which see(s).
°definition of "dialogue" remains open. "verball" is pertinent.
»»date of first dialogue - may 17, 69. number of dialogues enjoyed to current date - (13).
°°often giving occasion for pursuing investigation of information baths piece & pass-on-all-yr-ideas piece.

10

LEE LOZANO, JUNE 12, 69.

Lee Lozano, Dialogue Piece*, 1969*

von Bonin, Christopher Williams, and Mike Kelley, who referred demonstratively to their "discoveries" in their work, institutions also increasingly focused on these artist's artists. This is the fate of every artist's artist—to sow artistic seeds, which are later harvested by others, even if this takes the form of a homage to the originator, who thus retroactively benefits from the growing institutional recognition accorded to his younger advocates. But symbolic importance is also assured by (equally posthumous) theoretical analysis by critics and curators. Before lauding art institutions for their indispensable work of rediscovery, however, one should also recall that especially in times when market influence is strong, these institutions can only make an impact by devoting themselves to artists who would never appear in the rankings published by success-fixated art and lifestyle magazines.

One example of such successful revision that is not unrelated to the market is the recent "rediscovery" of Lee Lozano.[6] It demonstrates that knowledge produced by art institutions is often a motivating force within the sphere of the market. If critics and curators consider a particular artistic practice historically significant, the agents of the commercial market begin to pay attention, too. Finally, it was major-league gallery Hauser & Wirth that purchased the Lozano estate. Lozano's oeuvre has the distinction of including not only conceptual gestures that promise "negation," but also a body of (more marketable) paintings in which the radicalism of her "Language Pieces" resonates as a latent presence. Especially her *General Strike Piece* (1969) is still regularly interpreted as a radical rejection of the art world—a rejection seemingly reaffirmed by the biographical detail of her relocation to Texas in 1972, which was also read as a dropping out. In reality, things are more complicated. Alongside *General Strike Piece*, for which Lozano forbade herself, among other things, to attend "uptown gallery openings" in New York, she also produced *Dialogue Piece* (1969), whose instructions sought to establish contact with members of the art scene she "might not otherwise see." In Lozano's work, then, the fantasy of dropping out ran parallel to a slightly desperate-seeming effort to connect with key art-world players. But it is entirely in the interest of the market to style her as the ultimate artist of refusal—a refusal that, incidentally, takes material form in her "Language Pieces," and that therefore

6 In 1996, Lee Lozano was included in Ann Goldstein's "Reconsidering the Object of Art" at the MOCA, Los Angeles, followed by an exhibition in 1998 at the Wadsworth Atheneum in Hartford, CT.

doesn't disqualify it from a marketable commodity. Presumably on the assumption that the critical potential of *General Strike Piece* would automatically rub off on Lozano's tool paintings and tool drawings, the latter were shown—with no reference to the conceptual pieces made at the same time—at Documenta 12. The case of Lozano shows that not only symbolic but also economic capital can be made from the artist's artist, although in her case only posthumously.

But why is it that younger artists today barely consider the role of the artist's artist for themselves, and this despite the enthusiasm of institutions and among insiders? This trend is something I have observed in my capacity as a teacher at an art academy. Although students are fascinated by the model of the artist's artist, they themselves are more interested in striving for early market success. In the face of tighter economic constraints, the prospect of eking out an existence as an artist's artist no longer constitutes an attractive option. In addition, students are often confirmed in the belief that they must focus above all on marketing and professionalizing themselves by courses that attempt to provide them with personal market strategies. This increasing penetration of market constraints into art academies promotes isolation—instead of trying to gain the approval of a peer group, students tend to feel that they need to concentrate on looking after their own interests. This doesn't mean that art students have control over whether they end up in the position of the commercially successful artist or the artist's artist. Such positions are not the result of a willful act—they are attributed. Nonetheless, each individual artist does work toward his or her eventual position.

The decisive point here remains that the model of the artist's artist is the focus of boundless admiration at the same time as its attraction plummets due to the high cost of living in the world's art capitals. Today, few can afford to aim for (posthumous) recognition alone. Contenting oneself with the goodwill of esteemed colleagues is also especially difficult when the power of commercial success is manifesting itself so forcefully all around. Commercial success, it was whispered from all sides at the dawn of the new millennium, is key to the "good life." In this light, who would want to make do with purely symbolic recognition, or the acclaim of fellow artists? It would be better, instead, to ensure such recognition is transformed into economic capital *in one's own lifetime*.

Not only in practical terms, but especially under strained economic conditions, market success ranks above "mere" recognition. Even artists treated as artist's artists by those in the know during the 1980s and 90s—such as Michael Krebber—understandably have no objections if interest for their work now develops within certain segments of the market. Precisely because they have the reputation of being insider tips or underground figures, they arouse the interest of those segments of the market that value work that is complex and not hugely compatible with the demands of the commercial market. As a result of this heightened interest in figures formerly viewed as marginal, those once esteemed by insiders become figures everyone tends to agree upon.

This renewed enthusiasm for the work of typical artist's artists has not been limited to the knowledge-oriented segments of the commercial art market, however. Their stock has also risen in the market of institutions, as indicated by their many fans among those studying at art academies. But such tributes have not been translated into high auction prices. Often enough, the commercial market continues to ignore the artist's artist. This notwithstanding, the case of Lee Lozano shows how an artist's supposed distance from the market can be precisely what makes the market sit up and take note. But not every artistic offering deemed symbolically relevant by insiders is acknowledged by the market; some remain permanently on the periphery—further evidence that the dynamic interrelation between art and the market is more complex than the traditional art/market dualism would admit.

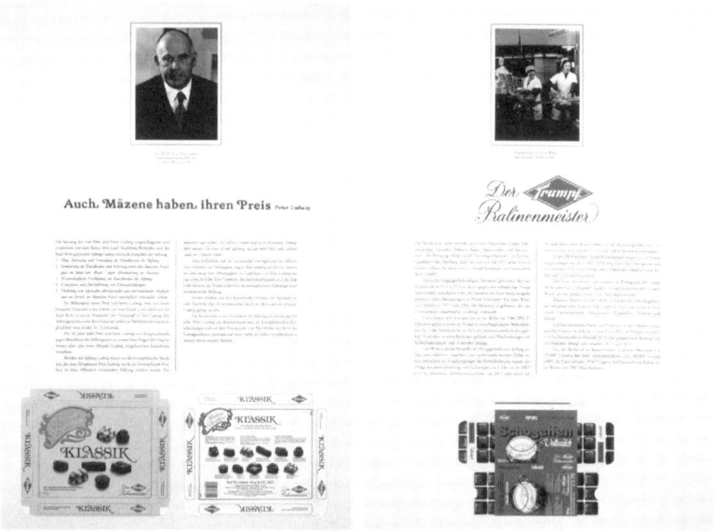

Hans Haacke, Der Pralinenmeister *(The chocolate master), 1981*

Art as Operation

"Everyone's just talking about money." – A.R. Penck (1989)

As part of the critique of modernism launched by Conceptual art in the 1960s and 70s and bolstered by poststructuralist art theory, the view became firmly established among progressive art historians that artworks must be understood as something that cannot be clearly demarcated and isolated. The interventionist practices of artists like Daniel Buren and Hans Haacke furthered the understanding of "art as operation," which originated in the 1920s with Russian Productivism.[7] The idea of a situational and interventionist aesthetic, dating back to the operative definition of art by an artist such as Sergei Tretyakov, was especially updated in the interventions of Buren and Haacke.[8] The key structural property of every operation is to be seen in its relational nature. Understood as operations, artworks must therefore be conceived of *in relation to* something. From this point of view, the dividing line between what "actually" constitutes an artwork and that which is seemingly external to it—contextual, historical, but also economic factors—has become fundamentally unstable. For art theory, this has far-reaching consequences. First, it has meant that since the 1960s, formal artistic decisions must always be located, that is, positioned with respect to historical, local, and economic conditions. And secondly, aspects apparently external to the work, such as institutional and economic conditions, must now always be included in the viewing of art, since they cannot in fact be external to it. If one wished, for example, to get to the core of a classic work of Institutional Critique by Michael Asher or Hans Haacke, one would arrive at institutional, architectural, or economic conditions that are not usually considered part of art, but which here are used as material in specific ways, and made to undergo specific aesthetic procedures. The converse also applies: What at first glance appears to be a purely formal detail with an exclusively immanent function in a picture that does not come across as interventionist—such as the muted color scheme of the early "Weltbilder" (World pictures) by painter A. R. Penck—proves on closer inspection to be an operation in which economic and social conditions resonate after all.

Penck's reduced color scheme was certainly dictated in part by the immanent needs of the picture—anything else would be economic determinism. But his restriction to four colors also reflects the artist's economic situation at the time. In an interview, Penck commented that living in the former East Germany in 1960s, he simply didn't have the means to afford a broader range of colors.[9] This biographical explanation, which seeks to emphasize the productive

7 See Daniel Buren, "Beware!," in *Theories and Documents of Contemporary Art: A Sourcebook of Artists' Writings,* eds. Kristine Stiles and Peter Howard Selz (Berkeley: University of California Press, 1996), 142: "Any production, any work of art, is social, has a political significance."

8 On the operative definition of art, see Devin Fore, "The Operative World in Soviet Factography," *October,* issue 118: 95–131.

9 A.R. Penck, interview by Wilfried Dickhof, *Kunst heute*, issue 6: 18. Penck said the following: "The painterly had no part to play here. I only had three colors, red, black and a bit of blue and a bit of white, four colors then. And that was what I had to work with. So the economy was a decisive contributing factor."

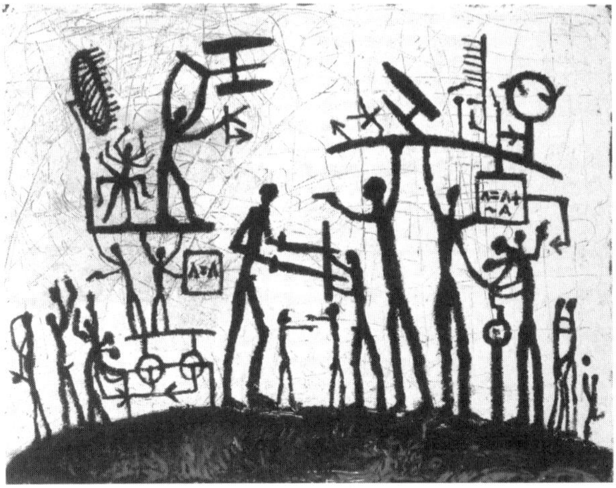

A.R. Penck, Weltbild 1 *(World picture 1), 1961*

influence of a planned economy marked by shortages, may be a case of retrospective truth-bending—it is possible that he had more colors at his disposal. But the crucial thing here is that a concrete (or fictitious) lack in Penck's work is transformed into an element of artistic style in which the specific economic conditions of a planned economy reverberate, but without being its sole *raison d'être* or providing an exhaustive explanation. To borrow a term from Walter Benjamin, one might say that the market based on a planned economy imprinted itself on Penck's early "Weltbilder" like a "hidden figure."[10] If one acknowledges such relations as *constitutive* of the artwork, then a different definition of art arises. The restrictive notion of "art in and of itself" must be abandoned in favor of a relational and operational definition. This kind of relationality, however, has nothing in common with Nicolas Bourriaud's much-discussed concept of "relational aesthetics." Instead of idealistically imagining art as a "state of encounter" that facilitates interaction and generates collectivity, it is a matter of abandoning the idea of art as a fixed variable.[11] Rather than forming the basis for relations, à la Bourriaud, art itself must be conceived of as a system of relations—a system of relations able to operatively negotiate the social and economic ties that constitute it, and to do so in a specifically artistic manner in each individual case. Use of the term "operation" can easily evoke an image of the artist as a "smooth operator" who leads the life of a cultural official. In the relational-operative definition of art, however, the operative aspect applies solely to the artwork itself. It has an inherently operative quality, but this does not diminish it to a function. The advantage of such a relational-operative definition of art is that artworks are not substantialized—no essence is ascribed to them, but they are also not reduced to mere economic (or communicative) functions.[12] Each individual artwork may be conceived of as a specific system of relations that are also capable of a wide range of connections. And the conditions to which they are related also include the conditions of the market.

It was art historian Michael Baxandall who envisioned a comparably relational understanding of artworks, and one that was neither deterministic nor reductionist. In his view, the paintings of the Renaissance were always ("among other things," as he specifically emphasizes) "fossils of economic life."[13] They should be imagined, in other words, as *traversed* by deposits of economic life, but not exhaustively characterized by them. Besides these and other deposits, they also contain many art-inherent peculiarities that cannot be reduced to external facts and conditions.

Must one then conclude that the artistic and the economic inevitably overlap in artworks, even if the two are not identical? Yes and no. First, as Penck's palette shows, the overlap is a matter of *isolated details*. Artworks are affected by economic conditions in certain ways, while remaining entirely autonomous in others. Just as they contain aspects that reflect the encroachment of the market, other aspects provide striking evidence of their specific and peculiar semantics. This paradox must be grappled with, especially under the conditions of an increasingly powerful art market.

10 Walter Benjamin, "On Some Motifs in Baudelaire," in *The Writer of Modern Life: Essays on Charles Baudelaire* (Cambridge: Harvard University Press, 2006), 180.

11 See Nicolas Bourriaud, *Relational Aesthetics* (Paris: les presses du réel, 2002), 18.

12 On the substantialization versus the functionalization of art, see also Helmut Draxler, "Die Substanz der Kunst," *Gefährliche Substanzen. Zum Verhältnis von Kritik und Kunst* (Berlin: Reihe Polypen 2007), 33–55.

13 Michael Baxandall, *Painting and Experience in Fifteenth-Century Italy* (1972) (op. cit.), 2.

Attempts to capture the radical specificity of an artwork, however, are best made on the basis of a recognition of the inherently porous divide between art and the market. Walter Benjamin, following Baudelaire, appealed for acknowledgement of the market as an "objective court of appeals."[14] In Benjamin's eyes, one of Baudelaire's strengths was to have "observed" the market without illusion from early on. The market is declared to be something that must be reckoned with and unavoidably *observed*. With this visual metaphor, however, Benjamin also brings in a certain degree of distance, as if it were possible to cast one's eyes over events on the market from some elevated vantage point, external to the artist. However topical Benjamin's appeal for market realism has proved, his demand for distance must be reviewed. Only by viewing the activities of the market soberly and *without considering oneself to be excluded* is it possible to establish a perspective that leaves behind the common (and false) alternative between market phobia and market euphoria.

Beyond Market Phobia and Market Euphoria

Diagnosing an increased influence of the market on artistic matters since the 1990s, sometimes coupled with the gestures of regret that have become common of late, clearly doesn't go far enough. However little I wish to voice a lament in the alarmist, time-honored tones of cultural criticism, I also have no desire to praise the triumphal progress of the market and the attendant expansion of its sphere of influence as guarantors of individual freedoms.[15] Whereas the market-phobic viewpoint tends to totalize the market and associate it only with evil, the market-euphoric viewpoint tends to simply deny the inequalities it produces, and thereby cement them. Notorious references to the healing powers of the market indeed ignore its structural violence, which usually lacks any justice concerning distribution; the brutal arbitrariness with which winners and losers are declared is played down; one is told, with a shrug of the shoulders, that it is simply the law of supply and demand at work.

However ruthless this market logic may be, it is also too easy to simply demonize it, to situate the market in some imaginary outside, or even style it as a totally evil Other. Instead, I would join sociologist Nico Stehr and appeal for the market to not be understood as a socially detached reality.[16] For we are all, in our own ways, linked to market conditions. But whereas Stehr tends to work with a concept of the market as uniform, it is important to emphasize the multi-faceted nature of the art market in particular. Even from an empirical standpoint, it makes more sense to differentiate between the art market's various segments.

It should by now have become clear that these various markets operate independently, while at the same time increasingly overlapping. Depending on the market segment, attitudes toward the market may be characterized by suspicion or enthusiasm. Whereas in large sections of the art world, a mood of reconciliation and de-stigmatization has been felt for quite some time, the economic crisis has naturally led to a growing number of gestures of rejection and lamentation over the market's speculative excesses. But these two tendencies—glorification and vilification—cannot be seen in isolation: they belong together. In a brief interview with German women's magazine *Amica*, gallerist Philomene Magers noted with regret that the emphasis in collecting today has shifted too far toward investment, and that everything is being sucked up as if by vacuum cleaners.[17] Of course, Magers's complaint, randomly chosen from many similar laments, may be an expression of genuine unease. And she is perfectly entitled to be worried about current developments. The problem is

14 Walter Benjamin, *The Writer of Modern Life: Essays on Charles Baudelaire* (op. cit.), 142.

15 See Peter Richter, "Wann platzt die Blase? Marktbereinigung: Auf der Biennale in Venedig kehrte die Kunst zum Kerngeschäft zurück," *Monopol* (April 2005): 20–21; and Niklas Maak, "Was Miami weiß," *FAZ*, October 31, 2006. On the subject of praising the market, see Rupert Walser / Bernhard Wittenbrink, *Ohne Auftrag. Zur Geschichte des Kunsthandels, Beispiel München.* In the preface, Siegfried Hummel claims that the "freedom of the market" guarantees "individual freedom." The author goes so far as to praise the art market as a "neutral mediator."

16 See Nico Stehr, *Moral Markets* (op. cit.), xii.

17 See *Amica* (May 2007): 156

the way she exempts herself from the development she incriminates, as if she weren't contributing to it, as if, as co-owner of Sprüth Magers, a large gallery with several branches, she didn't also profit from it. By regularly posing for lifestyle and fashion magazines, she also helped to promote the popular image of the art world as a place where money is just as much at home as connoisseurship, good taste, style, and fashionable self-presentation. And this is an image which has held a positively magical attraction for affluent young collectors in recent years.

But voicing such reservations with regard to those who collect for purely speculative reasons is also part of art trade etiquette. The art trade has a professional interest in preserving art's reputation as something very special, something that cannot be compared to stocks or shares. Mary Boone—one of the most successful gallerists of the early 1980s—was already complaining that more and more people only collected art because they hoped it would be a way to make a fast buck.[18] The more persuasively she is able to convince people that artworks are more than objects of speculation—which they really are—the greater the positive impact on her business, as a gallerist, will be. Those aspects of an artwork that cannot be reduced to marketing categories are the best argument for its marketability.

During the art boom, alongside this attitude of skepticism toward the market cultivated by successful market players in particular, voices expressing unbridled enthusiasm for the market also became louder. It was possible for a gallerist surrounded by friends at his own birthday party to announce that he *believed* in the market—not in art, as he might once have said, which would not have been any less of an ideological statement. Another open display of market euphoria was made in February 2008 by New York-based gallerist Leo König, a scion of the König dynasty. In a portrait in the German weekly newspaper *Die Zeit*, he spoke excitedly of a recent purchase of a Julian Schnabel painting whose potential for appreciation he considered a foregone conclusion—after all, Schnabel's latest film, *The Diving Bell and the Butterfly* (2007), had been nominated for an Oscar.[19] König's stated reason for optimism points to another crucial change. Whereas Andy Warhol found his reputation damaged by his rise to the status of notorious celebrity and his preference, especially during the 1970s, for frequenting a politically dubious international fashion jet set, today, glamorous contacts followed by Hollywood ennoblement no longer jeopardize artistic credibility. On the contrary—kudos from the cultural mainstream leaves the art milieu far from cold.

The Celebrity Artist as a Target for Hostility (Julian Schnabel)

In the 1980s, it was still possible for an artist like Julian Schnabel, pampered by the lifestyle press and blessed with record auction prices, to draw the anger and rejection of the entire progressive critical community. His pictures were dismissed as "reactionary" and "regressive." But Schnabel was also an ideal target because he stood for everything then considered worth fighting against: gestural painting coupled with an overconfident attitude, early commercial success, media hype, and celebrity posing. Even today, Schnabel is anathema to academic art historians. He is thought to epitomize the "eighties artist," a decade often totalizingly associated with the "art boom" and nothing else. In fact, commercial success was enjoyed only by very few, and by the end of the 1980s, the period of exploding prices for contemporary art was already coming to an end. A differentiated look at this period confirms once more the principle of the non-contemporaneity of the contemporaneous, as it is characterized by developments that move in different directions. The same is true of the reception of Schnabel's work, which has been anything but uniform. For in spite of his rapid rise to star status in the media

18 See Phoebe Hoban, *Basquiat: A Quick Killing in Art* (New York: Penguin, 1998), 191.
19 See Anita Blasberg, "Wir hier oben," *Die Zeit*, February 14, 2008.

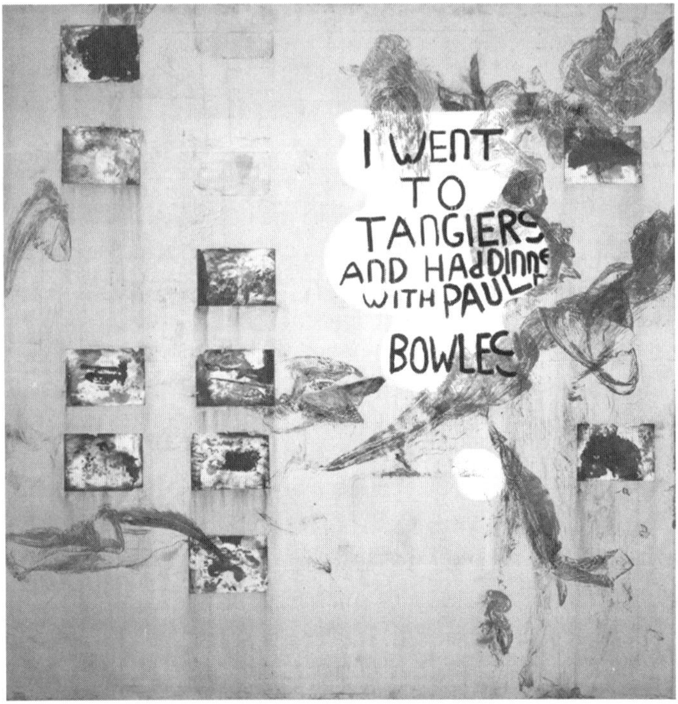

Julian Schnabel, I Went to Tangiers and Had Dinner with Paul Bowles, *1990*

and in the auction houses, progressive critics considered him the enemy incarnate. Although it was one of his "plate paintings" which in 1983 set the auction record thought to have triggered the 1980s boom,[20] Schnabel's name stood for the rise of the kind of "Neo-Expressionist" painting that progressive critics fought against so passionately because they viewed it as an attack on the conceptual practices they supported. The term "Neo-Expressionism" was used as a weapon in this fight, a pejorative label under which a wide range of painterly practices were subsumed in an unduly generalizing way. From Penck to Salle, from Oehlen to Chia and Clemente—all this was supposedly "Neo-Expressionism."[21]

But what offense was this "Neo-Expressionism" meant to have committed? It had returned to a unified artist-subject and the associated essentialization of painting.[22] Benjamin Buchloh argued, not unjustly, against the resurgence of the idea that "excited brushwork and heavy impasto paint application" should be seen as "painterly" or "expressive." And this although artists like Stella, Ryman, and Richter had proven that painted marks could not be transparent, and thus could not be unmediated expression.[23] What this justified criticism of the expressive paradigm overlooked, however, was that many of the artists considered part of this "movement" made just such a critique. In the early pictures of Schnabel, Kippenberger, and Oehlen, painterly codes are used for "authentic expression" in a way that undermines any hope of authenticity. When Schnabel and Oehlen applied smears, dripping, or violent gestures to their canvases, it was always a deliberate rhetoric. This approach can be characterized as "conceptual expression."[24] Rather than immediacy or authenticity, the emphasis here is on demonstrating that the seemingly authentic is in fact always based on an experimental setup. In this context, authenticity is highly contrived.

But Schnabel also caused lasting damage to his reputation by regularly posing in lifestyle magazines as a berserk renaissance man, stripped to the waist while painting.[25] Far from garnering respect, Schnabel's tendency toward media self-display, styling himself as a *plein-air* painter at his grand residence, reinforced his detractors' rejection of him.

Today, it is possible to laugh about such self-portrayals as amusing exaggerations of the cliché image of the artist-genius, but at the

20 See Phoebe Hoban, *Basquiat: A Quick Killing in Art* (op. cit.), 183.

21 See Benjamin H.D. Buchloh, "Figures of Authority, Ciphers of Regression: Notes on the Return of Representation in European Painting," in *Art After Modernism: Rethinking Representation,* ed. Brian Wallis (New York: Museum of Contemporary Art, 1984), 127. Buchloh speaks here of a "'movement' of neoexpressionism."

22 See Douglas Crimp, "The End of Painting," in *On The Museum's Ruins* (Cambridge: MIT Press, 1995), 84–106.

23 See ibid., 99.

24 On the notion of "conceptual expression," see also Isabelle Graw, "Conceptual Expression: On Conceptual Gestures in Allegedly Expressive Painting, Traces of Expression in Proto-Conceptual Works, and the Significance of Artistic Procedures," in *Art After Conceptual Art* (Cambridge/Vienna: MIT Press/Generali Foundation, 2006), 119–133.

25 On the cover of *Wolkenkratzer Art Journal*, eds. Roman Soukup and Lothar Krauss (Frankfurt am Main: October 1985), Schnabel is pictured wearing an undershirt and sunglasses with star-shaped lenses.

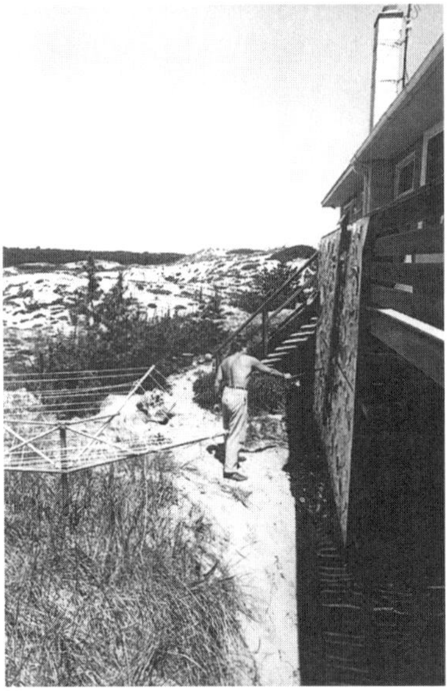

Julian Schnabel in Amagansett, N.Y., 1981

time, the conditions for such a humorous reception were nonexistent.[26] The main reason for the huge controversy surrounding Schnabel lies in the structure of the New York art world in the late 1970s and early 80s—two irreconcilable camps facing off, battling each other on the basis of clearly defined notions of who the enemy was. On one side were the advocates of the "Pictures Generation," influenced by poststructuralist theory and favoring media such as photography and video; and on the other, their ultimate bugbear, the Neo-Expressionist painters. Progressive critics were occupied primarily with denying the artistic legitimacy of the kind of painting that they believed was flooding the market. Another factor contributing to the escalation of this situation was the way Schnabel's supporters—curators associated with the "New Spirit in Painting," including Norman Rosenthal and Christos M. Joachimides—used a rhetoric as undifferentiated as it was reactionary, celebrating his paintings as a return to authentic expression or a farewell to Conceptual art, which they once again accused of being "overly-intellectual" or "austere," thus doing justice neither to its political significance within the art context nor to its aestheticized formal idiom, which undeniably appeals to the senses as well as the intellect.[27] Both Schnabel's opponents and his advocates, then, tended toward polemic shorthand, which is always the sign of an extremely polarized situation.

Since then, the polar structure of the art world has been replaced by a plural one. Whereas Bourdieu characterized the artistic field as a field of combat, defined by opposing poles of "traditionalists" and "avant-gardists," this warlike domination of the field by "the very struggle" can no longer be upheld.[28] Instead, the art world today presents itself to us as a "network world" (Boltanski/Chiapello) that has broken into different segments existing side by side in peaceful competition—a whole host of micro-universes illustrating the transition from antagonistic to pluralistic structure. As a result, no group is likely to feel vexed if artists belabor the expressive paradigm, or group together to form an all-male "Kommando Friedrich Hölderlin."[29]

And no one gets upset when an artist as omnipresent in the media as Jonathan Meese has another photo session or interview published in German gossip magazines, like *Bunte* or *Gala*. Working with the lifestyle and gossip press no longer necessarily represents a threat to one's artistic prestige. In the 1980s, the hostility between "high art" and mainstream culture, between specialist art publications and the tabloids, was far more pronounced.

One example of the relaxed approach now taken toward the lifestyle press is the day in 2007 that the now defunct German *Vanity Fair* summoned the Frankfurt art scene to a photo shoot, and everyone (me included) turned up on time, and perfectly styled.[30] All of

26 See Thomas Lawson, "Last Exit: Painting," in *Art After Modernism* (op. cit.), 153–164. Lawson criticizes the "pseudoexpressionists" for their "self-importance" and says they have no humor.

27 See Christos M. Joachimides, Norman Rosenthal, et al., "Preface," in *A New Spirit in Painting* (London: Royal Academy of Arts, 1981), 11; and Christos M. Joachimides, "A New Spirit in Painting," in ibid., 15.

28 Pierre Bourdieu, "The Market For Symbolic Goods," in *The Rule of Art: Genesis and Structure of the Literary Field* (op. cit.), 253.

29 See Isabelle Graw and André Rottmann, "Still gestanden," *Texte zur Kunst*, issue 66 (June 2007): 38–41.

30 See Sebastian Frenzel, "Sind im Bild," *Vanity Fair*, 25/2007: 107–119.

a sudden, everyone was available, as if fully booked schedules and difficulty in appointment-making had never existed. Whereas in the 1980s, cooperating with mass media was like playing with fire, many galleries now prioritize maintaining visibility in the tabloid press. What once was viewed as potentially damaging to business is now often equated with the hope for popularization and new clients.

In many respects, however, the 1980s can be viewed as a kind of trial run for the structural changes still taking place today. Galleries like Michael Werner and Mary Boone entered into early cooperative mergers, although only for short periods at a time. Auction houses began to manage themselves like credit institutions by offering guarantees. And the celebrity potential of artists was demonstrated once and for all by figures like Schnabel and Jean-Michel Basquiat, with prominent cover stories in *The New York Times Magazine*.[31] From then on, attention focused less on art itself and more on those who produced and sold it, and the image they projected in the media. Granted, Jackson Pollock had already excelled at this kind of image projection, of course, but the pressure to stage oneself in this way grew more pervasive, also affecting dealers. Mary Boone, for example, candidly compared her role with that of "the girl in the bathing suit standing in front of the car to sell the car."[32] She was clearly aware of the importance of her appearance, on which she seems to have worked hard. Despite her inadmissible equation of the artwork with a consumer item, she was perceptive of the metonymic relationship between her self-presentation and the product she was selling. If Boone herself looked sexy and stylish, it automatically rubbed off on the artwork she offered for sale.

Expanded Professional Profiles

The example of Mary Boone shows that the dividing line between art and the market has shifted and now runs through the people involved in this market. They now articulate this tension, upholding the idealistic belief in art as Other to the market, while at the same time trying to do justice to the commercial demands of this market in a pragmatic fashion. In the role of a dismayed idealist, Boone denounces the profit-striving among collectors, and in the role of a market expert, emphasizes the importance of her own appearance, knowing that it reflects back on the art she sells. This dual-track rhetoric translates the contradictory relationship between art and the market. Another symptom of how conflicting "art market" demands (stretching between the term's inscribed poles) influence the self-image of the individuals involved is the expansion of professional profiles since the 1990s. Jobs and fields of expertise that were once mutually exclusive in theoretical terms now overlap more and more, even becoming hopelessly mixed up with one another. In the past, this would have been called "accumulation of offices." Cultural commitment and economic interest join hands.

This kind of mix-up occurs, for example, when museum trustees try to influence the institution's acquisitions policy in such a way as to enhance the perceived value of works they themselves own. Another example is the now-pervasive figure of the "collector-dealer," who tends to claim the additional functions of a curator or publicist. He collects and deals in art, speculating on the appreciation of his purchases, which he buys at attractive prices, possibly splitting resulting resale profits with the gallerist.[33] Practices that in other fields would be denounced as criminal or insider-trading are commonplace in the art market. In 1984, Warhol commented dryly that "dealers put the stuff in [to auctions] and bid it up."[34] Further evidence of this trend is provided by campaigns of expansion on

31 See the cover of *The New York Times Magazine*, February 10, 1985.
32 Phoebe Hoban, *Basquiat: A Quick Killing in Art* (op. cit.), 232.
33 See Anthony Haden-Guest, "Drawing on a Noble Tradition," in *Financial Times*, August 18/19, 2007: "But Nyehaus also deals on the secondary market, and ambitiously"; see also Tim Nye (ed.), *Martin Kippenberger – Bermuda Triangle* (New York: Foundation 20 21, 2005).
34 Pat Hackett (ed.), *The Andy Warhol Diaries* (New York: Warner Books, 1989), 573.

the part of auction houses like Sotheby's, buying shares in private galleries to get closer to the "raw material."[35]

Every widening of a particular field of activity resonates not only with economic but also with symbolic interests. While the critic who also acts as a consultant is trying to secure his economic survival, the collector who also publishes catalogs is concerned, conversely, with distinguishing himself as an intellectual. When a collector like Harald Falckenberg buys a majority share in Merve, a small, prestigious publisher of theoretical works, it reflects his own fascination with art theory as well as his desire to be considered a thinker. Incidentally, no collector whose activities were purely speculative would be taken seriously in the long term. His seriousness is demonstrated by his activity as a publicist. Even New York-based collector-dealer Tim Nye, who collects art, deals in art, *and* runs his own exhibition space, produced an elaborately designed publication on Martin Kippenberger after purchasing many of his pictures from the Paris Bar in Berlin.[36] And Friedrich Christian Flick commissioned DuMont Buchverlag to produce a series of monographs on artists whose work he collects, helping to finance the project himself.[37] In this way, his collection, which is associated with tainted money (having been built up using funds derived indirectly from his grandfather's arms business where, during the Nazi period, 40 percent of the staff were forced laborers, prisoners of war, and concentration camp inmates) is ennobled by art history. The collector buys himself credibility by advancing into the realm of art theory and publishing. His desire for symbolic capital meets with the notoriously under-funded field of cultural production.

The final barrier between criticism and commerce seems to fall away when an art magazine such as *frieze* organizes an art fair. Under these conditions, it is no longer possible to clearly distinguish between institutional and commercial spheres. But this is precisely what is required here—an insistence on the separation between art criticism and art trade, on keeping their divergent interests apart. Although it is essential to break with the usual art/market dualism that declares art and market irreconcilable opposites, this does not mean that all attempts to establish their differences are illegitimate. In certain situations it may be absolutely necessary to do so, for example, when insisting on the ideal of independent criticism or when recalling the historic figure of the non-dealing collector as a patron of the arts. Precisely because economic interests and cultural capital are so closely interwoven in an expanded professional profile, the categorical differences that once made it necessary to keep them apart should be emphasized. Within such a profile, two value systems overlap—artistic and economic—which must be singled out and subjected to functional analysis on a case-by-case basis.

In this light, it is significant that no one thought to associate Lisa Dennison's move from the directorship of the Guggenheim in New York to Sotheby's with a loss of prestige.[38] Instead, it seemed to go without saying that she would not reject the auction house's lucrative job offer. No fear was expressed that it might damage her reputation as a serious art scholar—it was interpreted as a vital career move. Does this mean that transitions between the institutional and economic spheres have become so fluid that even the editor of an art magazine taking the position of manager of the Art Basel fair is interpreted as business as usual?[39] One reason such expanded spheres of activity meet with understanding is that all players seek to bridge the art / market divide. All are under pressure to "professionalize"

35 See Ulrich Clewing, "Wie sich Auktionshäuser in Galerien verwandeln," *Zeitmagazin Leben*, 31 / 2007: 45.

36 See Nicolás Guagnini, "Golden Spat: The primary Primary and the Secondary Tim Nye," *Texte zur Kunst*, issue 61 (March 2006): 124–127.

37 Including the first monograph in German on Rodney Graham: Dorothea Zwirner, *Rodney Graham* (Cologne: Friedrich Christian Flick Collection, 2004).

38 See Claudia Bodin, "Schwunghafter Wechsel. Nach insgesamt 29 Jahren am New Yorker Guggenheim Museum, die letzten zwei Jahre als Direktorin, wechselt Lisa Dennison zum Auktionshaus Sotheby's," *Art. Das Kunstmagazin*, August 1, 2007.

39 See Adriano Sack, "'Meine Sicht auf Kunst ändert sich täglich.' Cay Sophie Rabinowitz leitet ab Januar 2008 die Art Basel," *Welt am Sonntag*, June 17, 2007. In this article, no mention is made of the fact that Rabinowitz was editor of *Parkett* magazine before being appointed artistic director of the Art Basel fair. On her subsequent resignation from this post, see Ute Thon, "Cay Sophie Rabinowitz tritt zurück," *Art. Das Kunstmagazin*, April 30, 2008.

themselves, where "professional" means adjusting one's actions to economic requirements.

At this point, I should mention that I also have a broad professional profile, having worked as a freelance critic, salaried lecturer, and publisher of a magazine that produces and sells editions as a way to ensure its economic survival. Few figures in the art world are entirely free of such conflicting roles, although now these conflicts are hardly experienced as such. But it makes a difference whether one cultivates an awareness of these compromises in order to consciously set limits on them, or whether one simply neglects the problem, considering oneself separate from the conditions of market.

Multiple jobs always become a problem when the supposedly independent judgment of the critic is transformed into a sales argument from which the critic himself also profits. There are critics who simultaneously write about artists, run a gallery, and make art themselves. Their gallery business profits directly from the symbolic power of interpretation attributed to them elsewhere. I am not appealing here for a return to the rigid, classical division of labor—the problem is rather a lack of awareness, the absence of a self-reflexive analysis of functions. In fact, one could argue in favor of such an expanding professional profile in the direction of the critic-dealer, on the grounds that critics usually derive no benefit from the symbolic surplus value that they generate for artworks. Viewed like this, the fusion of critic and gallerist contains some poetic justice, with the critic siphoning off a share of the value to which he makes a considerable contribution, but for which he is usually insufficiently remunerated.

But what about the "critic-artist" who unites critical and artistic skills in a single person? Thanks to Conceptual art, the figure of the writing artist no longer arouses suspicion. Although, as Tom Holert recently pointed out, an artist who writes must still reckon with the charge of intellectualism, his expanded field of activity corresponds to a post-Fordist culture in which flexibility and mobility are writ large. Today, multitasking is a profile as identity-forming as it is market-compatible.[40] The artist who writes fully satisfies the prevailing demand for transdisciplinarity, while at the same time finding himself faced with the skepticism of a market that values clarity and definability above all else.

But every art boom is accompanied by a restructuring of the art system, reflected in expanded demands made on artists and in hybrid identities such as the artist/gallerist/curator/critic. Just as the Dutch artists of the late sixteenth and especially seventeenth centuries broadened the spectrum of their painting, committing themselves to interiors or still lifes, in the early twenty-first century, an expanded job profile for artists has now become the rule, bridging the gap between art and the market. They are now responsible not only for their work in the narrow sense, but also for the production of meaning, self-promotion, and marketing. In the wake of every new advance by the market, then, come expanded profiles and altered artistic identities.

Cooperate ’til You Drop

Expanded professional profiles also reflect the “networking imperative,” which obliges members of the art world to cooperate unceasingly. By operating in different roles, one stretches oneself in all directions, as it were, so as not to let even the slightest occasion for cooperation go unused. In a networked world, cooperation is the first duty of every citizen. According to Boltanski and Chiapello’s “network capitalism,” all individuals are dependent on one another.[41] Anyone who turns down an offer to cooperate, however compromising it might be, runs the risk of being branded a spoilsport. It is far better to take the opportunity presented by such a contact, especially considering its high value in a “connectionist world.”

40 Tom Holert, “Expansion of Praxis or the Ends of Writing,” *Texte zur Kunst*, issue 70 (May 2008): 60.

41 Luc Boltanski and Eve Chiapello, “The Formation of the Projective City,” in *The New Spirit of Capitalism* (New York / London: Verso, 2005), 103–163.

But the pronounced tradition of cooperation in the field of art is also directly linked to the precarious nature of value. Artworks are not valuable "in themselves" or "per se." According to Marx, the value of one thing is expressed in another. While value is attached to products resulting from concrete and useful labor, this labor becomes irrelevant as soon as the product is exchanged. It is because of the specificity of value as an "equivalent form" (Marx) that it can transform "concrete and useful labor" into its opposite—"abstract human labor." From this it follows that value is an abstraction, disconnected from intensity or duration of labor. Due to this lack of rootedness, value is the result of a permanent process of negotiation that never comes to a conclusion. Applied to the issue of cooperation, the quality of value as a "social relation" (Marx)[42] means that for value to be created, a considerable level of interaction must first take place—without cooperation, no value. In this light, the constant networking typical of the art world can be understood as both an expression and a consequence of the relational character of value. Precisely because the value of an artwork stands on clay feet, it must be the subject of endless communication. But this is also what makes it so susceptible to economic fluctuations. If the question of value on the art market is governed by "maximum insecurity," then this is directly linked to the fact that value is always located elsewhere, making it subject to agreement by necessity. But value is also threatened, because of its essential lack of foundation. Moreover, the process of value creation never achieves closure, and in order to get a sense of the current state of this process, one must gain access to the valuations of others. It is precisely because value is not where one expects it to be, that the need to find out about its current status grows. It is thus the fundamentally metonymic quality of value that drives the desire to network, just as, conversely, interaction and communication make a vital contribution to value creation.

Cooperation is overemphasized in a networked world, while the especially pronounced "cooperation imperative" in the art world is also directly connected to its segmented, plural character. If the artistic field no longer defines itself in terms of camps and rivalries, there is also no reason to refuse to cooperate with anyone. In the absence of clearly defined opponents, going about it alone or abusing others in public makes no sense. As a result, few are prepared to write a well-founded negative review, as I know from my work as an editor. People are unwilling to make unnecessary enemies, especially as their support might one day be needed. Today's rival could be tomorrow's crucial cooperative partner. For this reason, hardly anyone today fights out in the open. It is inconceivable for artists to tear each other down in public—a form of behavior that was part of the standard repertoire of every avant-garde from Dada to Situationism. While I do not argue for a nostalgic return to these brutal struggles, I nevertheless consider it telling that, if there is criticism today, it is made quietly or pseudonymously.

From this point of view, the segmentation of the artistic field is the other side of the obligation to cooperate. Geographical separation is cultivated to avoid stepping on one another's toes. A city like Berlin provides a good illustration of this tendency: Every new gallery that opens seems to be at pains to establish itself with a few others in a location as far off the beaten track as possible.[43] What happens in one such gallery cluster is not experienced by other galleries as a threat to their artistic identity, even if in theory it does call this identity into question. Instead, each gallery develops its own social context that has few points of contact with other scenes, like so many micro-universes. In such a situation, competition is not abolished, it is just more likely to take place covertly. Just as every gallery has its own social milieu, the constraints of a globalized market have caused galleries to rely on international partners for cooperation. Artists are exchanged, the world is carved up into geographical zones for representation, booths at trade fairs may be shared, and joint branches

42 Ibid.
43 Galerie Baudach moved to Berlin's Wedding district; Galerie Giti Nourbakhsch opened a space in Schöneberg; Johann König at Potsdamer Platz, etc.

are opened—in recent times most often in Berlin. In such a strongly networked world, anyone who understands himself as a lone wolf is lost. Ultimately, however, the pressure to cooperate has paradoxically also pushed people apart. They don't want to spoil their relations, as one day globalized markets may make it necessary to share a branch with those potential rivals with whom one has made it a point of coexisting peacefully for years.

Why Did Art Become So Popular?

In the late 1990s, as an art critic one still had to face accusations that the art world was an elitist crowd, not very accessible, with openings especially offering repulsive examples of rigid hierarchies and perfidious methods of exclusion. In the years 2004–2008, on the other hand, one could hardly open any German lifestyle or fashion magazine (*Amica*, *Bunte*, *Vanity Fair*) without seeing multi-page reports about art fairs, opening night parties, and portraits of commercially successful artists.[44] Never before had the principle of "contemporary art" enjoyed such popularity,[45] a principle that amalgamates notions of novelty and zeitgeist with expectations of timelessness and immortality.

But how exactly can one explain the increased focus of media enthusiasm on social events in the art world? Was it only the news of auction records being broken again and again that drove up the art world's stock in the eyes of the media? In the case of this phenomenon, such economistic explanations are too simple. To begin with, it is important to mention that only certain celebrity-compatible players were featured on this level—the usual suspects included Jay Jopling, Thaddaeus Ropac, and "celebrity artists" like Rachel Feinstein and Sam Taylor-Wood, who appeared in the party pages of German women's magazine *Bunte* and British and American *Vogue,* and who also seemed to have actively promoted their presence on this level.

But sensational auction records alone cannot explain the cross-media enthusiasm for contemporary art. Some new element must have been added for supposedly more "high-brow" outlets like *Der Spiegel* to obligingly seek out a rich Russian oligarch collector, or to publish a report on the decline of the Venice Biennale to a fashion and party zone —a development of course mourned in the classic tone of cultural criticism, while at the same time being furthered by the article itself.[46] And in the weeks leading up to Documenta 12, the arts and culture editors of Germany's major broadsheets *Frankfurter Allgemeine Zeitung* and *Süddeutsche Zeitung* tried to outdo each other in being the first to publish fresh installation views. The number of pages devoted exclusively to reporting on this one large-scale exhibition went far beyond anything before seen.[47]

Initially, this popularity of fine art in the media was based on the assumption by publishers that it was a popular subject. The huge increases in visitor numbers (achieved, incidentally, only by blockbuster exhibitions) were taken as a sign of increased cultural significance. Once again, symbolic authority had been attributed to economic data—as if to say: the figures speak for themselves. But this still doesn't explain the curious fact that media interest focused primarily on the *social dimension* of this world. For the kind of personality-oriented reporting that forms the staple diet of lifestyle

44 Since the emphasis has shifted to the crisis of the art market, there has been a marked decrease in reporting on art-world social events in the lifestyle press.

45 See commentary by Rose-Maria Gropp, "Die große Kunsttour," *FAZ*, June 1, 2007.

46 See Ulrike Knöffel, "Club der Königinnen," *Der Spiegel*, 10/2008: 192–195; and Ulrike Knöffel, "Die große Modenschau," *Der Spiegel*, 24/2007: 164.

47 See "Wenn die Documenta fertig ist, ist sie tot. Mit dem Knüppel auf die Birne? Auf der Documenta soll Komplexität massenkompatibel serviert werden. Die Kuratoren Ruth Noack und Roger M. Buergel gewähren erstmals gemeinsam Einblicke in Details der Kasseler Weltkunstschau." Interview by Holger Liebs, *Süddeutsche Zeitung*, June 15, 2007; "Das war die Documenta – Eine kurze Geschichte der Kasseler Ausstellung," *FAZ*, June 9, 2007; ibid., "Was so in Kassel alles zu sehen ist"; ibid., "Ruth Noack, Kuratorin der documenta 12"; ibid., Niklas Maak, "So wird die documenta – Ein Kurzführer"; Christian Demand, "Der Wille zum Vagen. Je mehr man hört, desto weniger weiß man, worum es geht – Was will Documenta-Chef Roger M.Buergel?," *FAZ*, June 10, 2007; and Thomas Wagner, "Angriff auf die Zeit. Nun wird es ernst: Wagt die documenta 12 einen neuen Blick auf unsere Gegenwart?," *FAZ*, June 13, 2007.

and fashion magazines has long since expanded beyond its native terrain into the specialist art press.

With its much-visited gossip website "Scene and Herd," American art magazine *Artforum* assured itself a permanent place in the talk of the town—an ingenious piece of marketing. In these gossip-oriented reports on fairs and exhibitions, artworks naturally don't receive adequate treatment even on the level of description, as interest is focused on the names and looks of the people in the pictures. These reports reveal not only who was where, but also who was considered worthy of being photographed. And who willingly posed for the site in return for such recognition—after all, anyone could refuse their presence on this level, although this opportunity is only taken by a very few.

When art is reported on in this way, the people involved take center stage, while the artworks act merely as negligible pretexts. At the same time, these people become object-like, acting as advertisements for themselves. Countless pictures of artists posing and flaunting themselves to the market recall the observation by Boltanski and Chiapello that "human persons as such" are now being engaged "more deeply than before in the profit dynamic."[48]

In my view, however, the main reason for the strong interest in the art world shown in recent years by fashion and lifestyle magazines in particular lies in the many "attractive modes of inclusion" (Urs Staehli) it offered. Parties, dinner invitations, drinks and excess, fashionable scenes, eccentric characters, but also cultivation and connoisseurship, all contributed to the image of an attractive milieu that offered the additional promise or prospect of inclusion. As if it were possible for anyone to participate here and experience something out of the ordinary. The enthusiasm of journalists often seemed to know no bounds and some even claimed that "a Friday-night marathon tour of exhibition openings in Berlin" was about the most interesting thing that could happen to a person.[49] This is where "glamour" is to be found in large amounts, with glamour figuring once again as the ultimate empty formula for all that is desirable.

No mention here of how tedious and depressing such openings can be, or of the sometimes underwhelming quality of the work on view. According to the version presented to readers of magazines like *Glamour* and *Amica,* by simply flying to the Art Basel Miami Beach fair they could become part of an international jet set living the high life and partying the nights away.

What this promise of inclusion failed to address was the very real exclusion mechanisms at work in this milieu. Like any other, the art system regulates itself by means of both inclusion *and* exclusion.

But it would be wrong to essentialize this exclusive side, as if exclusion were an intrinsic, irrevocable fact, along the lines of "once excluded, forever excluded." The many mythical accounts of unexpected ascendancy and sudden acceptance so eagerly circulated by the media are meant to prove again and again that this milieu has a high degree of mobility and fluctuation. But there is a grain of truth to these myths, if one thinks of the meteoric careers observed especially in Berlin in the wake of German reunification—in the case of Klaus Biesenbach, from art-loving amateur to curator of MOMA.[50] Clearly the tide can turn even for those who were once considered hopelessly excluded.

This opening up of the museum sector to staff from non-typical backgrounds was due in part to a liberalization of previously more rigid career structures. This reflected new economic requirements, calling above all for entrepreneurial skills. But the media image of the art world as one big career-boosting, integration-driving, quick-buck-making machine was also related to the fact that people are not usually interested in stories of exclusion, marginalization, and lack of success. Failure does not make good copy. Whereas unsuccessful artists arouse little interest and remain underrepresented, success is extraordinarily present in the media. But this also means that our

48 Luc Boltanski and Eve Chiapello, *The New Spirit of Capitalism* (op. cit.), 464.
49 See comment by Peter Richter and Claudius Seidl, *FAZ,* June 10, 2007.
50 See Anja Lösel, "Unser Mann in New York," *Stern*, January 16, 2007.

idea of success is always media-defined: we know success only in the sense of what is represented as successful in the media.

The Artist as a Prototype of the Entrepreneurial Self

One reason for the particular fascination exerted on the media by the commercially successful artist was the fact that he not only possessed the mythical power of money, but also corresponded to the no less mythical image of the "free artist." In this doubly mysterious light, he represents someone capable not only of working in a self-determined, creative way, but of living in prosperity at the same time. Two societal norms enter into an irresistible combination here: just as success is one of today's "modern duties" (Neckel), creativity has taken the position of a "salvatory concept of the present" (Bröckling). The commercially successful artist perfectly fulfills both requirements—he has money, the "omnipotent being" (Marx) whose magic powers are usually attributed to its owner,[51] and also embodies the prototype of the "creative worker" so coveted on the employment market today, especially in the service sector.

The times when artistic production offered a counter-image to the world of labor seem to be well and truly over. Today, it is impressed upon every service-sector employee that he or she must display initiative and creativity. Correspondingly, sociologist Pierre-Michel Menger has shown that the "central values of artistic competence," such as (supposedly) responsible or self-determined action, have long since been transferred to other fields of production.[52] As the description of a trend, this is surely accurate. But even if the ideal of the creative worker prevails in the service sector, this should not cause us to forget the countless employees still in dependent situations who experience their work as extremely heteronomous, repressive, and regimented. The deregulated working life of the artist—which comes, it should be remembered, at the price of maximum insecurity—is still far removed from the reality of those employed in the cheap-labor sector. Here too, then, the non-contemporaneity of the contemporaneous. But Menger is right insofar as the image of the innovative and original artist really was the blueprint for the "entrepreneurial self" (Bröckling) that is now ubiquitous in the creative industries and the service sector. A set of requirements that formerly applied exclusively to artists has advanced to the status of a general ideal: everyone is supposed to be as flexible and creative as possible, to work on their own initiative, and to have a high degree of mobility. The more deregulated conditions become, the more likely it is that the artist will become a model, epitomizing as he does the "creative nonconformist" everyone now wants to be.[53]

The artist's rise to the status of a prototype for the ideal creative worker, whose origin can be traced back to the reception of Rubens or Rembrandt, thus forms the blueprint for the generalization of such an artistic self-image. These two developments reinforce each other and help explain the increased media interest in the commercially successful artist. Because the profile of the artist brings together generally required characteristics, he becomes a point of reference at the moment when the ideology of creativity is dominant across many fields. This "self-determined" artist is the norm that inspires the model of the creative worker.

Does this mean, by implication, that the call for self-determination typical not only of artistic avant-gardes, but also of social movements, has now been wholly absorbed, made useful, and thus neutralized by the market? This transformation of an emancipatory ideal into an entrepreneurial one has been analyzed by Boltanski and Chiapello, who consider that the key demands for emancipation formulated during the 1960s have been co-opted by capitalism.[54] In

51 See Karl Marx and Friedrich Engels, "The Power of Money," in *The Marx-Engels Reader* (New York: Norton, 1978), 103: "The extent of the power of money is the extent of my power."

52 Pierre-Michel Menger, *Portrait de l'artiste en travailleur: Métamorphoses du capitalisme* (Paris: Seuil, 2003).

53 See Ulrich Bröckling, *Das unternehmerische Selbst. Soziologie einer Subjektivierungsform* (Frankfurt: Suhrkamp, 2007), 124.

54 Luc Boltanski and Eve Chiapello, *The New Spirit of Capitalism* (op. cit.), 425.

the new spirit of capitalism, they write, the demand for autonomy and self-determination is fulfilled, but in the sense of a new set of requirements. From this point of view, capitalism is a perfidious machine that co-opts everything and is capable of totally absorbing even the most extreme emancipatory endeavors and the most eccentric characters. What their rather schematic account overlooks, however, is the reactive potential of the artist, who is quite capable of evading the current emphasis on creativity and resisting the paradigm of self-realization. Furthermore, the emancipatory movements made lasting achievements that should not be underestimated. However perfidious the norm of self-determined creative work may be, it is still preferable to the merciless rhythm of punching a clock. Despite deeper involvement of the human person in the profit dynamic, the new spirit of capitalism might still be considered better than the old one. Ubiquitous calls to "take responsibility for oneself" may ultimately mean that the individual, like the free artist, must make do without social security, even being made liable for structural problems with which it actually burdens itself. But a return to alienated working conditions and the command of the boss do not seem to be a desirable alternative. Perhaps self-exploitation is the lesser evil after all.

The art world also attracts projections on account of its correspondence to the ideal of a "society of pure competition," like something dreamed up by a neoliberal. Few other sections of society display such a pronounced inequality of distribution. In this winners-take-all market, the gulf between commercially successful and unsuccessful artists is extreme, reflecting today's concentration of wealth in the hands of the few superrich.[55] As well as its tradition of wildly divergent incomes, the art world can also be seen as a model in its apparent anticipation of neoliberal calls for a "dismantling of the welfare state." For the art world officially knows no safety nets for catching any artist defeated by the imperative of commercial success (except perhaps Germany's *Künstlersozialkasse*, an insurance plan for artists covering the share of health and pension contributions that employers pay for their employees, and that non-artist freelancers must pay for themselves). It is only unofficial niche economies that enable less successful artists to secure their livelihood as studio staff, technicians, artistic assistants, and so forth. During the latest art boom, there was a noticeable growth in these niche economies, employing and supporting more and more people. Whereas it was customary in this field to arrange jobs for each other and practice solidarity, commercially successful artists were naturally forced to be increasingly competitive.

All of these factors taken together (attractive modes of inclusion, tough competition, the artist as a prototype for the entrepreneurial self and epitome of the creative nonconformist) were responsible for the art world's becoming such a rich source of material for success-fixated media (especially German *Vanity Fair*), which sought to position themselves on the side of the "movers and shakers"—meaning those who take risks without state support and who "make things happen," and meaning, above all, artists. In the mythical form of the successful artist as a radically individualized, exceptional being, the neoliberal mandate for people to please take responsibility for themselves has found a perfect model. In view of the most recent developments, it should be added that when the ostentatiousness of art-world social life fails to take place (be it for lack of money or because of a general mood of crisis that decries wasteful behavior as obscene), then media interest also dwindles.[56] Times of crisis typically breed a mood that is generally hostile to the market. But this doesn't affect the recognized validity of the neoliberal system. It is true that during the banking and economic crisis, even the most convinced proponents of a market economy expressed doubts in the

55 See Stefan Theil, "Special Report," *Newsweek*, special issue on "Unsinkable Luxury" (May / June 2008): 48–52: "Indeed, top-end luxury consumers seem almost invigorated by the rest of the world's economic woes."

56 See Isabelle Graw, interview by Brigitte Werneburg, "Fluchtpunkt aller möglichen Interessen," *taz*, February 7 / 8, 2009: Werneburg: "Since the autumn auctions proved to be an economic disaster, reporting on fine art in the lifestyle press has completely collapsed."

blessings of the market.[57] But the call for state regulation and the massive state interventions of current times do not represent a break with neoliberalism, even if this has often been claimed. If neoliberalism is understood less in terms of the radicalization of an unbridled market, and more in terms of the state caring for and cultivating the market, then state intervention can be seen as a genuinely neoliberal politics.[58] The state, one might say, creates the best possible conditions for a return to the "natural" course of market activity. As such, the genuinely neoliberal side only manifests itself in the way the state deals with the crisis. The fact that belief in the market is capable of surviving even the near collapse of that market is illustrated by a comment by Tobias Meyer, who explained away the 30-percent drop in prices at the fall 2008 auctions by simply stating that the market had "regulated" itself.[59] This notion of "poetic justice" operating in the market is widespread. People paint the crisis in pretty colors and rejoice that it will separate the wheat from the chaff at last. No need to worry, the market will take care of things—once again, this notion of self-regulation reproduces a belief in the market as a natural corrective. In truth, there is no such poetic justice in the market, which proceeds arbitrarily as a matter of principle. Although some of what was hyped during the boom may lose some credibility during the downturn, every economic crisis always also claims innocent victims. And in hindsight, the boom did have a good side, as the cake that was being divided up was large enough to spare a few crumbs even for those operating at the fringes of the market. With the crisis, however, a major shift in mentality took place, away from unbroken market euphoria and toward a greater degree of skepticism.

57 See Holger Stelzner, "Rettung der Wallstreet," *FAZ*, September 20, 2008.
58 See Lars Gertenbach, "Jenseits der Krise des Marktes. Anmerkungen zum Neoliberalismus," in *Texte zur Kunst*, issue 72 (December 2008): 160–163.
59 See "Der große Höllensturz," in *Der Spiegel,* 48 / 2008: 174–178.

Chapter Three

Art World and Artwork in the Age of Market Conformity

The End of the Fixed-Profile Gallery

In a situation characterized by both breaks *and* continuities, the true extent of change can only be fully appreciated from a historical perspective that seeks to grasp the specificity of the present by contrasting it with the past. However, there is always the risk of writing a history of demise, merely listing negative losses. It seems more sensible to look candidly at the changed conditions and to analyze them as the expression of a "new spirit of capitalism" (Boltanski / Chiapello), thus avoiding a cultural-critical lament. Rather than nostalgically mourning the "good old times," this study aims to avoid nostalgia in discussing a changed situation, from which new lines of conflict emerge.

What must therefore be addressed are the problems cultural producers face as a consequence of these new lines of conflict. For example, what has become of the "dealer-critic system" (Harrison and Cynthia White), which emerged in the late nineteenth century and replaced the academic Salon system? In the Whites' analysis, the dealer-critic system was the emerging art-world structure within which the task of establishing an artist was no longer performed by the official authority of the state art academy's Paris Salons, but by the art trade as part of an interplay with critics.[1] Rather than go unnoticed amid the mass of work on show at the Salon,[2] artists began to organize themselves into movements and, with the help of art dealers, to stage programmatic group exhibitions, as was the case with the Impressionists. With growing inadequacies in the academic Salon system, this dealer-critic system proved better suited to the distribution needs of a new type of artistic production. In other words, avant-garde groups called for a specific presentational framework. For the art of modernism this was provided by the dealer-critic system,

1 Harrison White and Cynthia White, *Canvases and Careers: Institutional Changes in the French Painting World* (New York/London/Sydney: Wiley, 1965), 194.

2 Courbet criticized the Salon of 1848, saying that with 5,500 pictures it was impossible to be noticed. See Petra ten-Doesschate Chu (ed.), *Letters of Gustave Courbet* (op. cit.), 77.

with groups of artists clustering around a dealer. From figures such as Durand-Ruel, Vollard, and Kahnweiler to Michael Werner, who to this day presents "his" artists (Baselitz, Immendorff, Lüpertz, Penck) as a circle of friends, this framework appears as a family-like structure promoting itself as a clan or gang.

Such program-galleries with specific profiles, championing a particular, programmatic vision of art, are characterized by their loyality to one artistic formation over a span of decades. At present, this is changing in two respects: Not only is the dealer-critic system eroding to make way for a different constellation, but the fixed-profile format of galleries is now also disappearing. The long-term pact between artist and gallery on which this system was based has been replaced by temporary partnerships, watering down the original programmatic profile.

Under the conditions of global competition, gallerists must also reckon with their commercially successful artists being lured away by bigger galleries with greater financial clout. Most recently, Richard Prince broke off his relationship with Barbara Gladstone, the gallery that represented him for many years, and declared his wish to work "independently" from now on, pointing to a future partnership with the Gagosian empire that lures artists with high transfer fees and an infrastructure with which mid-level gallerists simply cannot compete.[3]

But the pact is also crumbling from the other side. Artists whose market position is uncertain have less hope than ever of enjoying the unconditional, long-term loyalty of their gallerists. Whereas the fixed-profile gallery once seemed to offer protection against economic fluctuations and abrupt mood swings, current partnerships between artist and gallery are characterized by their transience. They can be cancelled at any time and are highly susceptible to the vicissitudes of fashion. Most artists can no longer count on their galleries to stand by them during tough times. The fixed-profile gallery is simply not sustainable, as few galleries can afford to stubbornly preserve their original program and simply ignore new trends and changes. Those wishing to remain competitive must be prepared to compromise, bringing commercially successful artists into their stable, for example, or dropping unsuccessful ones. Galleries today are also well advised to look for fresh talent in good time, as they are very likely to lose their commercially successful artists.

The result is an uncertain outlook for all involved. One must always reckon with the worst, which generates a feeling of permanent vulnerability and pressure that recalls Italian philosopher Paolo Virno's description of the "post-Fordist situation." For Virno, this situation is characterized by a direct relationship to the world, to which one is thus more exposed: in this world, the separation between "inside" and "outside" has largely been erased, resulting in a sense of not feeling at home.[4] Though this vision of being constantly exposed and under threat may sound a little overdramatic, it actually describes the crux of the modern artist's situation, especially today, but also in the past. After all, the court artist was already entirely at the mercy of his employer, the price he paid for being freed from the constraints imposed by his fraternity.[5] Today, it is market constraints that extend more or less directly into the sphere of artistic production, although this by no means implies that artistic production is completely determined by them. It is heteronomous and autonomous at the same time. Due to the structural changes described here, however, the gallery is no longer able to act as a buffer zone.

Artists are also finding themselves obliged to take care of their own business, as well as the administrative functions formerly delegated to galleries. As a result, they are more directly exposed to the vicissitudes of the market. For Virno, opportunist behavior becomes an "indispensable resource" under post-Fordist conditions,

3 See Sarah Thornton, "Freudian Analysis," www.artforum.com, May 14, 2008 (accessed June 20, 2008).

4 Paolo Virno, *A Grammar of the Multitude: For an Analysis of Contemporary Forms of Life*, (New York: Semiotext(e), 2004), 33.

5 See Martin Warnke, *Hofkünstler. Zur Vorgeschichte des modernen Künstlers* (op. cit.), 33.

a kind of strategy for survival.[6] What is called for, he writes, is a "sensitivity sharpened by the changeable chances." The opportunist knows how to take chances and to adjust flexibly to unexpected developments. These qualities have been in demand within the artistic sphere for a long time; in fact, they have traditionally been expected of the artist.[7] One might therefore say that the art world is a prototype for Virno's post-Fordist situation.

Even the classic image of friendship between artists—like that between van Gogh and Gauguin—is a manifestation of the combination of unselfish companionship and professional contact, which has become the rule in a "network world."[8] The chief reason for such a friendship is mutual professional interest. This instrumental trait, which exists in every relationship to a certain degree, conversely implies that there is no longer any private sphere exempt from profit motives. The more personal the contact, the better for business.

Restructuring the Dealer-Critic System

But the fixed-profile gallery is not alone in having outlived its usefulness as a result of precarious market conditions. The structure to which it belonged—the dealer-critic system—has also ceased to function within the present constellation. For it is no longer dealers *in conjunction with* critics who stimulate value-creation processes and launch careers. This vision was already problematic for the way it simply bypassed the artist and his specific work, as if that were no longer important. In the dealer-critic system, as the name suggests, the artist goes by the board. This implies an imposition on the artist's freedom not least because it is based on a restrictive vision of artistic creation. The artist is supposed to be responsible only for artistic concerns in a narrow sense, while everything else—production of meaning, marketing—is dealt with by the critic and the dealer. But relegating the artist exclusively to the role of picture-supplier ignores the historical fact that artists like Rembrandt and Courbet already took an active role in the marketing of their work.[9] Courbet even went so far as to attempt to control the production of meaning himself when he fed critics like Champfleury with interpretations of his paintings.[10]

But the dealer-critic system has also broken down in terms of those involved. Since the 1990s at the latest, it was replaced by what should perhaps be called the "dealer-collector system." Today, alongside gallerists, collectors and their buying habits influence the processes of value creation much more than critics do. And these increasingly influential collectors have long since ceased to follow the path set down by critics when shaping their interests and preferences. Instead, they look to their own preferences—and those of other collectors—which fuel their own desires.

When visiting an art fair, it is possible to gain the impression that everyone is chasing after precisely those works that they know or believe are on the wish lists of "key" collectors.[11] In such behavior, the mimetic and identificatory aspect of desire is displayed in exemplary form, to a degree otherwise seen only in fashion. As postulated by Lacan, desire proves to be desire of the Other,[12] a longing for that which one assumes is desired by the Other.

One clear indication that collectors now keep their own company and act as each other's points of reference is the strictly hierarchical organization of openings and advance viewings at events like the Art

6 Paolo Virno, *A Grammar of the Multitude: For an Analysis of Contemporary Forms of Life*, (op. cit.), 86.

7 This was already clear to Courbet, who in 1854 wrote in a letter to Max Bouchon: "You must be aware that, when opportunity presents itself, one must take advantage of it." See Petra ten-Doesschate Chu (ed.), *Letters of Gustave Courbet* (op. cit.), 126.

8 Luc Boltanski and Eve Chiapello, *The New Spirit of Capitalism* (op. cit.), 123.

9 See Paul Crenshaw, *Rembrandt's Bankruptcy: The Artist, His Patrons, and the Art Market in Seventeenth-Century Netherlands* (Cambridge / New York: Cambridge University Press, 2006); see also Jörg Zutter and Petra ten-Doesschate Chu, *Courbet: Artiste et promoteur de son oeuvre* (Paris: Flammarion, 1998).

10 See Courbet's letter to Champfleury from 1854, furnishing the critic with a text on *L'atelier du peintre* (The artist's studio), Petra ten-Doesschate Chu (ed.), *Letters of Gustave Courbet* (op. cit.), 131–133.

11 See Olav Veltuis, "Accounting for Taste," *Artforum* (April 2008): 308: "A large number of buyers are going after a small number of artists."

12 See Jacques Lacan, *Écrits* (Paris: Seuil, 1966), 823f.

Basel fair. Besides the previews reserved for mere VIPs, there are also more exclusive appointments for super-VIPs. At these previews open only to the truly major collectors with private jets, neither critics nor artists are welcome. Whereas in the 1980s, a typical collector was still interested in engaging directly with artists and intellectuals, considering himself lucky to sit at the same table with them, today's collectors prefer to remain among their own kind,[13] avoiding rather than actively seeking contact with critical intellectuals.[14]

Elsewhere, on the other hand, intellectuals are more welcome than ever—at symposia, for example, or as authors of catalog essays. The flipside of the hostility toward discourse that characterizes the milieu of mega-transactions is the demand for theorists to generate meaning. Never before has the art world employed and commissioned work from so many theorists, from such a range of disciplines. And this although they do not figure at all in the uppermost spheres of the commercial world.

Despite this bunker mentality, which is now especially prevalent among super-rich collectors, there is no reason to return to the old "dealer-critic" times when critics from Champfleury through to Greenberg still appeared to have unchallenged dominion where judgments of taste were concerned. For a start, it should not be forgotten that dealers literally come first in the "dealer-critic system," and it is the dealers who ultimately call the shots. In the Whites' account, legendary gallerists like Durand-Ruel are heroized as exemplars of a new kind of entrepreneur.[15] Critics, on the other hand, are reduced to the role of mere communicator in this model, and expected to diligently explain the artist's position and instruct viewers as to how to appreciate his pictures. In other words, they pay for their direct influence on value-creation processes by having their work reduced to a function. Critics lose the last remnants of the independence traditionally accorded to them, which always did have to remain fictitious to a certain degree, but which also possessed great potential.

Moreover, the attitude of the critics who operated successfully within this system was overtly self-confident and authoritarian—a stance that, from today's point of view, schooled in critiques of the subject, hardly seems desirable. Who would want to find themselves in the role of a Clement Greenberg, who certainly excelled at communicating the aesthetic program of his favorite brand of painting, but who remained blind to the questionable nature of his own self-assuredness, dealing out arbitrary, subjective judgments left, right, and center?[16] There can be no return to the kind of apodictic statements so characteristic of Greenberg, nor to the absolutist claims of an arbitrary, subjective judgment that is usually based on a position of unquestioned authority. Certainly the critic was more influential within the dealer-critic system, more directly involved in value-creation: when Greenberg visited Pollock's studio, for example, he is supposed to have passed judgment as to whether a given picture was finished or whether the artist should continue working on it; he also occasionally acted as an advisor to collectors and dealers. But since critical self-reflection is not among the strengths of this type of critic, he usually positions himself in a space outside of the market. This self-perception as someone remote from the market reveals a fundamental problem of criticism, which traditionally tends to exclude itself from the conditions it questions.[17] This prompted conservative historian Reinhart Koselleck to make the polemic comment that the constant unmasking of others leads to blindness in the unmasker himself.[18] It is true that criticism has often been blind to its own involvement, and especially when it comes to criticizing market

13 See also Alan Bowness, *The Conditions of Success: How the Modern Artist Rises to Fame* (New York / London: Thames and Hudson, 1989), 39. Bowness assumes a type of critic who enters the scene on account of his friendships with artists, whose advice he gladly accepts.

14 See Isabelle Graw, "Im Griff des Kunstmarkts," *taz*, April 14, 2004.

15 See Ulf Wuggenig, "Kreativität und Innovation im 19. Jahrhundert. Harrison C. White und die impressionistische Revolution erneut betrachtet," in *Kritik der Kreativität*, eds. Gerald Raunig and Ulf Wuggenig (Vienna: Turia + Kant, 2007), 219–236.

16 See Florence Rubenfeld, "Imperial Clem," in *Clement Greenberg: A Life* (New York: Scribner, 1997), 259–281.

17 See Reinhart Koselleck, *Kritik und Krise* (Frankfurt: Suhrkamp, 1989). Although Koselleck plays down criticism's emancipatory achievements, he does point out the structural problem that criticism excludes itself from its own critique.

18 Ibid., 100.

conditions, the critic tends to consider himself exempted from them. Denying his involvement is the prerequisite for such criticism.

In this light, the fact that the dealer-critic system is no longer among the defining structures of the art world is not entirely regrettable. If we are going to weep at all, it would be more appropriate to lament the passing of the good old fixed-profile gallery. For every gallery that once fitted this description—examples in Germany include Galerie Max Hetzler and Galerie Christian Nagel—has long since departed from a clearly-outlined program. Cases such as Galerie Michael Werner must be considered as the structural exceptions that prove the rule.

External, Internal, and Self-Imposed Purposes

We have already identified a dual character as an important structural feature shared by art-as-commodity and commodities in general. Where ordinary commodities oscillate between "consumer item" and "commodity," art-as-commodity splits into a symbolic value that supposedly has no price and a market value embodied in its price. And we have seen, in the example of Courbet, how market and symbolic value directly influence one another: In the nineteenth century, high prices were already capable of generating artistic credibility. We attributed the special quality of art-as-commodity to the fact that its price is based on the (not entirely unjustified) assumption that it is in fact priceless.

But what sets artworks apart from brand items, which also legitimate their price in terms of pricelessness and the promise of a unique experience? Are there other historical explanations for the association of artworks with epistemological gain? Is their symbolic charge ultimately justified, or does it amount to mere idealization?

One might say that a pricing scale based on pricelessness applies to greater numbers of consumer items. But while Marx assumed that "socially necessary labor-time" was an index of value, the price of brand items in particular is now calculated more or less independently of how many labor hours go into producing them.[19] While premium prices are linked to good quality, as when we pay for the amount of engineering that has gone into a luxury car, the price of this car will nevertheless far exceed its production cost. This emancipation of exchange value from labor hours also seems to speak in favor of an increasing affinity between artwork and consumer item. Is it still possible to draw a clear line between art-as-commodity and commodities in general? Take, for example, a luxury-class Mercedes, which functions as a consumer product and a status symbol, not unlike an artwork. Such a car legitimates its exchange value via a symbolic dimension that can be described in terms of "style," "good taste," or "classiness." This emphasis on experiential value ensures further detachment from the car's use-value, from which, according to Marx, it had already become abstracted by the process of exchange, which ignores use-value in favor of the commensurability of commodities as values.[20] Does this mean that the use-value of the commodity goes by the board during the process of exchange in a way that recalls the departure from the utility principle in art? Yes and no. Unlike purchasing an artwork, buying a car is still governed by considerations of utility, which render the price plausible in the eyes of the buyer. Use-value has a part (however secondary) to play in rationalizing the purchase. In the case of the luxury Mercedes, for example, one might point to its particular roadworthiness or the high quality of its fittings—some of them useful—to explain the price to oneself. The price of a new model appears legitimate due to all the new features that it offers. And this especially since installing these features was labor-intensive. Such rationalization is justified and has a calming effect even if one is aware of the inferior role use-value actually plays here. The notion of use-value adheres to the luxury Mercedes even when it is not its usefulness that stands into the foreground. The art-

19 See Michael Heinrich, *Kritik der politischen Ökonomie. Eine Einführung* (Stuttgart: Schmetterling, 2004), 40.
20 Ibid., 47.

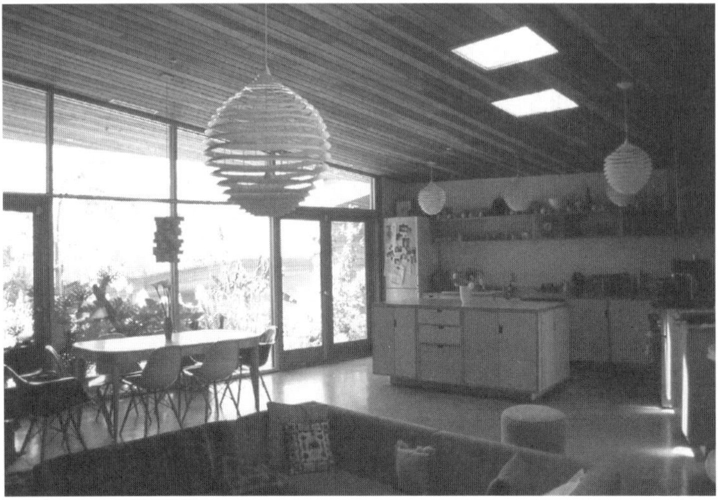

Jorge Pardo, 4166 Sea View Lane, *1998*

work, by contrast, has traditionally served to formulate expectations that project it far beyond the role of a service provider, thoroughly detaching its exchange value from its immediate use-value. It is to this detachment from the utility principle that art owes its special status. If artworks have a utility, a use-value, then it is the fact of their not being directly useful. But surely this raises major problems: What about the purposes and uses that artworks undeniably do serve, such as status enhancement, decoration, and speculation?

In this context, sociologist Niklas Luhmann has suggested distinguishing between intrinsic and external purposes. A purpose such as status enhancement is considered "purely external usage," which ultimately has no effect on art's claim to uselessness and purposelessness.[21] According to Luhmann, the external harnessing of the artwork to a purpose does not infringe on the purposelessness that is integral to it. However productive this idea of distinguishing between inner and outer purposes may appear at first glance, it does not bear closer inspection. For it is based on the assumption of art's essential purposelessness, which is furthermore posited as being beyond question. It would be more accurate to speak of the privilege historically accorded to art, granting it the ability to set its own "intrinsic purpose," a privilege it still commands today. Viewed in this way, it is by no means essentially purposeless, as Luhmann suspects, nor can it be reduced to external purposes. Might it be possible, then, to modify Luhmann's distinction, no longer differentiating between "intrinsic" and "external" purposes, but between those that are self-imposed and those brought to art from the outside? This distinction, too, is difficult to uphold, not least because it has long been abolished by artistic practices. From Russian Productivism through Conceptual art and the service models of the 1990s, explicit and distinct attempts have been made to give art back its external purpose—in the form of a function within society. Many artists have declared harnessing art to a purpose as their aim. The rendering of service (to a client, for example) from which "autonomous art" was freed in the eighteenth century, was voluntarily reclaimed by the service art of the 1990s.

This development has been given a further turn by contemporary artists like Jorge Pardo, who produces items of use-value—decorative lamps—which also claim for themselves the privilege of the autonomous, purposeless artwork. Clearly the line between "intrinsic" and "external" purposes cannot be drawn as clearly as Luhmann imagined. It is possible for the inner purpose of the artwork to be that it serves an external purpose. Today, an artist like Jorge Pardo need have no qualms about aiming for an external, decorative purpose, because the status of his work as art elevates it above the sphere of the applied. Its inner purpose, one might say, is to aim for an external purpose, which does not compromise its reputation as an ultimately purposeless work of art. As the owner of such a lamp, one kills two birds with a single stone: One owns a functional, decorative lamp, which at the same time radiates the aura of the purpose-free artwork. While a consumer item—such as the luxury Mercedes—bears the shadow of its use-value as part of its essence, art-as-commodity has long since cast it off and transcended it. Where general consumer articles remain harnessed to specific external purposes, works of art

21 See Niklas Luhmann, *Die Kunst der Gesellschaft* (Frankfurt: Suhrkamp, 1995), 247.

possess the privilege of dictating their own purpose. But this does not mean that they are immune to unintended purposes. Just as they cannot be reduced to external purposes, they are equally capable of being harnessed to them.

The Artwork as Precursor to the Commodity

The symbolic charge of art-as-commodity prefigures the transformation of general commodities into branded goods. The more consumer items are transformed into brand items, the greater the defining role of their "cultural-informational dimension," bringing them closer to the artwork in ontological terms.[22] From this point of view, artworks (though special commodities) can be viewed as precursors to branded goods.

Branded goods really do seem to be based on artworks, not least because of the parallel ways they generate experience and produce individuality. The consumer of a brand can imagine himself to have done something good, to have made a display of taste, or to have demonstrated his membership in the caste of the knowledgeable and the cultivated. Today, the consumer's individuality is defined primarily via consumer goods that help him find his identity. Artworks, too, have an identity-forming dimension: They situate the viewer and supply him with emotions and meanings via a communicative function similar to that performed by brands.[23] If they manage to send a message that marks difference and generates confidence, the resulting sense of community and belonging is not unlike that evoked by branded goods. Whether the focus is "Prada" or "Mike Kelley," this feeling is similar. Artworks and branded goods both shape identity, then, acting as "central bearers of meaning for self-positioning and outward demarcation."[24]

Like branded goods, artworks also aim to monopolize the minds of their viewer / consumer. And the sensation accessed via these "experience and identity goods" is supposedly unique. Branded items aim to develop a personality (YSL, KL, Marc Jacobs), recalling the way artworks circulate on the market as names (a Koons, a Hirst, etc.). The personalization of brands correlates with the personalization of artworks, just as the consumer experience is based on the experience of art.

In his exploration of the commodity's potential to fascinate, Marx already referred to the model of aesthetic experience as imagined by the idealist aesthetics of Schiller and, to an even greater degree, by Kant. For instance, when Marx elaborated on the table-as-commodity in his treatise on "The Fetishism of the Commodity and its Secret" (1864) and defined it as "a thing which transcends sensuousness,"[25] it recalls the quality of *je ne sais quoi* traditionally attributed to beauty, as well as Kant's paradoxical definition of art as something judged in terms of "purposiveness without a purpose."[26]

By analogy with the artwork, Marx raised the commodity to the status of a para-religious phenomenon that was beyond reach. The metaphors of evasion and withdrawal used in deconstructive aesthetics are also foreshadowed by this choice of words: art is defined as that which eludes intelligibility. Ultimately, "transcending sensuousness" means that the commodity, while still being perceived as something sensuous, cannot be grasped, that it is always elusive. Present and absent at the same time, within and beyond the reach of the senses—such is the unity of opposites that aesthetic theorists from Kant to Adorno have used in order to describe art. Despite having a concrete presence that can be experienced in material terms, artworks are assumed to go beyond this sensory dimension, thus making

22 See Maurizio Lazzarato, "Immaterial Labor," in *Radical Thought in Italy: A Potential Politics*, eds. Michael Hardt and Paolo Virno (Minneapolis: University of Minnesota Press, 2006), 133–150.

23 On the communicative power of brands, see Kai-Uwe Hellmann, *Soziologie der Marke* (Frankfurt: Suhrhkamp, 2003), 89.

24 Ibid., 101.

25 Karl Marx, "The Fetishism of the Commodity and its Secret," in *Capital: Vol. 1: A Critique of Political Economy* (op. cit.), 163.

26 Immanuel Kant, "Critique of Aesthetic Judgment" in *Critique of Judgment* (Oxford / New York: Oxford University Press, 2007), 57.

them comparable to Marx's commodity. It is the transcendental dimension of the commodity that, conversely, makes it resemble the artwork. The puzzle faced by Marx concerning the "mysterious" commodity also seems to be borrowed from the aesthetic topos of art's enigmatic quality. For Adorno, works of art are enigmatic simply because they "say something and in the same breath conceal it."[27] In Marx, a similar dialectic of revealing and withholding is at work when the commodity casts its spell over us by keeping something from us. There is clearly much to suggest that Marx based this characterization on the artwork. But if the experience of the commodity takes its lead from aesthetic experience, shouldn't that make art-as-commodity the ultimate commodity? And under these circumstances, how can the claim of art's status as a special kind of commodity be maintained?

I would propose a distinction here. Not only in its marketing, but also from the point of view of reception theory, art is equipped with a particular capacity that makes it a special kind of commodity. But viewed in terms of these special properties attributed to it—epistemological gain, within / beyond the reach of the senses, enigma—it represents a seminal version of the commodity. It is both a special kind of commodity and the prototypical commodity at the same time.

Making the Conditions of Production Transparent?

Marx identified the source of the commodity's peculiar attraction in the fact that the process of labor used to produce it is hidden: "The mysterious character of the commodity-form consists, therefore, simply in the fact that the commodity reflects the social characteristics of men's own labor as objective characteristics of the products of labor themselves, as the socio-natural properties of these things. Hence it also reflects the social relation of the producers to the sum total of labor as a social relation between objects, a relation that exists apart from and outside the producers."[28] Consequently, the commodity is not visibly a product of labor. Rather, the labor expended to produce it appears to be part of its essence. For commodities also possess the "fixed quality of natural forms of social life."[29] In them, a genuinely social process is naturalized. A "definite social relation" takes on the "fantastic form of a relation between things."[30] In his *Kritik der politischen Ökonomie: Eine Einführung* (*Critique of Political Economy*: an introduction), Michael Heinrich casts this commodity problem in Marx's work as one of value: For Marx, he writes, the fetishization of the commodity means that, within the context of society, it is automatically accorded a value that cannot actually be grasped via the commodity itself.[31] This metonymic trait of the commodity is an expression of the relational character of value. If value is a social relation, then no thing can be valuable in and of itself. But, he adds, as a comment on Marx's characterization of its "transcending sensuousness," the commodity makes this social relation *appear* to be its "thing-like property."[32] This deceptive quality was long a bone of contention for cultural critics who accused commodities of dealing in falsehood. For Heinrich, this view—commodity fetishism as a kind of "false consciousness" that only veils the true situation—is a "reduced view of commodity fetishism." And yet, this "reduced view" has been used as the basis for entire theoretical constructs—from critical theory to critiques of the spectacle. Guy Debord, for example, certainly had false consciousness in mind when he denounced the commodity as "notre vieille ennemie." This personalization also recalls the sexist aversion to all that is feminine.[33] Like the perceived threat of a woman whose use of fashion and makeup give her seductive powers, the commodity is conceived of as something that casts a spell with its deceptively alluring packaging.

27 Theodor W. Adorno, *Aesthetic Theory* (op. cit.), 160.
28 Karl Marx, "Commodities and Money," in *Capital: Vol. 1* (op. cit.), 164–165.
29 Ibid., 168.
30 Ibid., 165.
31 See Michael Heinrich, *Kritik der politischen Ökonomie. Eine Einführung* (op. cit.), 70–71.
32 Ibid., 37–77.
33 Guy Debord, *La Societé du Spectacle* (1967) (Paris: Gallimard, 1992), 35.

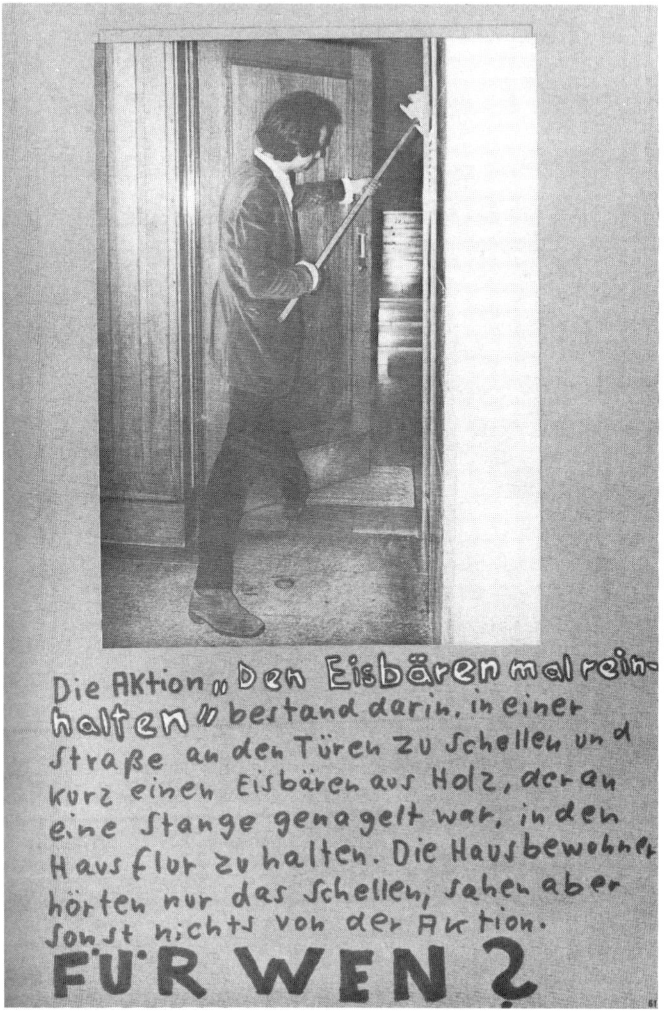

Jörg Immendorff, "Den Eisbären mal reinhalten," *1968, from the artist's book* Hier und Jetzt: Das tun, was zu tun ist *(Cologne/New York: Gebr. König, 1973)*

For proponents of this theory, the commodity's seductive power was doomed from the moment the labor processes concealed within it were laid bare. This wish for demystification was the basis of ideological critique, but it also motivated many art projects—from 1920s Russian Productivism to the Process art and Institutional Critique of the 1960s and 70s—which loosely followed Marx in trying to render the conditions of production transparent. Understandability was already emphasized in Rodchenko's objects, with their deductive structures.[34] Since then, many attempts have been made to reveal and reflect on the conditions of artistic production in artworks themselves, often with a positive result. One example is Jörg Immendorff, whose performance-actions of the 1960s tried to playfully account for his working methods, but did so in a way that humorously exaggerated the enforcement of "self-criticism" then common in Maoist groups. Precisely because his early work contains the history of its making, for instance, pointing to his belonging to a specific social context (as in "LIDL") or revealing traces of his political activity (as in the artist collective Mietersolidarität [Tenant solidarity]), it has retained its urgency and relevance. This suggests that making an artwork's conditions of production transparent does not annul its commodity character. On the contrary, art-as-commodity is capable of adding such a gesture of demystification to the sum total of its mystery.

The same is true, incidentally, of branded goods. When a designer like Stella McCartney assures the public that she has used only materials with the best ecological credentials for her clothes, this information, aimed at providing transparency, does not reduce attractiveness in the slightest.[35] In fact, the consumer's desire for unfalsified goods is satisfied by such an offer,[36] as demonstrated by the trendy jute bags with the slogan "My Bag Cares," which became fashionable in the course of the battle against plastic bags. This "commodification of the authentic" (Boltanski / Chiapello) is something Marx could not have predicted. For him, the problem lay in the fact that the object-like appearance of the commodity concealed the social character of labor. But the line between "fake" and "real" is no longer as clearly defined as Marx postulated. It is no longer possible to assume

34 See Hal Foster, Rosalind Krauss, Yve-Alain Bois and Benjamin H.D. Buchloh, *Art Since 1900* (New York / London: Thames & Hudson, 2004), 178.

35 See Jill Danyelle and Stella McCartney, "Vegan Fashion," www.inhabitat.com, November 26, 2006 (accessed July 21, 2008).

36 See Boltanski and Chiapello, *The New Spirit of Capitalism* (op. cit.), 441–443

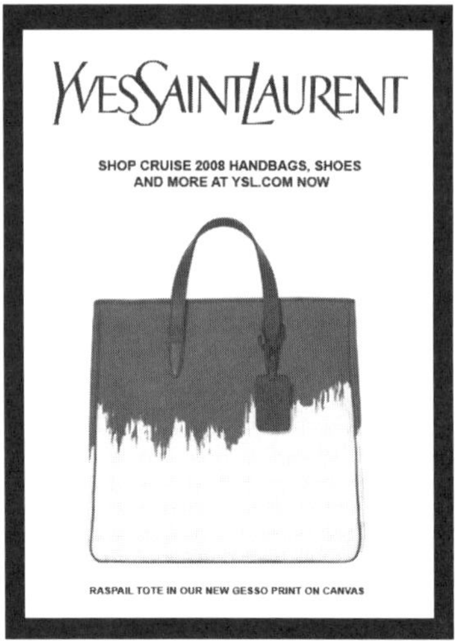

Canvas YSL tote bag from the Cruise 2008 collection

"authentic" social conditions of production, undistorted by any kind of representation and contrivance, which only need to be made transparent. Neither can one assume commodities based purely on appearances, devoid of any trace of their social character. Not only are commodities evidently capable of transforming the desire for revealing their "true" conditions of production into a commodity—in addition, these unveiled, supposedly authentic conditions prove to be highly artificial constructions.

Artworks and Luxury Goods: Close Relatives or Distant Acquaintances?

Artworks and luxury goods are growing more similar, making it difficult to distinguish between them. Like art-as-commodity, luxury products seek to demonstrate uniqueness by means of limited editions. The legendary Hermès Kelly bag, for example, is produced in small numbers only, giving it an aura of mega-exclusivity, which seems to be inspired by the artwork's promise of originality.[37] Such measures designed to generate scarcity and prestige, which include the ubiquitous waiting lists for exclusive luxury goods, have found their high point to date in bespoke luxury goods specially tailored to their buyers.[38] The owner of such a made-to-measure handbag can be sure that no one else is carrying one. Added to this is the feeling of a direct connection to the designer, who, after all, made the bag as a personal commission. What is praised as the ultimate luxury is inspired by the singularity of the artwork, which is also one-of-a-kind or issued only as a limited, signed edition.

Art production and the luxury goods industry also increasingly overlap as business sectors, on both structural and personal levels. Buyers of luxury goods tend to purchase art and design objects, just as art collectors usually have a weakness for luxury goods. It is no wonder, then, that art booms have traditionally been accompanied by a growth spurt in the luxury and premium goods industry.[39] This was already the case in the sixteenth century—when the dividing line between artwork and artifact was less pronounced—and it is the case again today. The close ties between the art market and the luxury sector are also apparent in times of crisis: if the art market slumps, demand for luxury goods also usually dwindles. For an unmistakable sign of the close relation between the two universes, one need look no further than major-league French collector François Pinault. If the notorious hit lists are to be believed, he is one of the most important collectors in the art world—important in terms of money and power. He is a lynchpin and uncrowned king of both worlds insofar as he owns not only an auction house (Christie's) but also one of the biggest fashion empires (the PPR Group), including brands such as Gucci and YSL. Moreover, in keeping with current trends, he has built up a collection of contemporary art, for which he purchased the Palazzo Grassi in Venice. Pinault also closes the gap between art-

37 See Tanja Wolff, "Die Kunst der Knappheit. Ein Hauch von Planwirtschaft: Wie die Hersteller von Luxustaschen den Wert ihrer Ware durch begrenzte Stückzahlen noch steigern," *Süddeutsche Zeitung*, September 11, 2007.

38 See Sameer Reddy, "Special Report: There's Nothing Else Like It in the World," *Newsweek*, special issue on "Unsinkable Luxury," (May/June 2008): 54–59.

39 See Elisabeth Alice Honig, *Painting and the Market in Early Modern Antwerp* (New Haven / London: Yale University Press, 1998), 13.

as-commodity and the world of luxury goods in that the money he spends on art is likely to flow back into his own boutiques. After all, wealthy artists are enthusiastic buyers of designer fashion. When Pinault buys contemporary art, he could be said to be investing in his fashion empire, furnishing potential customers with money to spend in his shops.

This connection between luxury goods and the art world does not alter the fact that the artwork possesses a degree of cultural and social prestige to which luxury goods can only aspire. For all the efforts that have been made (made-to-measure, waiting lists), luxury goods have not managed to establish a comparable aura of cultural importance. No collector amassing luxury goods can hope for a level of cultural cachet to match that of the art collector. The German edition of *Vanity Fair* referred to this iron rule with its claim that collecting art is the greatest source of prestige.[40]

But what does the artwork have that luxury goods lack? The initial impression is that the similarities outweigh the differences. Like the artwork, a Cartier watch functions primarily as a status symbol, performing a function as an afterthought. No one would buy a Cartier watch if all they needed was a new timepiece. Debord rightly noted that use-value had been eroded by the "overdeveloped commodity economy," as he called consumer capitalism.[41] Where use-value is eroded, it is fair to assume that criteria such as wearability or comfort, which refer to a logic of utility, become less important. This is the case with designer shoes by Louboutin, the key feature of which is their recognition value, ensured by their trademark red soles. Fashionistas can immediately spot a pair of Louboutins, just as an art lover can identify a Rothko at a hundred yards. With luxury goods, use-value clearly takes a back seat. But unlike the Rothko picture, the Louboutin shoes are put to immediate use: they are worn, trodden on, walked about in. This usability even applies to the cream jar encrusted with 2,400 Swarowski stones for the La Prairie luxury cosmetics line Crème Caviar—the ultimate decadent product that seems to have taken its lead from artworks like Hirst's skull, which return to an emphasis on material value. The main point of this cream, as a piece of jewelry, is certainly not its anti-wrinkle effect. But even the glittering cream jar has a remnant of use-value because its contents can be applied directly to the skin. It is this inherent practical dimension of luxury goods that sets them apart from artworks, even when the latter venture into the realm of the applied, as in the example of Pardo. The direct use of wrinkle cream is not the same as the indirect harnessing of art to the ends of prestige or decoration.

The line separating luxury goods from artworks is clearly a thin one, with both sides actually at pains to resemble the other ever more closely. Many artists—from Warhol, with his diamond dust paintings, to Hirst, with *For the Love of God*—have applied the lesson of the luxury product. Not to mention an artist like Sylvie Fleury, whose practice demonstratively equates artwork and luxury article, as if dismissing art's historical claim to autonomy as pure illusion, as if voluntarily foregoing the scope of action that results from this claim. Conversely, a symbiosis between artwork and luxury product is evident in the monumental handbags of the spring/summer 2007 season, "tote bags" carried about by their wearers like signs. Their size corresponded to that of a medium-size painting, underlining the structural proximity between owning art and owning accessories: both secure prestige, both are ornaments. As if to push this development to its limit, YSL included such a bag in its Cruise collection (2008) under the name "Raspail." At first glance, it seemed that this bag had mutated into a painting, especially as it fused formal idioms of Clyfford Still and Morris Louis. Still's typical frayed edges and his harsh-looking division of the picture into different color zones met with Louis's watercolor-like pouring technique and the resulting impression of a canvas sodden with deep red paint. Even in 1955, Greenberg found the boundary between the painterly and the decorative to be fatally unstable—it is a boundary that, in this bag, once

40 See *Vanity Fair*, 26/2008: 59.
41 Guy Debord, *The Society of the Spectacle* (London: Rebel Press, 2005), 23.

again proves to be fluid.[42] The strength of "Raspail," however, is its exaggeration of the structural similarities between artwork and luxury product, while upholding the small differences between them. It is and remains a bag, which can only dream of the intellectual potential ascribed to art since the eighteenth century. At the same time, it offers itself as a picture in bag form, the ultimate picture accessory. Both handbag and canvas painting owe their conquest of the market not only to the social prestige associated with them, but also to transport-related considerations. Just as bags can be carried and used for a variety of purposes, the status of the canvas as the most commercially successful art form is based, among other things, on the fact that it can be easily transported. Despite its mimetic orientation toward the pictorial language of Abstract Expressionism, "Raspail" finally admits its inability to grasp the symbolic-cultural dimension it tries to assimilate by quoting the visual idioms of Still and Louis. It is a bag that comments on fashion's desire for art. Instead of commissioning an artist to design a bag, as many labels from Vuitton to Puma have done in recent years, in the case of "Raspail," fashion paints its own picture of art—a picture that is immediately and necessarily identifiable as a clichéd image of modern art.

The Market and the Autonomy of Its Product

The art market relies on a belief in the remoteness of its products from the market. It is obliged to emphasize this autonomy for the simple reason that it forms the basis of the product's marketability. From a historical point of view, the push by aesthetics for an understanding of art as something radically special and irreducible to purposes had a largely positive impact on its market potential. There is a link between the late-nineteenth-century emergence of the art market as we now know it and the modern definition of art from the second half of the eighteenth century. Only once art was liberated from use-value and named a higher principle by aesthetics could it be marketed. A product tied to a specific purpose, possibly governed by the rules of a given trade, cannot be compatible with the demands of the art market. It has therefore been rightly observed that the autonomous aura and the market value of art are mutually dependent to this day.[43]

The typical reason given for the emergence of the art market is that art gradually detached itself from the directives of craft and trade guilds. Only once this separation took place, and art moved toward the court and the academy, was the market able to establish itself as an important distributional structure.

Although forms of art trade can be traced as far back as classical antiquity, and although commerce in art flourished during the Middle Ages, the origins of today's art market are located in the sixteenth century.[44] At that time, the centers of art were Venice, Antwerp, and Rotterdam. It was here that the first shops run by dealers dedicated specifically and exclusively to art were opened. This progressive freeing of art from its direct ties to the directives of the guilds was also what allowed aesthetics to label art as free of purpose. And this assertion of purposelessness was also grist for the mill of its marketing. The more detached from purpose and function art appears, the more potential scope it has. It is this attestation of potential for freedom that makes art the ideal surface for the projection of all manner of symbolic content. It seems appropriate to see the autonomy claimed by idealistic aesthetics as a kind of ennoblement strategy that gave the marketing of art a huge boost.

However questionable the claim of autonomy may be in its pointed idealism—as when it elevates art above all purposes and all

42 See Clement Greenberg, "'American-Type' Painting" (1955), in *Art and Culture: Critical Essays* (Boston: Beacon, 1961), 208–229.

43 See foreword in Michael Müller et al. (eds.), *Autonomie der Kunst. Zur Genese und Kritik einer bürgerlichen Kategorie* (Frankfurt: Suhrkamp, 1972), 7.

44 See Elisabeth Alice Honig, *Painting and the Market in Early Modern Antwerp* (op. cit.); or Michael North, David Ormord (eds.), *Art Markets in Europe 1400–1800* (Aldershot/Brookfield: Ashgate, 1998).

functions—it does contain some truth: Artworks possess a distinctive language, logic, and set of laws that cannot be explained away in terms of external realities. In this context, it is interesting that the notion of art's autonomy (that it is governed by its own rules) emerged at the same time as political economy—in the eighteenth century. Both aesthetics and political economy were systematic sciences; each conceived of its object as being governed by its own rules.[45] In this light, it is no wonder that aesthetics has traditionally showed no interest in economics, and that economics came up against the limits of its explanatory models where art was concerned. Anyone who claims to operate by their own rules can tolerate no other master. In the concept of the art market, however, these two claims to exclusivity are welded together, and as a result artists feel their freedom to be threatened by the market, just as economists cannot help being provoked by the impossibility of explaining art in terms of economic categories.

Of course, "autonomy" can mean a number of different things, from self-governance, to freedom from external constraints, to lack of purpose. What these ideas of autonomy have in common, however, is that they have always been more wishful thinking than fact.[46] It is an ideal state, never fully achieved, always kept in check by external constraints and conditions.

From Relative Autonomy to Relative Heteronomy

But how precisely should one imagine this blend of autonomy and heteronomy, which I maintain is characteristic of the artist's situation in general? In this context, it is helpful to refer to Bourdieu's model of "relative autonomy," according to which the field of art is a relatively autonomous, relatively independent universe.[47] The great advantage of this model is that it conceives of autonomy and heteronomy together. For Bourdieu, although the field of art develops its own rules, it never remains entirely untouched by what is happening in other fields, such as the economy. It is relatively autonomous insofar as it possesses its own criteria and standards without being totally immune to the effects of external events such as economic crises. External events do encroach on the field of art, but for Bourdieu, the decisive point is that they are refracted through the field's specific rules and conditions—they impact art, but on art's own terms.

In view of the delocalization of the market, whose logic now prevails in all segments of society, it now seems appropriate to modify Bourdieu's model of "relative autonomy" toward one of "relative heteronomy." By relative heteronomy I mean that external constraints prevail, but only in a relative fashion. It is crucial to note that these constraints can be fought against, and what artists tend to fight for is not relative but total freedom from them. While the concept of "relative autonomy" still has the advantage of taking into account the historical process of ongoing differentiation of the art field into a world of its own without denying the influence of external events, it places too great an influence on autonomy. And this autonomy is no longer the dominant structural characteristic of the field of art. Considering the dominance of the economic system within society, it is necessary to shift the emphasis toward a definition of the artistic field as "relatively heteronomous." In concrete terms, this means that the external constraints are placed in the foreground, and this even more so when being driven by economic considerations has become a prevalent mindset within the art world. One has only to recall how often economic constraints are invoked as if there were no cure for them. Their power is presented as overwhelming, a force of nature. And so it comes about that man-

45 On the notion of the economy as an autonomous entity in the eighteenth century, see Lars Gertenbach, *Die Kultivierung des Marktes. Foucault und die Gouvernementalität des Neoliberalismus* (op. cit.), 27.

46 See Horst Bredekamp, "Autonomie und Askese," in *Autonomie der Kunst. Zur Genese und Kritik einer bürgerlichen Kategorie* (op. cit.), 92–93.

47 See Pierre Bourdieu, "The Market for Symbolic Goods," in *The Rules of Art* (op. cit.), 248.

agement consultants like McKinsey are commissioned to assess art academies and the Goethe Institute, as if it were possible to draw up a balance of their yield, and measure their performance according to criteria of economic efficiency.[48]

The point of "relative heteronomy," however, is that it conceives of the power of external economic constraints not as absolute, but as relative. They impact only to a limited degree because individuals can relate to them, can put them in their place. In the model of relative heteronomy too, then, the power of the economy reaches its limits. If it is relative, then it can also be contradicted or even rejected. Nevertheless, it is external constraints that are considered the dominant structural feature, and not freedoms, as in Bourdieu's model. On the basis of recognizing these constraints, however, certain freedoms can be negotiated. Admittedly, the relative heteronomy of the field of art is something different from the juggling between heteronomy and autonomy that characterizes artistic production. Despite this, it makes sense to apply the simultaneity of an immanent specificity and external influences proposed by Bourdieu to works of art, which also display this mix of outside influence and autonomy.

As another indication of the relative heteronomy of art, the art market reacted very sensitively to the recent collapse of the global economy. At first it seemed that it would remain largely unaffected by the financial crisis: auctions continued to achieve record sales, prices skyrocketed.[49] Everything appeared to confirm Bourdieu's theory of relative autonomy for the art world. On closer inspection, however, the art market's apparent immunity was being bolstered by external factors. It was still benefiting from the money flowing directly in from the oil emirates and from Russia's new industrial magnates. Once again, it was events outside of the field of art, in the economy, to which the art market owed its vitality and apparent trend-bucking. In the meantime, the financial and banking crisis hung over the heads of those in the art world like the sword of Damocles. Outwardly, they were at pains to maintain an impression that all was well. But within, there were fears that confidence in the excessive market values of particular commercially successful artists might (rightfully) begin to wane. To prepare themselves for this crisis, many galleries tried to expand their programs, adding fewer commercial positions, as experience shows that work associated with "critique" or "content" gains status in times of recession. Even those who had before relied exclusively on commercial success and media presence, and performed extremely well with this approach, seemed to sense that the tide was turning. One example is the director of Munich's Haus der Kunst, Chris Dercon, who complained about power being taken away from public museums by private collectors, while completely exempting himself from this development, in which he played a contributing role.[50] But his evocation of apocalyptic scenarios (abandoned private museums, destroyed art collections) was symptomatic insofar as it signaled an about-face, from exhibition maker guided by the dictates of popularity to thoughtful critic of the market. Once cultural-critical laments and academic profundity are back in demand, then no one wants to be last in line. Crises have traditionally been a breeding ground for apocalyptic visions. When slump is in the air, art market players adjust their convictions accordingly, and in good time. That this mental shift is dictated by economic factors provides further proof that the art world has lost its "relative autonomy," exchanging it for "relative heteronomy."

The most persuasive evidence of the art world's relative heteronomy is the intensity with which it finally suffered from the global financial crisis. The cutoff point of its immunity to market events is the collapse of Lehman Brothers (in September 2008), after which the stock

48 See Thomas Steinfeld, "Der Narr als Betriebswirt. Grober Unfug: McKinsey reformiert das Goethe Institut," *Süddeutsche Zeitung,* June 27, 2007.

49 See Deborah Brewster, "Contemporary Art Defies Doomsayers," *Financial Times*, June 28/29, 2008.

50 See Chris Dercon, "Indiana Jones und die Ruine des Privatmuseums," *Süddeutsche Zeitung,* July 4, 2008.

market plummeted. The art market did not remain unaffected by these "corrections," as manifested in dwindling sales and declining prices. Above all in America, there were times during the steadily worsening economic crisis when art trade almost came to a standstill. Some gallerists said in confidence that they had not sold anything in months. A wave of mental paralysis seemed to be taking hold, so that even those who could still have afforded to spend money on art were now reluctant to do so. It was as if the abyss over which value is always stretched had suddenly opened up, and it became clear that an artwork's claim to value can be disputed at any time. At its heart, this crisis was a crisis of confidence, a lasting blow to confidence in symbolic and market values. Art's claim to value, one might say, revealed its true face—pure abstraction that can collapse at any time. The more unstable this value appeared, the more zealously art market players tried to call attention to art's "true" and "actual" value. In view of the metonymic quality of value, this insistence on intrinsic value amounts to a fantasy—but an enormously powerful fantasy all the same. The notion that art has some inherent value is the central (and most productive) illusion of the art market. Correspondingly, in times of crisis, market players regularly express their satisfaction that the "circus" is over at last, and as such, the crisis is actually "good" for art:[51] Now, they claim, it is possible to return to real art, to seriousness, content, and so forth. In the face of the recession, the art / market dualism is clearly at a climax—on one side, the "evil" market, on the other, "good" art. The tendency to style art and market as absolute opposites becomes even more pronounced in such times of crisis. People seek refuge from the impositions of the market and hide behind their ideal of art. But this collective refocusing of attention on "Art" is also a manifestation of relative heteronomy. An idealistic belief in art acts as a fortress from which to defy external economic constraints. A comment made by artist Brice Marden and quoted (approvingly) by Jerry Saltz is especially revealing in this context: "It's not the art that's suffering, it's the market that's suffering. They don't have anything to do with each other."[52] Any connection between art and the market is phobically contested, as if art existed under its own momentum in an economy-free zone. Once again, it is a commercially successful artist who banishes the market to some imaginary outside. Of course Marden's comment contains some truth, that is, the fact that artistic production is not completely subject to the dictates of the market. Historically, it has been furnished with "a logic of its own," enabling it to develop its own rules. But at the same time, it is kept in check by market conditions, a fact Marden chooses to ignore. Although it makes little sense to view art outside the context of its market conditions, there is scope for an oppositional stance. Artists who take market conditions into consideration are often those who fight for the (if only theoretical) possibility of an alternative to the capitalist status quo. Art is part of the market and, at the same time, a potential opponent to it. This is the nature of art's relative heteronomy.

The Art World as an "Industry Engaged in Producing Visuality and Meaning"

Ultimately, my proposed characterization of the field of art as "relatively heteronomous," a modification of Bourdieu, leads to a break with the sociological postulate of the functional differentiation of social systems. For differentiation has been replaced by a relative de-differentiation, which implies a structural alignment of the art world to other social systems. There is much evidence of such a development—artist types are now in demand everywhere, and eccentric, bohemian identities have arrived at the center of society. Everyone is an artist, the whole world is an art world dedicated to creativity. In a parallel development, the formerly retail-based "art

51 See Holland Cotter, "The Boom Is Over. Long Live the Art!," *The New York Times*, February 15, 2009.
52 Jerry Saltz, "Morality Play," http:/www.artnet.com/magazineus/features/saltz (accessed March 7, 2009).

business" has mutated into an industry that more and more resembles other cultural industries such as film and fashion.

In the fashion world, the push to form large-scale enterprises began in the early 1990s.[53] Nearly a decade later, in the first years of the new millennium, the replacement of the retail model by corporate structures à la Gagosian took place in the art world. Here too, the tendency toward monopolistic concerns with a simultaneous presence in several cities is becoming more and more pronounced. And the "celebrity logic" that plays a constitutive role in the worlds of film and fashion is also making deeper inroads into the art world. In the 1970s, a fixation on famous people, like that practiced by Warhol's inner circle, was a minority position aimed above all against the dominant artistic self-image as underground artist, provoking this consensus by frequenting politically dubious members of the international jet set. These days, the entire art world goes into raptures when Brad Pitt is spotted at Art Basel. Formerly, this fawning over celebrity was not widespread, only a marginal phenomenon. But the focus on celebrities has since transformed itself into a worldview from which no one can totally escape. Although the art world is moving toward other cultural industries in structural terms, this does not mean its peculiarities are completely lost. In this social universe, one still encounters archaic rituals, unusual business practices, and behavior that is difficult to explain, incompatible with the media, or even bizarre. On the one hand, the art world has developed into what I have referred to (by analogy with the culture industries) as an industry producing visuality and meaning. And this development is the key feature in its "relative heteronomy." On the other hand, alongside celebrity logic and corporate culture, one still finds remnants of a society based on exchange: lavish festivities, the principle of "one good turn deserves another," payment in kind, local folklore, and so forth. The decisive point here, however, is that these two sides of the art world go together: they enter into a productive relationship, they assist each other—which, considering that capitalism tends to retain previous forms of production, is far from being a contradiction.

Give and Take

Anyone entering the art market as a novice will inevitably be confronted with business practices that would be quite unthinkable in conventional business relationships. As if it were the most natural thing in the world, collectors cancel orders, payments are delayed, and invoices simply ignored. Not to mention the large amounts of "dirty" money that circulate in this field on account of the many transactions made "off the books." The reason why this market has developed its own, unorthodox practices (practices capable of plunging any accountant into despair) lies in its product—the work of art—which itself eludes economic categories. This incalculable aspect of artworks calls for art-world players, too, to act unpredictably. Only behavior that elsewhere would be considered bizarre, if not unprofessional and detrimental to business, can do justice to the special status of art.

If the players in this special market are not receptive to its regulation and codification (in the form of contracts, for example), then this recalls the rites of exchange in archaic societies, which were also based on unwritten rules, as described by anthropologist Marcel Mauss.[54] Like the exchange of gifts in such societies, art trade is not contractually regulated whatsoever. It is governed by unwritten laws only, such as the principle of "one good turn deserves another." When someone renders a certain service, he can be repaid in kind or in the form of a favor in return. Even the most generous gifts must be reciprocated. This apparently non-economic, but in fact very deeply economic, principle is mentioned by Mauss. Compared to those practices he describes for archaic societies, it could also be said that art-world deals are embedded in a potlatch-like system of "total services," consisting of invitations to lavish meals, glamorous parties,

53 See Alicia Drake, "Epilogue," in *The Beautiful Fall: Fashion, Genius and Glorious Excess in 1970s Paris* (London: Bloomsbury, 2006), 360–377.

54 See Marcel Mauss, *The Gift: The Form and Reason for Exchange in Archaic Societies* (1950) (New York/London: Routledge, 2002).

and the like. Indeed, in prosperous times, art market players try to outdo each other in throwing the most extravagant dinners and parties at the most original locations. Such lavish displays of wealth and largesse are interpreted by Mauss as gestures of superiority, with the aim of forcing others into submission by overwhelming them.[55] For demonstratively extravagant art parties, one could use less aggressive terms and soberly observe that even the most generous invitation ultimately seeks to charm the guest. After attending an opulent opening gala, one may be more positively disposed toward the exhibition as a whole. The courtesy owed to a host is often enough to keep most guests from openly expressing criticism, even if complaints flow unabated behind the host's back. The obligation to reciprocate identified by Mauss still exists, then, operating in the art world in more subtle, subliminal ways.

Mauss explains that the obligation to reciprocate a gift stems from a view of the received item as something not inanimate, and which therefore has to be passed on.[56] One might consider this a relapse into animism and superstition. But below the surface, it is just such a belief in "magic property" that continues to motivate the gifting of art collections, for example, to this day. Recently, former gallerist Anthony d'Offay described his "gift" to the Tate Gallery in just such terms of obligation: Everything one owns in life, he said, is only on loan, and must therefore be handed on.[57] In the societies Mauss studied, this practice was based upon the conviction that objects have a spiritual dimension: "To accept something from somebody is to accept some part of his spiritual essence, of his soul. To retain that thing would be dangerous and mortal."[58] In this light, the art collector has no choice but to part with his property. Ownership of an artwork is already associated with the notion that it facilitates contact with some spiritual being. The collector can revel in the feeling of possessing an artist's thoughts, even his person and his life. This impression that something is alive in artworks, is what fuels trade in them. The more "life" they evoke, the busier the process of exchange becomes, fittingly characterized by Mauss as a "constant give and take."

Mauss also observed that subjects involved in such transactions were in the habit of treating each other like objects. To the same extent that they consider the things exchanged as "animate," they themselves take on thing-like traits, creating a "mixture of spiritual ties between things that to some degree appertain to the soul, and individuals, and groups that to some extent treat one another as things."[59] This tendency to subjectify objects, accompanied by an increasing objectification of subjects, sounds familiar. In the art market, too, artworks are immediately subsumed under the name of their author, thus filled with life and made to resemble subjects. Artists, for their part, are expected to stage themselves as credible personalities, becoming more object-like. Marx deduced this correlation from the commodity form: it is the commodity's immanent opposition of utility and value, of special and abstractly general work, that results in a "personification of things" and a "reification of persons."[60] While the commodity mutates into a person and takes on a life of its own, those exchanging it assess each other like commodities.

So how does this archaic system of gift exchange, with its obligation to reciprocate, its animation of objects, and its reification of people, relate to the above-mentioned transformation of the art world into a global industry producing visuality and meaning? We are dealing here with two sides of the same coin. The raucous singing and late-night table-dancing at a restaurant after an exhibition opening, which looks archaic or strange to an outsider, is the *necessary counterpart* to the attempts for economic expansion by many galleries that continually open new branches and join forces with international partners to form large-scale enterprises. In their quest to expand,

55 Ibid., 95.
56 Ibid., 72–73
57 See Gina Thomas, "Ortstermin. Zum Tee bei dem Londoner Galeristen Anthony d'Offay, der Großbritannien seine Kunstsammlung überlässt: Jeglicher Besitz ist doch nur Leihgabe," *FAZ*, March 15, 2008.
58 Marcel Mauss, *The Gift* (op. cit.), 16.
59 Ibid., 18.
60 Karl Marx, *Capital: Vol. 1: A Critique of Political Economy* (op. cit.), 209.

they have internalized the doctrine of economic growth hammered into the head of every entrepreneur that he must grow his business to remain competitive. Marx noted that "competition subordinates every individual capitalist to the immanent laws of capitalist production, as external and coercive laws."[61] Alongside this internalization of market requirements, the lavish parties and unorthodox business practices are also the expression of a belief in art as something for which no expense can be too great. This coexistence of economically rational and apparently irrational behavior reflects the special demands of art as something that is sold, but in a way that violates the laws of a free-market economy—exemplified by the way in which gallerists sell works not to the highest bidder but to individuals in whose possession they believe the work to be "in good hands." Sometimes the emphasis is on the pricelessness of art, for which no invoice is written as a matter of course. Other times, art is subjected to a base logic of profitability that asks only how much it will yield.

The Economy of Aesthetic Judgments of Taste

It is clear that there is no purely economic or purely aesthetic way of relating to art. Even "aesthetic experience" is permeated by economic motifs. In some cases, this may even appear in the guise of an aesthetic judgment of taste. Usually, an art dealer's aesthetic reservations are especially strong when problems with sales appear on the horizon. Young artists in particular are familiar with such economically motivated changes of opinion. At the slightest sign of economic fluctuation, the gallerist claims to have a problem with their work on account of its "form" or its "content." But as soon as the work is back in great demand, these aesthetic reservations vanish into thin air. Such value judgments are far removed from what Kant referred to as a "pure" or "subjective" judgment of taste. The vacillations of the gallerist show that aesthetic goodwill can be fueled by the prospect of economic gain, just as aesthetic reservations can be multiplied by a drop in demand.

According to Kant, the key feature of aesthetic judgment is that it makes a claim to universal validity.[62] Only where approval is won and everyone can be expected to share the same pleasure, Kant says, can one speak of a "pure" judgment of taste.[63] As such, the peculiarity of an aesthetic judgment lies in its normative power: it should be accessible to and shared by all. With this claim to "validity for everyone," however, it also claims authority. But an aesthetic judgment can only make this claim by referring to what Kant calls "common sense,"[64] by which he means a capacity for judgment as subjective as it is general, determined by feelings alone, not by concepts. This principle is as individual as it is general, amounting to a subjectively internalized norm. For Kant, a judgment of taste can only be made on the basis of such a common sense. For us, however, what is decisive here is that the authority to which Kant links aesthetic experience—common sense—is *internal and external at the same time*. He conceives of this experience as "autonomous." For without recourse to common sense, no judgment of taste could claim universal validity. But if a judgment depends on "common sense," this relativizes Kant's ideal of a "pure" judgment of taste made in complete freedom. Taken to its logical conclusion, "common sense" should tear down Kant's model of autonomous aesthetic experience. But he stubbornly insists on the autonomy of the judging subject, whose judgment should not be based on "a collection of votes and interrogation of others," as he explicitly emphasizes.[65] It should be based on "his own taste" alone, rather than being the result of "insinuations." This means that anyone passing an aesthetic judgment must "stop his ears" with wax like Odysseus's crew. Today, however,

61 Ibid., 739.
62 Immanuel Kant, "Analytic of Aesthetic Judgment" in *Critique of Judgment* (op. cit.), 46.
63 Ibid., 43.
64 Ibid., 68. Common sense is defined here as a subjective principle that uses only feeling and not concepts to determine, with universal validity, what is pleasing, and what is not.
65 Ibid., 111.

such a subject, who judges "for himself" without, as Kant so nicely puts it, "groping about among other people's judgments," comes more and more to resemble a fiction.[66] Even for Kant, this ideal of a judgment of taste arrived at independently seems to have been more like wishful thinking, causing him to defend it all the more doggedly. He makes a vehement appeal not to be forced to accept the opinions of others.

Today, especially under the conditions of the information and media society, it should go without saying that no one makes judgments "for himself," totally unaffected by what others say, think, or write. Never before has judgment-formation depended so heavily on the kind of "idle talk" so despised first by Kant and later by Heidegger. It is only Paolo Virno who has rehabilitated "idle talk" in the sense of a "contagious and prolific discourse without any solid structure" that offers orientation in times when it is hard to gain an overview. It "nurtures reassuring certainties" and "diffuses opinions that are always already shared."[67] What for Kant must be ignored at any price is recognized as a productive force by Virno, who declares it the core form of production within a society already ruled by communicative action.

If it is true that we are currently experiencing significant growth in the importance of communication, information, and gossip, then it is fair to assume that this will leave its mark on our perceptive behavior. Today, this behavior is further removed than ever from resembling something self-contained, not to mention a state of "monadically encapsulated perception" (Luhmann). For in today's "connexionist world" (Boltanski / Chiapello), the key is to have access to as much information capital as possible. And one can assume that this information capital, with its newly enhanced value, will help shape our aesthetic judgments of taste. What Kant condemned as invasive chatter now forms the basis of our capacity for aesthetic judgment. Someone who has heard or read about the record prices paid for works by Daniel Richter, for example, will pay them a different kind of attention than if the artist's name meant nothing to him at all. A crucial influence on the shaping of my judgment will also be whether and above all *by whom* the artwork in question was recommended to me. What sources does idle talk draw on? Do I value the opinion of those who claim to appreciate this work? Or, do I instead have an allergic reaction to consensus-building, especially within my own group of friends, so that work that is recommended is even more likely to meet with my reservations? One may decide to momentarily block out the many and varied social factors of any given aesthetic experience (prior knowledge, existing interests, knowledge of artistic hierarchies, recommendations from others, etc.) in order to concentrate purely on the experience of form. But this experience of form, too, is far from autonomous. It is tied to specific perceptive skills, just as every form must be viewed as something contextual that is traversed by external parameters.

66 Ibid., 112.
67 Paolo Virno, *A Grammar of the Multitude* (op. cit.), 88–89.

Chapter Four

Market-Reflexive Gestures in Celebrity Culture

Internalized Norms in the Neoliberal Regime

The relationship between art and the market is like the fraught interplay between two partners who are always arguing, but who ultimately depend on each other. Despite this close bond, artworks are by no means completely determined by events on the market. They may be held in check by specific market conditions in isolated instances, but thanks to the special status acquired by art since the eighteenth century, fine artists are also predestined to *relate* to such market constraints. They may even insist on imagining a different society, a society not ruled by market constraints. But in order to fight the notion that consumer capitalism is a given that we simply have to deal with, there is no way around addressing its specific conditions. Instead of considering artistic production as entirely subjected to the laws of economics, then, it makes more sense to examine its specific *market-reflexive* potential—a potential that, incidentally, can be of considerable interest to the commercial art market. But the market is not capable of totally monopolizing or neutralizing what I call "market-reflexive gestures," even if this is the tone struck by the most recent (and most interesting) critiques of capitalism. In the scenario envisaged in this study, art-market constraints do extend into artistic practices, but without neutralizing them or dictating all conditions. Or, put in systemic terms: A high degree of heteronomy does not rule out a certain degree of autonomy.

What form can this autonomy take under conditions of heteronomy in which the wider market has encroached to what German so cial scientist Thomas Lemke sees as an "unprecedented degree"? And is it admissible, as a critic, to focus exclusively on artworks when the personality and "life" of the artist have long since been sucked into the marketing machine?

In previous chapters, the intrusion of market mechanisms into the art world was discussed as a consequence and symptom of a "neoliberal" system that, according to Ulrich Bröckling, aims to regulate all social relations and ties between people via market mechanisms.[1] This means that even areas formerly considered private—the body, health, social relationships, appearance, friendships—come under economic pressures to optimize (via self-imposed regimes of dieting, excercise, surgery, therapy, etc.). This is most obvious in the media and in advertising, which call upon one to take responsibility for one's own health, to keep fit and slim, to look after one's relationships, to improve one's appearance, and so forth. Such invocations only find fertile ground because they do *not* directly correct, discipline, or coerce. The way they work is more subtle, aiming at internalization—neoliberalism does not produce submissive, disciplined individuals. Instead, it causes us to internalize its norms and objectives, which we then find "normal" or generally desirable.[2] Even once we identify the dubious nature of these ideals, we are still receptive to them, often submitting to them against our better judgment.

The Biopolitical Turn

When subjects are urged to optimize their entire lives, including their bodies, and orient them toward an ideal, then this is the expression of a biopolitical turn in the course of which politics has increasingly focused on life (Greek: bios).[3] Thomas Lemke has defined biopolitics as essentially a "political economy of life," meaning that life is not only politicized, but also economized.[4] Biopolitics therefore implies a bioeconomical dimension. It was Foucault who introduced the concept of biopolitics to describe a historically specific technique of power aimed at people's lives. Foucault, who situates the emergence of this regulatory power in the second half of the eighteenth century, always emphasized that biopolitics functions primarily by stimulation and not by submission or discipline. It is the power, as Foucault put it, to "make live and to let die."[5] Those who die are abandoned to their fate, while attention is focused fully on the form we give to our lives. In this scenario, the term "life"—which tends toward essentialization in any case—always remains a little vague. Foucault's main aim was to distinguish biopolitics from sovereign power by referring to its non-repressive impact on life.[6] To achieve this aim, one might say he was obliged to work with such a slippery concept as "life." According to Foucault, biopolitics exerts its influence indirectly, prompting people to give a particular form to their lives of their own accord. As an indication of just how pervasive its power has become, even the most intimate aspects of everyday life are subject to a pressure to optimize. These conditions are not new and I certainly don't mean to present them as a radical break. But since the 1960s, with the advent of a media society that tirelessly produces affect and aims at marketing life, these conditions have intensified noticeably, and their sphere of influence has expanded. Many theorists—especially Antonio Negri and Michael Hardt—presume that we now live in a "biopolitical context" in which "the production of capital converges ever more with the production and reproduction of social life itself."[7] This position has been disputed, especially among Marxists, as it tends to underestimate the ongoing importance in advanced global capitalism of production based on the exploitation of outsourced cheap labor. But Negri / Hardt were also right to point to a parallel shift in the economy where we are forced to throw our lives into the bargain. This increased focus on life is of course also due in part to the social movements of the 1960s and 70s, which insisted on a politicization of the private. Without belittling the enduring historical achievements of those movements, art historian Sabeth Buchmann rightly points out in a recent essay that an "erosion"

1 See Ulrich Bröckling, *Das unternehmerische Selbst. Soziologie einer Subjektivierungsform* (op. cit.), 76.
2 See Lars Gertenbach, *Die Kultivierung des Marktes. Foucault und die Gouvernementalität des Neoliberalismus* (op. cit.), 152–155.
3 See Thomas Lemke, *Biopolitik* (Hamburg: Junius, 2007), 9.
4 Ibid., 80, 16.
5 Ibid., 50.
6 See Maria Muhle, *Eine Genealogie der Biopolitik, Zum Begriff des Lebens bei Foucault und Canguilhem* (Bielefeld: Transcript, 2008), 9.
7 Michael Hardt and Antonio Negri, *Empire* (Cambridge: Harvard University Press, 2001), 402.

of the classical modes of production has since taken place: The difference between the fields of leisure and work has collapsed, as has the dividing line between the traditionally male sphere of production and the traditionally female sphere of reproduction.[8] If the world of private life comes to resemble the world of work ever more closely, then society as a whole can be viewed as a "factory" (Negri / Hardt) in which life goes to work.[9] Biopolitics and the neoliberal regime concur here in that they both exercise power indirectly. They opt for self-regulation, which also means that they view society as something structurally similar to the market, as something that is capable of regulating itself.[10]

Art and Artists as Purveyors of Life

Art has always considered life a productive force. One need only think of historical avant-gardes such as Futurism, Russian Constructivism, and Surrealism, which championed a merging of art and life. Did they not foster a situation in which life has become the privileged focus of our actions, and upon which the market tries to capitalize? Yes and no. It is not fair to accuse historical avant-gardes of biopolitical complicity; their calls for closer ties to life were explosive precisely because they were directed at a prevailing definition of the artist as ivory tower dweller. Today, we face a situation in which the artist embodies the ideal of the "entrepreneurial self" (Bröckling), and in which, equally, every manager wants to be "creative." In any case, where a self-image formerly attributed to artists has become a general ideal, one can say that the line between art and life, which the avant-garde sought to blur, has been largely erased. Today, self-realization is a near-universal priority. But we should keep in mind that "life" is an ambiguous concept, which the various avant-gardes interpreted in very different ways.[11] While it would indeed be farfetched to accuse them of promoting the biopoliotical turn, their focus on "life" does have a biopolitical and bioeconomical dimension, not least because of the massive boost it gives to its value. This enhanced value is also reflected in the classic art monograph with its claim to explore the artist's "life and work." Here, life is portrayed as a fundamental category at least as worthy of our interest as the work. Most artist monographs vehemently pursue this angle, giving them a biopolitical slant.[12] They are based, after all, on the assumption that the artist devoted his entire life to art, thus subjecting that life to a norm of artistic production. And, conversely, his life is proclaimed exemplary, not least because it was capable of bringing forth such an outstanding body of work. The status of the artist as a legendary figure also feeds on biographical information. In their pioneering study on the legend of the artist, Ernst Kris and Otto Kurz demonstrated that particular "preconceptions" run through artist biographies as leitmotifs.[13] These include the idea of the artist as an exceptional being enabled by talent to bridge the gap between art and life. The mythical artist possesses the ability to create "motion" and "life."[14] This is the basis for his special status. He has thus made something out of his life, just as his art has something inherently alive about it. Rembrandt's portraits, for example, have always been described as "animated," among others by Georg Simmel, who praised him for telling the story of a "stream of life."[15] The artist is clearly expected to give life form—to do so, however, he must also be capable of rendering every scrap of his own life productive.

8 See Sabeth Buchmann, "Biopolitik als Melodrama. Zu Yvonne Rainers Lives of Performers und Rainer Werner Fassbinders Warnung vor einer hl. Nutte," in *Der Einsatz des Lebens. Lebenswissen, Medialisierung, Geschlecht*, eds. Astrid Deubler Mankowsky, Christoph Holzhey, Anja Michaelsen (Berlin: b_books, 2009).

9 See Antonio Negri and Michael Hardt, *Labor of Dionysus: A Critique of the State-Form* (Minneapolis: University of Minnesota Press, 1994), 9–10.

10 Ibid., 278.

11 See Peter Bürger, "Lebensbegriffe der Avantgarden," in *Film, Avantgarde und Biopolitik*, eds. Sabeth Buchmann, Helmut Draxler, and Stephan Greene (Vienna: Akademie der bildenden Künste, 2009), 72–84.

12 See Martin Warnke, "Foreword," in *Rubens* (Cologne: DuMont, 2006), 6.

13 See Ernst Kris, Otto Kurz, *Legend, Myth, and Magic in the Image of the Artist: A Historical Experiment* (1934) (New Haven: Yale University Press, 1979), 3.

14 Ibid., 71.

15 Georg Simmel, *Rembrandt: An Essay in the Philosophy of Art* (1916) (New York / London: Routledge: 2005), 6.

Exceptional Beings and Celebrities

The figure of the "artist as an exceptional being" implies two things: the assumption of an outstanding personality, and the attribution of an extraordinary life. Both of these also apply to the now omnipresent figure of the celebrity, whose life and personality are supposedly exemplary and worth talking about. The celebrity, too, rises above the mass of ordinary mortals, lending him an exceptional aura. It was the "legendary" artist who provided the blueprint for the celebrity, formed in his image.

Current definitions of celebrity reflect this connection to the artist as an exceptional being. Cultural theorist P. David Marshall has described celebrities as "hyper-versions that express the potential and possibilities of the individual."[16] As such, this potential is theoretically available to all, but is significantly heightened in the image of the celebrity. Like the legendary artist who has supposedly given everything and devoted himself wholly to his work, media celebrities stand for an especially intensive exploitation of universal assets: They know just how to derive the most capital from these assets by giving their all. In the absence of general ethical guidelines, the celebrity serves as a fixed point capable of offering orientation, as living proof that it is possible to make one's life productive, profitable, and happy. Celebrities like Kate Moss and Amy Winehouse even seem to live through strokes of fate (separation, career setbacks, drug addiction) in exemplary form. Their celebrity status also benefits from the fact that they render comprehensible the possible failure of a universal potential. This is the reason for the worldwide fascination with the custody battles of someone like Britney Spears: Her legend grows with each new, all-too-human disaster. In addition, schadenfreude over a celebrity's failure provides an outlet for resentment and malice. Although they are quite obviously media constructs, celebrities are experienced as real people made of flesh and blood, people we know all too well.

How Much of a Product Is a Person?

One key difference between the celebrity and the artist as exceptional being is that the former has no body of work circulating independently of their person. Whereas it is possible in theory for a fine artist's life and work to be examined separately, in the case of the celebrity, person and product tend to become one. Describing this regrettable state of affairs, actress Angelina Jolie has said that today, her private life makes up 80 percent of her product, consisting of "silly, made-up stories and what I'm wearing."[17] Whereas for her father's generation (actor Jon Voight), private life was far less important, accounting for only 20 percent of the actor's product. Almost nostalgically, Jolie recalls a time when the focus was on acting skills, which now seem almost irrelevant. Film stars derived their importance from their screen roles, but in the case of celebrities the emphasis is on their way of life. And this regardless of the fact that movie acting is actually a difficult skill—a lot of labor and other people's work goes in to it. But this labor is forgotten when it comes to celebrities. Jolie is the best example of this; her product is her life, or rather what the media imagine her life to be.

Celebrities par excellence, like Paris Hilton, are simply famous for being famous.[18] Not so the artist, who usually has a product to show, a product that has the potential to circulate on its own whether or not it is highly dependent on his person. This is even the case for an artist whose position relies strongly on self-marketing, such as Yves Klein—there is a body of work to back them up.[19]

One exception is performance art, in which person and work naturally coincide. Artists whose work is performative put their physical selves on the line, and as a result, the distinction between their

16 P. David Marshall, "Introduction," *The Celebrity Culture Reader*, ed. P. David Marshall (New York / London: Routledge, 2006), 4.
17 See Rich Cohen, "A Woman in Full," *Vanity Fair* (July 2008).
18 See Graeme Turner, *Understanding Celebrity* (London / New York: Sage, 2004), 5.
19 See Benjamin Meyer-Krahmer's comparison between Paris Hilton and Tino Sehgal, *Texte zur Kunst*, issue 68 (December 2007): 160–163.

private and public identities is blurred. Artist Andrea Fraser recently referred to this fact, commenting that for her, there had rarely been any difference to speak of between "personal" and "professional."[20]

But apart from performance art, fine artists have the ability to adopt a position in relation to their product. This is also what gives artistic production an aesthetic advantage and forms the basis for its special status—the fact that artists can shape their relationship between life and oeuvre, between person and work, in a wide variety of ways. On this point, they are certainly better off than celebrities. The latter may retreat from the media, refusing to give details of their private lives and/or speaking only about their work. But since their work—modeling or acting—is completely filled by their person, they will be unable to completely shake off media interest in the "personal" dimension.

The relationship between "life" and "work" is fundamentally metonymic, marked by shifts and transfers. This applies to both artists and celebrities: life and work rub off on each other, the significance of one generates significance in the other. When an artist like Joseph Beuys stages himself as a patriarch in a photograph of his family watching *Star Trek* on television (*Familie Beuys beim Fernsehen von Raumschiff Enterprise*, 1972), then this conventional domestic setup must be taken into account when interpreting his work. But it would be reductive to discuss his work only in these biographical terms. Whereas it is almost impossible to clearly distinguish between Angelina Jolie's media image and her film roles, the drawings produced by someone like Beuys can certainly be viewed apart from his staged media image (as a shepherd in a floppy hat, for example).

But there is also a type of artist for which the constructed media "personality" is very much in the foreground—that of the "celebrity artist." Such an artist is encountered most often in fashion and lifestyle magazines, with the focus firmly on the person and the spectacle surrounding him or her. In such publications, artists like Rachel Feinstein or Sam Taylor-Wood are presented less as artists than as "It Girl," "party queen," or "muse." Privileging of the personal to the exclusion of the work is a particular problem for women artists. Traditionally, they have been confronted with a purely biographic interest fixated on their lives, loves, looks, and so forth—obliging them to invest a great deal of effort in refocusing attention on their work. Strikingly, a recent portrait of Rachel Feinstein in American *Vogue* was illustrated only by a picture of one of her mobile-like wooden objects, rather than the usual artist photograph.[21] It is possible that Feinstein herself attempted to bring about this shift in attention away from her person and toward her work. But the idea of it being possible to exert control over celebrity journal reportage is essentially an illusion. At best, one can influence the basic direction of an article. After all, no one forces the artist to pose for *W* magazine like a model and then chat, as Cecily Brown did recently, about upcoming hairdressing and waxing appointments.[22] Rather than playfully countering the magazine's celebrity logic in some way, she fulfilled every cliché from painterly "mastery" to "It Girl."

It is also possible for artists to counter the personalization of their product in less conventional ways. There is no need to allow themselves to be photographed in front of a painting in their studio with paint-stained jeans, on the one hand fulfilling media expectations (the artist as self-realized messy painter, resurrected painter prince, or transgressive drug-user), while, on the other, reproducing an image of the artist that has long become suspect within their own milieu, which they possibly see as a successful provocation. A more interesting approach would be either to reject a certain form of media coverage altogether, or to go further and attempt to address the conditions of celebrity culture in one's own work in a less predictable manner.

20 See Andrea Fraser, "Psychoanalysis or Socioanalysis: Rereading Pierre Bourdieu," *Texte zur Kunst*, issue 68 (December 2007): 139.

21 See *Vogue* (May 2008), unpaginated.

22 See Julie L. Belcove, "Brown's Eye," *W* (July 2004): 78–87.

From Market Expansion to Celebrity Culture

Now that the market encroaches on almost every aspect of our lives, and "life" serves not only as a theme for artists (as it always has), but also becomes an object of political intervention and economic valuation, then celebrity culture is the form of society best suited to this development. This may sound surprising and rather farfetched. But if one considers celebrity culture as a form of society in which individuals are selected at random and rewarded for the successful marketing of their lives (or what is presented as their life), then the neoliberal and biopolitical subtext becomes clear. The neoliberal regime, which aims at the economization of everyday life, can be said to have found its true expression in celebrity culture. In this light, the "spectacle culture" regularly evoked (and condemned) by cultural critics has long been replaced by a "celebrity culture" in which a massive personality cult is practiced. At first glance, the similarities between spectacle and celebrity culture seem to outweigh the differences. Debord's definition of the spectacle as "a social relation between people that is mediated by images" is certainly also applicable to celebrity culture.[23] Except that the concept of the spectacle assumes the possibility of contemplating the spectacle from some detached standpoint. But such a position of absolute distance becomes impossible as soon as market conditions encroach more profoundly and more directly into our lives, as in celebrity culture.[24] Here, these conditions have burrowed their way deep into individual lives that remain subject to an economic imperative of ever-increasing value. The whole world mutates into one big catwalk upon which life goes to work. Whereas Debord's spectacle manifests itself as a shift from "having to appearing,"[25] celebrity culture actually equates appearing with having: Whoever appears in the media as a celebrity has the only thing that matters—global fame.

In recent years, the cult of celebrity has grown to unimaginable proportions. The creation of many new magazines is evidence that the hunger for celebrity news cannot be sated.[26] From the aptly-named *Celebrity* to magazines like *InStyle*, a veritable industry has developed around the celebrity complex, including many online outlets. Today, the fabrication of celebrity is a key industry—an industry that profits from collective addiction to pictures of celebrities and keeps addicts supplied with fresh material. Even "up-market" magazines like *Vanity Fair* are giving over more and more space to celebrity features.[27] Broadsheets, too, are increasingly devoting pages to gossip or lowbrow content. The general yearning for celebrity status and visibility has grown proportionally to the degree to which it has been encouraged, exploited, and mobilized by these media formats.

The notion of celebrity culture is usually associated with the departure from an accomplishment-oriented society, where achievement was seen as something that could be objectively measured. Celebrities no longer perform any task in the conventional sense. If anything, what they achieve is fame: they have managed to achieve prominence for themselves—their life or personality—rendering them economically useful. Paris Hilton's accomplishments consist of allegedly having received no money from her parents and attaining fame and wealth by means of self-stylization and business acumen.

Celebrity culture is thus the true face of a neoliberal regime in which the individual is writ large. As everything now depends on this individual, it must optimize itself in every respect: maintain a tirelessly polished appearance, doggedly combat signs of ageing, continually improve its public image. Celebrities are taken as a point of reference because their work requires them to take these tasks especially seriously. They are at the mercy of the public and there-

23 Guy Debord, *The Society of the Spectacle* (op. cit.), 7.
24 On the problem of the concept of the spectacle, including its orientation toward a "problematic utopia of social authenticity;" see also Juliane Rebentisch, "Spektakel," *Texte zur Kunst*, issue 66 (June 2007) 120–123.
25 Guy Debord, *The Society of the Spectacle* (op. cit.), 11.
26 See Graeme Turner, "Celebrity: The Tabloid and the Democratic Public Sphere," in *The Celebrity Culture Reader* (op. cit.), 487–500.
27 Ibid., 490.

fore cannot afford neglect (of their teeth, for instance, which must be bleached).

The ideological function of celebrities is evident in the way they ceaselessly call out to us that we too can make it if only we take our lives, our looks, and so forth, into our own hands, if we work tirelessly on our fashionable appearance and physical fitness. But such reportage on celebrities regularly ignores the fact that it took specific conditions and a whole team of advisors and stylists to elevate them to celebrity status in the first place. To believe that one's own advancement is only a matter of willpower and perseverance is as tempting as it is illusory. Without a doubt, idolizing celebrities can have an encouraging, self-empowering effect. Why else would so many women immediately copy Kate Moss's latest hairstyle? The kind of radical makeover initiated by a shopping spree or visit to the hair salon can sometimes work wonders. But the celebrity press regularly gives the impression that the right haircut coupled with discipline and willpower is all one needs. Questioned about their success, many stars fall back on the stock answer that they were always just extremely "focused"; the message is that you can make it if you really want to, if you stick at training your body and concentrate exclusively on getting ahead.

Turning up our noses at the phenomenon of celebrity culture will not get us very far, however. Celebrity worship may be a new form of the cult of the saints, revealing a desire for comfort and redemption, and a hope for salvation that should be taken seriously. Just as a fan derives strength from his fandom, celebrity adoration can reduce feelings of isolation and confirm people in their actions: Here is someone else who has struggled with her figure after childbearing, someone else who relapsed after coming off drugs. The fan's identification with the celebrity has a hallucinatory quality insofar as it mentally blurs the difference between his own situation (in financial terms, for instance) and that of the star. The way celebrities deal with career setbacks and problems in their love lives or drug addiction can serve as a parable for our own lives.

Warhol Lives: Between Star and Celebrity

There is a widespread view, promoted by books (*Social Disease,* 1992)[28] and exhibitions ("Celebrities. Andy Warhol and Stars," Hamburger Bahnhof, Berlin, 2008), that Warhol's practice wholeheartedly embraced celebrity culture. This view lacks complexity and must be contested. As much as Warhol's practice imitated and reflected these conditions, it also distanced itself from them. Warhol both accepted *and* analyzed the laws of celebrity culture. As a consequence, one could indeed argue that the name "Andy Warhol" stands for the introduction of celebrity logic into artistic production. Not only do his pictures reflect the star system, as in his early silkscreen prints of popular idols like Marilyn Monroe, Liz Taylor, and Elvis, his life stories recounted by telephone, such as *POPism* and his *Diaries*, also pay tribute to the massive presence of gossip in a celebrity culture interested in even the most banal everyday acts. From the moment when life becomes a resource, it is subjected by Warhol to incessant examination. Who sleeps with whom, who has put on or lost weight—this is now valuable information on the subject of life and how it is lived. As a person, too, Warhol rose to the status of an influential celebrity during the 1960s, as revealed by numerous media reports on the "Factory scene." *The New York Times* even took notice when he made a perfectly staged visit to a department store with his entourage, during which Nico wore his *Fragile Dress* made of paper.[29] It is tempting to treat Warhol as a founding figure of celebrity culture, if only because his much-quoted dictum that everyone can be famous for fifteen minutes has proven so prophetic. After all, the desire for fame now supports entire industries. But in contrast to the promises of superstardom made by certain

28 Karl Steinorth, Thomas Buchsteiner (eds.), *Social Disease: Photographs '76 – '77* (Ostfildern: Hatje Cantz, 1992).

29 See Mark Francis and Margery King, "Silver Factory: The 1960s," in *The Warhol Look: Glamour, Style, Fashion* (Munich / Paris / London: Schirmer / Mosel, 1997), 128.

television shows such as *American Idol*, which end in bitter disappointment for most candidates, the fame in Warhol's work is something money can buy. Every industrialist's wife who commissioned a portrait from him in the 1970s found herself transformed into a star. Warhol's commercial portraits were a ticket to the world of the rich, the beautiful, and the famous, acting as a shortcut on the arduous path to glory. Instead of working hard to optimize one's looks, all one needed was the cash to pay for a Warhol portrait. Like a cosmetic surgeon, he teased the star potential out of every sitter, elongating necks, enlarging lips, and retouching wrinkles.[30]

The fabrication of stars and fame was a lifelong interest for Warhol. Legend has it that his enthusiasm for film stars began at the tender age of six, when he started collecting pictures of Shirley Temple and Judy Garland.[31] However, he did not stop at such worship—as encouraging and enabling as it may be. As a graphic designer for luxury shoes and a window dresser for department stores, he had ample opportunity to acquaint himself with the laws of the fashion industry that supplies stars with their armor. In his early silkscreen prints, Warhol referred directly to the star phenomenon, but without merely reproducing it. Warhol's identification with fame took an aesthetic turn at the moment when it became the focus of his artistic production as a whole. By concentrating exclusively on celebrities in his pictures, he claimed membership for himself in this sphere, a sphere that was actually closed to him.[32] When he used pictures of stars like Marilyn Monroe as his material, he metaphorically claimed to be on par with them. The fact that this logic of transfer worked is evident in the way images of the stars he portrayed now circulate under his name, as "Warhols."

It would be wrong, however, to reduce Warhol's project to an attempt to profit from the status of his subjects. He may have siphoned off fame for himself, but he also created it in equal measure—and he did so on his own terms. Alongside his official star portraits, Warhol also worked to produce his own underground stars during the 1960s, as exemplified by his screen tests, his movies, and the band The Velvet Underground. The screen tests alone were a form of casting based on highly idiosyncratic criteria, which can be read as a "litmus test of the subject's response to the unblinking camera."[33] In other words, they were used to test each person's celebrity potential.

However much Warhol participated in the general enthusiasm for stars, he also created his own version of stardom. Warhol's "superstars" (a term coined by Jack Smith) including Ingrid Superstar, Viva, Baby Jane Holzer, and International Velvet all had celebrity potential, although deviating from the smooth veneer of mainstream stars. Edie Sedgwick had a magical filmic presence that was certainly compatible with Hollywood, but when she was led to reveal her mental problems in front of the camera, as in *Kitchen* and *Poor Little Rich Girl* (both 1965), the break with Hollywood conventions became obvious. Many of Warhol's superstars were drag queens, posing a challenge to the bigotry of Hollywood's heterosexist norms. Warhol's own star business was flanked by the creation of a star magazine, *Interview*, to take care of PR.

After the attack by Valerie Solanas in 1968 and Warhol's withdrawal from the underground milieu began the period of his commissioned portraits, whose function can also be seen as supporting the production of "underground stars." Rich people's aspirations to stardom financed the dreams of fame of people who could never have afforded a Warhol portrait and who were, incidentally, very badly paid. Here, the Factory proved representative of a neoliberal regime that erased the line between "working hours" and "leisure," exploiting life around the clock. The increased willingness to work

30 See Pat Hackett, "Introduction," in *The Andy Warhol Diaries* (op. cit.), xvi.
31 See Barry Paris, "15 Minutes, But Who's Counting? Andy Warhol and His Icons," *The Warhol Look: Glamour, Style, Fashion* (op. cit.), 58.
32 See Jonathan Flatley, "Warhol Gives Good Face," in *Pop Out: Queer Warhol*, eds. Jennifer Doyle, Jonathan Flatley, and José Munoz (Durham / London: Duke University Press, 1996), 113.
33 Quoted from Steven Watson, *Factory Made, Warhol and the Sixties* (New York: Pantheon, 2003), 131.

for nothing corresponds to celebrity culture's view of fame as a means to survive—one only lives if one is famous.

But while the Factory produced life, exemplifying what Maurizio Lazzarato has rather pointedly termed the capitalist "command over subjectivity,"[34] it also allowed different sexual identities and life concepts to find expression and gain recognition.[35] New constraints were imposed, but new possibilities were created as well.

Moreover, Warhol's works of the 1960s and 70s embody a shift from the old star system to the emergence of celebrity culture. While stars, as mentioned above, were admired on the basis of their performative achievements (as an actor or rock singer for example), the attraction of the celebrity is based purely on personality and the way they supposedly live. Stars live through their roles, while celebrities are admired for simply existing. The underground stars fabricated by Warhol can be read as the beginning of the transformation of the star into a celebrity. When stars are connected with life, they become celebrities. Accordingly, Warhol's artistic production always aimed for the person as a whole, or even for that person's whole life.

Authentically Staged Life

Taken as a whole, Warhol's film oeuvre is proof that it was "life" he was after. Basic activities such as hanging out, arguing, taking drugs, having sex, sleeping, staying awake, and mercilessly interrogating others were his raw materials. Jonas Mekas aptly described these films as "meditations on life, [...] almost religious, [...] a looking at daily activities like eating or sleeping."[36] In the films, these activities were accorded the "real time" they take in life, but by projecting them at the silent movie speed of sixteen frames per second, the artist opted to slow life down, as if to subject it to a carefully scrutinizing and classifying gaze. Warhol himself acknowledged that his films aimed to capture life when he once pointed out the impossibility of distinguishing between them and the lives of the actors.[37] In a comment on the shooting of *Chelsea Girls* (1966) he laconically remarked: "Everybody went right on doing what they'd always done, being themselves."[38] But this claim to authenticity does not alter the fact that it was a highly mediated, extremely artificial, and technologically produced authenticity—if only due to the technological apparatus of film. Life in film is mediated by definition, comparable with life under the conditions of celebrity culture, which is itself a product of the media.

Just as celebrity culture tries to market life, Warhol's films try to capture the lives of their performers. While the aim is to "get close" to life, this cult of the authentic should also be seen in the context of an anti-illusionist aesthetic that was not only widespread in the underground films of the 1960s (Hollis Frampton, Kenneth Anger, Jack Smith), but also found expression in avant-garde dance experiments (like those of the Judson Dance Theater), which clearly influenced Warhol.[39] Simple everyday activities like running, walking, hanging out and communal drug use, as well as nudity, sex, and arguments became art-worthy subjects. But even in view of the fact that anti-illusionism was an artistic convention of the time, we should not forget how shocking this cult of "mere existence" seemed at first—not only in the eyes of the general (puritanical) American public, but also to those closely associated with the Factory, who were equally baffled. Stephen Shore, for example, who photographed the scene at a young age, was allegedly astonished by the way people

34 Maurizio Lazzarato, "Immaterial Labor," in *Radical Thought in Italy: A Potential Politics* (op. cit.), 134.
35 See Douglas Crimp, "Getting The Warhol We Deserve," *Social Text* 59 (summer 1999): 49–65: "A whole motley crew of artists, actors, writers, drag queens and other sexual deviants worked on one another's projects and generally found mutual inspiration in a shared countercultural milieu."
36 Quoted from Robert Rosenblum, "Saint Andrew," *Newsweek*, December 7, 1964, in Alan R. Pratt, *The Critical Response to Andy Warhol* (Portsmouth, NH: Greenwood, 1997), 10.
37 See Andy Warhol and Pat Hackett, *POPism: The Warhol Sixties* (New York: Harcourt Brace, 1980), 219.
38 Ibid., 180.
39 See Yvonne Rainer, *Feelings Are Facts: A Life* (Cambridge/London: MIT Press, 2006), 243.

at the Factory just sat around in a daze: "It is not like they're reading, it is not like they're meditating, it's not even like they are sitting watching, they're just sitting—staring into space and waiting for the evening festivities to begin."[40] The members of this scene, then, don't do anything in the conventional sense, they don't even engage in relaxation exercises or observe what's going on. They don't sleep either, as a result of their speed-fuelled lifestyle, portrayed in Warhol's novel *A*. Insomnia was a cinematic topos at this time in any case, as illustrated by Hollis Frampton's interest in the subject. What members of the Factory offered, however, was lived time. They only became active when it was time for the evening's events. The parties formed the stage on which they put their lives on show. But what was presented in this nightlife framework was far from an authentic "self." Parties demand role-play; they are strongholds of theatrical identities whose fundamentally contrived and artificial nature comes into play as a key quality.

Against this backdrop, the Factory of the early 1960s can be understood as a machine that not only staged transgressive ways of life, but also profited from people's willingness to perform them. Especially Warhol's early films like *Sleep, Eat, Blow Job, Kiss* (all 1963), and *Drunk* (1964) can be said not only to have created a space for different concepts of sexual identity or transgressive behavior—one need only think of the overtly sexual kisses between homosexual *and* heterosexual couples in *Kiss*—but also to have capitalized on these identities. The actors' way of life is both honored and exploited. There was in fact a great deal of literal exploitation in Warhol's film productions: the actors were not paid. One might argue that the Factory profited from a willingness to work without pay that grew in direct proportion to the symbolic capital and fame that could be expected in return. When labor potential can no longer be separated from the person or the body—as is the case in post-Fordism, according to Virno—then a certain degree of self-exploitation is unavoidable. The Factory can be compared to a bio-political theater that stages and cannibalizes life. But it also offered something in exchange:

space for the development of different sexualities and the prospect of underground fame and notoriety. The latter is a precious commodity in celebrity culture, not least for those who have no product to offer other than themselves.

Life and Work

By all appearances, Warhol's own life revolved entirely around parties. In any case, the dividing line between his work and what might be called the public performance of his "lifestyle" is fundamentally unstable and cannot be clearly defined. It is impossible to confine Warhol's artistic production to objects, paintings, and films alone. Not only the statements he made in his *Philosophy* (1975) and his *Diaries* (1989), but also the way he designed himself as a public persona, should be viewed as integral to his artistic practice. Of course, statements by artists must always be taken with a grain of salt—the "true meaning" of their work is not to be found here. Instead, such statements must be decoded and interpreted, as they are part of a carefully choreographed pose that is in equal parts staged and authentic, deliberate and accidental, strategic and unconscious. The innumerable eye-witness accounts of Warhol (by ex-assistants, ex-It Girls, ex-collaborators) should also be treated with caution, as they, too, are personally motivated projections that create an illusion of proximity. However, they do reveal something about the attitude Warhol adopted toward life and work.

One such eye-witness is Bob Colacello, according to whom Warhol was incapable of relaxing and had no concept of "vacation."[41] He converted pleasure into work, using every social occasion as an opportunity for "'getting ideas,' 'getting portraits,' or 'selling ads'" for *Interview*.[42] Colacello's account is of course tendentious and

40 Andy Warhol and Pat Hackett, *POPism: The Warhol Sixties* (op. cit.), 111.
41 Bob Colacello, *Holy Terror: Andy Warhol Close-Up* (New York: Harper Collins, 1990), 167.
42 Ibid.

tainted by his own frustration—as if he had to retroactively justify why he stopped working with Warhol. But this anecdote sheds light on a pose that Warhol actually cultivated, one in which life goes to work. As well as recording all of these networking activities, his diaries present "going out" as a way to meet rich people who would eventually, when they had had enough to drink, buy his art.[43] What was once called "fun" or "leisure time" is quite explicitly represented as work. Even intimate relationships sooner or later mutated into working relationships, as Billy Name recalled.[44]

This instrumentalization of formerly private activities and friendships recalls Paolo Virno's description of the "post-Fordist condition," in which "remunerated life and unremunerated life" (corresponding to the old distinction between labor and non-labor) can no longer be distinguished.[45] But Warhol's merging of the private and the professional is also in line with portrayals of the "legendary" artist, at least since Giorgio Vasari's famous accounts of Renaissance artists. They, too, were represented as exceptional beings—celebrities *avant la lettre*—who allegedly consecrated their entire lives to their work.[46] Warhol was also prescient in recognizing the art world's networking imperative, fulfilling it to the point of excess. But he had a nose for its pitfalls too. During the 1970s and even more in the 80s, he constantly increased his party-going activities, as his diaries show, recording every visit to a newly opened club. But the need to dose one's public appearances is also mentioned. Too much media presence is damaging: "Because also, they use you up. And it's scary."[47] According to Warhol, fame is not everlasting for the simple reason that the media eventually grows tired of the people it promotes. This weariness was something he found genuinely frightening. Here, as elsewhere, he proves to be both a theorist and a practitioner of celebrity culture, whose principles he studied, used as his artistic material, *and* lived out himself. The iron law of celebrity culture that stars, especially female stars, wear out with time, was something he positively internalized: unmoved and with great regularity, he dropped one It Girl (Edie Sedgwick) in favor of another (Viva), only to lose interest in her too after a while.[48] In his own production, too, he drew consequences from a market in which personalities, unlike artworks, become worn out—for despite a busy social life, Warhol made sure his paintings were in steady supply. To the same extent that the Factory provided a space for people to "perform themselves" (Steven Watson), it also remained a place where products were made. And however seriously Warhol pursued "going out" as work, he seems to have been very much aware of the advantages of separating artistic output from the artist's personality. At least that is the implication of the following dictum from his *Philosophy* (1975), a kind of *dictionnaire des idées reçues* of celebrity culture: "You should always have a product that's not you."[49] Consequently, relying on selling one's own personality—showing up at countless parties, collecting contacts, and networking intensely—is not enough: those who market only themselves are left empty-handed. His advice to actors and models, in whom product and personality coincide by definition, is to count their films or photographs. Only then will they know how much they are actually worth. For Warhol, what counts ultimately is the product, the only thing that is credited with a capacity for value creation.

Warhol himself was far from being the kind of artist who withdraws to his studio to dedicate himself solely to the manufacture of these supposedly all-important products. On the contrary, he led a life more or less completely exposed to the public, just as celebrities do today. But unlike celebrities, Warhol had a product—his artworks. Of course, this product was certainly "enriched" with "life." The time Warhol spent at parties and in the Silver Factory and the hip fashionableness and coolness associated with him definitely generated

43 Pat Hackett (ed.), *The Andy Warhol Diaries* (op. cit.), 646: "Here's how it all works: You meet rich people and you hang around with them and one night they've had a few drinks and they say, 'I'll buy it!'"
44 See Steven Watson, *Factory Made: Warhol and the Sixties* (op. cit.), 128.
45 See Paolo Virno, *A Grammar Of The Multitude* (op. cit.), 102–103.
46 See Giorgio Vasari, *Lives of the Artists* (London: Penguin, 1987).
47 Pat Hackett (ed.), *The Andy Warhol Diaries* (op. cit.), 272.
48 See Bob Colacello, *Holy Terror: Andy Warhol Close Up* (op. cit.), 69.
49 Andy Warhol, *The Philosophy of Andy Warhol* (San Diego: Harcourt Brace: 1975), 86.

value that flowed into his product. This product carries life embedded within it, but is capable of circulating independently of the artist as a person: The artist can avoid over-exposure by sending a product ahead, so to speak. Or he may also hide behind his product, especially as it will outlive him in any case.

Despite the advantages of an independently circulating product, Warhol always showed his face to a degree matched by few other fine artists before him. Does this mean that by exploiting every personal encounter, he was the perfect embodiment of the neoliberal ideal of a totally deregulated working life? Certainly. But it is interesting that the unbearable nature of a life shaped by the dictates of optimization was also a theme for Warhol. "Life's too hard" was his personal way of putting it, a phrase he dropped into conversation at every opportunity like a mantra. It captures the unreasonable demands made by a life that instrumentalizes each and every private encounter. Nonetheless, Warhol led just such a life.

The Flipside of Celebrity: Warhol as Productive Fan

Warhol also proves to be a theorist and practitioner of celebrity culture by shedding light on the dark side of celebrity life. His paintings both examine and generate the celebrity phenomenon, especially the early portrait motifs of Jackie Kennedy (*Twenty Jackies*, 1964), Liz Taylor (*Blue Liz as Cleopatra*, 1963), and Marilyn Monroe (*Marilyn Six-Pack*, 1962), which Thomas Crow has convincingly argued must be read as an investigation of the connections between celebrity, death, crisis, and mourning.[50] He points to the way in which *Sixteen Jackies* (1964) allows us to see Jackie in different poses, smiling, with her head lowered, nearly crying but attempting to keep up appearances. Indeed, this work comes close to being a study of what Aby Warburg referred to as "pathos formulas"—formulaic signifiers of different emotional states, in this case stages of grief. As a widow,

Jackie also functions as the prime witness to the unstable border between life and death. If biopolitics is also "thanatopolitics," as Giorgio Agamben has suggested,[51] amounting to a decision between life and death, then Jackie also serves as an allegory for the fundamental instability of this threshold. The more abstract and blurred these images appear due to the technical process of screen printing, the "truer" they seem. The work's seriality also means that Jackie's singularity is both emphasized and annulled. We see her sixteen times—confronting us with an observation characteristic of celebrity culture, that is, that the impression of singularity and uniqueness can be further enhanced under conditions of mass production. An existential and singular event in life—the loss of a person and the act of mourning—is captured and carefully examined, at the same time as it is rendered meaningless and lifeless.[52] In addition to exploiting and cannibalizing life, Warhol also empties it. He seems to have also worked on a kind of democratization of the celebrity principle via his choice of motifs. Benjamin Buchloh has rightly pointed out that in a single year, 1963, Warhol confronted pictures of the most famous and glamorous stars with the most horrific and anonymous everyday images.[53] In this approach, stars and disasters have equal right to artistic treatment. Whether famous or anonymous, even the most un-portrait-worthy subject—the nameless accident victim or the criminal sought by the FBI in the "Most Wanted Man" series (1964)—is declared portrait-worthy in Warhol's work.

It is not just a matter of depicting and generating fame, however—that alone would be too simple. In Warhol's work, the celebrity's

50 Thomas Crow, "Saturday Disasters: Trace and Reference in Early Warhol," in *Andy Warhol*, October Files #2, ed. Annette Michelson (Cambridge: MIT Press, 2001), 49–66.

51 Giorgio Agamben, *Homo Sacer. Sovereign Power and Bare Life* (Stanford: Stanford University Press, 1998), 122f.

52 On "lifelessness," see Benjamin Buchloh, "Anniversary Notes for Andy Warhol," in: *Andy Warhol, Shadows and Other Signs of Life* (Cologne: Buchhandlung Walther König, 2008).

53 See Benjamin H.D. Buchloh, "Andy Warhol's One-Dimensional Art: 1956–1966," in *Andy Warhol: A Retrospective*, ed. Kynaston McShine (New York: The Museum of Modern Art, 1989), 26.

claim to rise above the masses is both fulfilled and denied. As a serial process, screen-printing both heightens and erases singularity. Repetition impresses the special quality of an image upon us, while also presenting it as a non-exclusive manufactured item.[54] This quality of being singular and mass-produced is that of the human being as commodity under the conditions of celebrity culture. But serialization also highlights the fact that Warhol was obviously taken with his motifs. The "Flower" paintings, for example, he repeated endlessly.[55] The series is thus a vehicle for sustained, even obsessive interest, to which it also gives expression—as if Warhol were unable to stay away from particular motifs, as if he were compelled to approach them again and again via endless variations and color combinations.[56] This desire for the same pictures over and over again, with interest focused on the tiniest detail, or the smallest deviation, is also the driving force behind the celebrity industry. Warhol occupies a double viewpoint, that of the culture industry *and* that of the consumer. His paintings satisfy a desire and document that desire. As such, Warhol stands for the fan as "active producer," as redefined by cultural studies in the 1980s: Rather than being a passive victim of manipulation, the fan was considered to be an active protagonist creating identity via identification (in some cases, the fan's consumer behavior was even given the weight of a political act). Warhol's approach stands for a reconciliation of these opposing concepts of fandom. His screen prints of the 1960s show evidence of an actively producing fan, as Warhol always selected particular images, defined specific crops, and made decisions concerning color. At the same time, they reveal the passive position of a devotedly admiring fan, as the artist abandons himself to the material of celebrity culture. Not only in pictures, but also in word and deed, Warhol never left any doubt as to his belonging to a celebrity culture, by whose visual materials he was obviously touched, and by whose ideals of beauty he himself was kept in check.

The Tyranny of Looking Good

Warhol's high esteem for "beauties" is itself an indication of the increasing importance of "looking good" in celebrity culture. It has often been pointed out that he distinguished between "beauties" and the rest of the world.[57] Concerning the appearance of those he encountered, nothing escaped his notice. Be it weight gain, the same Halston dress worn twice, or the first signs of aging—everything was mercilessly registered, classified, and logged in his diary.

In addition to applying them to his surroundings, however, Warhol also subjected himself to strict criteria concerning appearance. He was constantly trying to optimize his own looks by means of nose jobs, facials, and fitness trainers, as his diary tells us. At times, it is as if he anticipated the universal internalization of "looking good" in celebrity culture. How clearly aware he was of these norms is illustrated by his explanation of an "early appointment with Dr. Linda Li" (his dermatologist): "This is all to keep myself beautiful for business."[58] What Warhol openly acknowledges here (and actually condones, although in a slightly resigned manner) is the fact that, in a labor market that wants all of us—body and soul—external appearances can be crucial. In Warhol's artistic production, however, the internalization of this norm is always accompanied by its analysis. (Once again, "artistic production" is used in an expanded sense here to include statements and public appearances.) An obvious example of such an analysis would be *Before and After I* (1961), a picture based on an advertisement for the visible

54 On the difference between repetition and difference in Warhol's work, see also Rosalind Krauss, "Carnal Knowledge," in *Andy Warhol* (op. cit.), 117.

55 See also the following statement by Leo Castelli in John Wilcock, *The Autobiography and Sex Life of Andy Warhol, by John Wilcock and a Cast of Thousands* (New York: Other Scenes, 1971), unpaginated: "He gets enthusiastic about a certain screen, lets say the flowers. He did more of those than of other things."

56 See Bob Colacello, *Holy Terror: Andy Warhol Close Up* (op. cit.), 267: "Andy painted every subject until he had exhausted his range of appropriate color combinations—he thought about color a lot it seemed to me."

57 Ibid., 88.

58 Pat Hackett (ed.), *The Andy Warhol Diaries* (op. cit.), 569.

benefits of a nose job. The work clearly distances itself from these norms of beauty, if only by virtue of image cropping and dripping as evidence of artistic manipulation. But the picture also captures the hope associated with such an ad, hopes for personal betterment due to radical makeover. It refers to and reflects upon the "tyranny of looking good."

It is also important to realize that in the art world of the 1970s, Warhol's personal obsession with beauties, models, and celebrities was a marginal position, directed provocatively against what was then still a relatively intact consensus, with most artists considering themselves left-wing and thus identifying with an egalitarian ideal. But Warhol's ostentatiously hierarchical and classifying mindset also touched on a painful subject. It's no secret that even under cover of formal equality, gross inequalities flourish, especially in the art world. What at the time was the minority position of an art and fashion jet set developing around figures like fashion designer Halston and his muse Bianca Jagger—the glorification of youth, beauty, and money—is now common in large sections of the art world. While only a small circle shared Warhol's fascination with models like Jerry Hall, today the assembled art-world tribe grows ecstatic when Claudia Schiffer is spotted shopping at Frieze Art Fair. The fashion world played a pioneering role in this respect, especially as it had already left behind egalitarian ideals in the 1970s. Fashion designers mutated into universally admired stars and fashion's ongoing enthusiasm for celebrities was also just beginning.[59] Not only in the formation of corporate empires, but also where self-marketing and celebrity obsession were concerned, the fashion world was some three decades ahead of the art world.

Through his experience as a graphic designer for fashion, Warhol became familiar with the laws of this industry. By worshipping "beauties" and models, he transferred these laws to the art world. Although this amounted to provocation at the time, today it seems prophetic, as the art world too, now celebrates models and fashion designers.

Significantly, Warhol's final public appearance was as a model in a fashion show (at the Tunnel Club), just a few days before his death. Photographs of the event show him pacing along the catwalk with a delighted but suffering expression. Although he must have been in severe pain from an enflamed gall bladder, he seems to enjoy the situation as someone who has finally triumphed. A dream had come true—presenting a collection as a model, belonging to the genus of "beauties," at last![60] But his appearance is also an unequivocal reminder of the toll taken by staking one's whole body and personality.

Unlike a model, however, Warhol had a product—a product called art, that is traditionally defined via a symbolic value that lifts it above the sphere of the applied. The symbolic value of art is based on the not entirely unjustified assumption that artworks generate a symbolic surplus that can be reduced neither to "history" nor to the artist's biography. Nevertheless, speculation about the artist's personality—how he supposedly lives, whether his work can be linked to bohemian or glamorous contexts—does become part of the art's symbolic value and may even enhance it. But ultimately, the product's advantage is that it cannot be reduced to the person, while not remaining entirely separate from it. Warhol's work is a ceaseless demonstration of how product and person infiltrate one another—especially when circulating in the neoliberal and biopolitical context of celebrity culture—while potentially also leading separate existences. And yet, despite his willingness to expose himself to these conditions as a person, he did not permit his work to be governed by them.

For and Against the Market: Andy Warhol

Warhol's work explores the constraints and opportunities of an emerging celebrity culture, in which the market figures as something

59 See Alicia Drake, *The Beautiful Fall: Fashion, Genius and Glorious Excess in 1970s Paris* (op. cit.), 256.
60 See Bruce Hainley, "Model," in *The Warhol Look: Glamour, Style, Fashion* (op. cit.), 296.

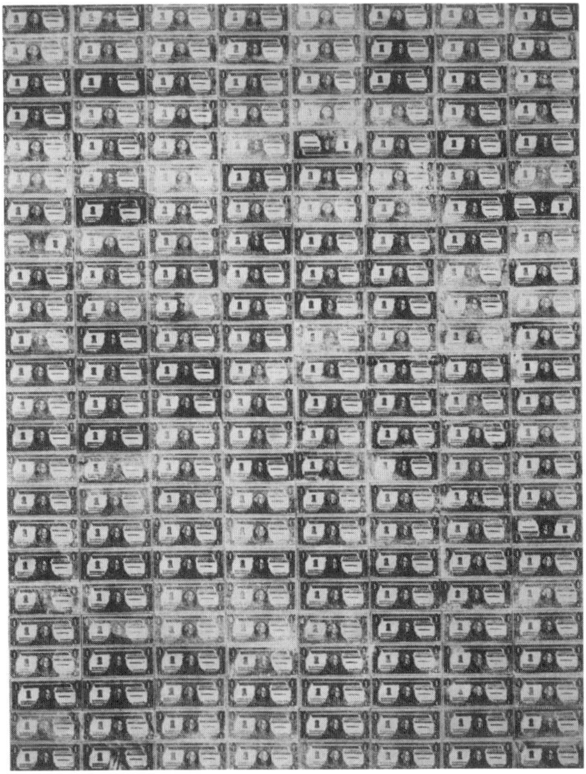

Andy Warhol, 192 One-Dollar Bills, *1962*

that must be reckoned with, albeit without totally submitting to its demands.

This awareness of his product's conformity with the market is illustrated by the motif for his first screen-prints from the early 1960s: one-dollar bills. Significantly, money was Warhol's first portrait subject. As well as occupying this prominent position in Warhol's oeuvre, money was also accorded a privileged place among commodities by Marx, according to whom it functions as a "general equivalent." It is a measure and an expression of value in one, making it comparable to the artwork, to which value is also ascribed and which can also serve as a method of payment. The credibility of an artwork, like that of money, depends on collective agreement. People must have agreed in advance that it expresses a particular value. In Warhol's *192 One-Dollar Bills* (1962), this structural similarity between art and money—which, incidentally, has occupied many artists from Rembrandt to Klossowski—is taken to the point of a literal fusion. The picture consists of (screen-printed) banknotes arranged in series, so that money value and artistic value appear to become one, exaggerating the widespread tendency among art-world players to mistake the price of an artwork for an expression of its value. In this case, however, confusion between price and artistic value originates in the work itself, which not only portrays money, but also provides information about its monetary value. If its artistic value did not exceed the value of the money depicted, then it would correspondingly be worth $192. The picture anticipates the position of someone whose only aim is to earn money with it, making no secret of the fact that possessing art always also means possessing money. Indeed, the picture's future owner will have dollars mounted on his walls.[61] But if art is ultimately a pile of dollar bills, as Warhol suggests, then all hope of its "symbolic surplus value" must be abandoned. In this light, Warhol's first screen-prints are like bombshells, deflating the excessive expectations placed in art once and for all.

In spite of this, the picture cannot help generating a kind of "surplus." Some of the dollar bills are printed faintly and appear faded, an effect created by Warhol's specific screen-printing process and his receptiveness to resulting errors and imprecisions. These washed-out areas of the picture seem to escape the viewer's grasp, dissolving into an abstractness that can be read as an allegory for the operation of abstraction performed by money. Obviously, these pictures cannot be reduced to their money function, and this precisely because they suggest a reading of themselves as just money. In this way, Warhol once again proves himself to be an artist who both conformed to and resisted the market. On the one hand, his dollar bill screen-prints

61 See Pat Hackett (ed.), *The Andy Warhol Diaries* (op. cit.), 34: "I'm trying to get some dollars on his wall."

take the art / money analogy to absurd lengths, making available what everyone wants—money—and thus disappointing traditional expectations that art should be "more" than this. But as a result of his specific aesthetic procedure, in the end, the dog gets its bone after all.

This balancing act between satisfying and disappointing the expectations of the art market runs through the whole of Warhol's artistic production. The typical image of Warhol as an artist who conformed to the market is too narrow and must be corrected. It is true that he constantly promoted this image, as when he ostentatiously referred to himself as a "commercial artist." In the art milieu of the 1960s, this declaration of an attitude not averse to selling amounted to self-stigmatization. As members of the avant-garde, artists wanted to be all manner of things—except commercial. This self-description was a gift to Warhol's detractors, who could feel justified in finding him "too commercial." The label endangered his reputation as a serious artist to the same degree that it secured him a unique selling point, signaling his break with the traditional image of the artist. Finally, the model of the "commercial artist" is a reminder that artistic production is usually also guided by economic motives.

Such a mixture of resistance to the market and commercial opportunism is a feature of Warhol's behavior on the art market in general. In an interview in the late 1960s, for example, he started a rumor that Brigid Polk actually painted his pictures.[62] The statement can be read as a provocative break with the principle of "authorship," continuing the legacy of Duchamp and Fluxus. But those in the art world were not amused. Warhol's German collectors in particular were immediately alarmed and feared for the authenticity of their paintings. Warhol was obliged to issue an official declaration correcting this claim in order to avoid works being returned.

It cannot be stated often enough that from the point of view of the established art market, Warhol was an unsafe bet, especially in the early 1960s.[63] This is suggested by an anecdote recounted in *POPism*, according to which his dealer Ivan Karp eventually stopped visiting the Factory on the grounds that it wasn't his world, the scene Warhol surrounded himself with being just too destructive.[64] Karp's comment represents the viewpoint of a puritanical America that could not approve of the Factory's sexually transgressive climate. The gallery scene, too, was apparently irritated by his insistence on openly keeping company with freaks, drag queens, transsexuals, and drug addicts. In this respect, Karp's apologetic explanation for being so taken aback is symptomatic: He only felt comfortable, he said, in the "art community." This demarcation bears witness to the distance that still separated the world of underground film and music from the "official" art world at the time. Although Warhol himself had ties with both milieus, in the 1960s they had few points of contact with each other. If Karp had had his way, this social segregation, which he considered jeopardized by Warhol's Factory, would have remained in place. By opting for the underground and its transgressive practices in the 1960s, Warhol risked alienating the established art milieu. But he also paved the way for the now ubiquitous recuperation of the underground by the mainstream.

In Warhol's art, market conformity and resistance to market conditions always go hand in hand. When, for example, he announced in 1965 that he was giving up painting in favor of filmmaking, with the characteristic explanation that he was more fascinated by "people,"[65] it had two effects: Besides raising doubts among buyers about the dependability of his artistic output, which seemed to be in danger of slowing, the prospect of a reduction in the number of pictures caused a price increase.[66] At the time, it was reportedly impossible to lay hands on a Warhol. Once again, a measure taken to irritate the market actually fuels the market, turning up the commercial heat.

62 See Andy Warhol and Pat Hackett, *POPism: The Warhol Sixties* (op. cit.), 248.
63 See interview with Ivan Karp in John Wilcock, *The Autobiography and Sex Life of Andy Warhol, by John Wilcock and a Cast of Thousands* (op. cit.), unpaginated.
64 Andy Warhol and Pat Hacket, *POPism: The Warhol Sixties* (op. cit.), 83.
65 Ibid., 113.
66 See interview with Sam Green in John Wilcock, *The Autobiography and Sex Life of Andy Warhol, by John Wilcock and a Cast of Thousands* (op. cit.), unpaginated.

The decisive point here, however, is that in Warhol's case, events on the market are always acknowledged in his work as affecting his position. He closely followed art auctions, for example, not least out of personal interest.[67] In his diary, he noted the exact prices fetched by his paintings, but not without expressing dismay that works by fellow Pop artists like Lichtenstein and Johns had been valued far more highly. This makes it quite clear that the auction market, too, is not external to the artist. Warhol constantly emphasized the encroachment of the economy into life and work, at the same time as attempting to emancipate himself from the authority of the commercial art market—by developing other commercial outlets, for example, via his film production or *Interview* magazine. But in direct negotiations with gallerists, such as Ron Feldman, Warhol could also be decidedly uncompromising, even dictating terms and conditions.[68] One might say that he took the requirements of the art market into account without dancing to its tune. Warhol epitomizes the market-reflexive artist insofar as he took market activity as his material at the same time as opposing it. Instead of opportunistically playing to commercial art-market expectations, he regularly thwarted them.

Art as Market-Reflexive Gesture?

Speaking of a market-reflexive "gesture" implies an aspect of performance. Gestures are used to communicate via body or sign language. Etymologically, the word "gesture" is derived from *gestus* (facial expression, gesticulation), highlighting its origins in acting. When artworks are discussed as gestures, the emphasis is on their theatrical dimension. Insofar as they portray or show something, they resemble a performance. The painter Henri Michaux, known for his "gestural" vocabulary, is said to have claimed he was only able to associate with the world via gestures. The gesture, understood as genuinely artistic, thus represented the only possibility for him to enter into a relationship with his surroundings—which brings us to its fundamentally communicative function, allowing one to relate to social conditions.

Art in general, and fine art in particular, is a privileged field of activity for the gesture. Besides theater and performance—its preferred territory—it can also be found in painting and Conceptual art. Painterly practices have a media-specific gestural repertoire: more or less powerful brushstrokes, differing styles of applying paint, and so forth. But many gestures have also emerged in Conceptual art—written declarations or ritual transactions in the form of checks or certificates—forming a vocabulary that can always be invoked. What does it mean, however, to attribute market reflexivity to a mere gesture? Is it not asking too much? I do so here on account of the gesture's ability not only to represent or symbolize, but to enter into a reflexive relationship with its surroundings. By "market-reflexive gestures," I mean reflection upon market activities from which the individual making the gesture does not exclude himself. This market activity is addressed in its specific historical form—be it a claim of the art market's structural proximity to the financial market, or an exploration of the impact of the celebrity principle on artistic production. Decisively, the market-reflexive gesture does not claim absolute distance from market events. Its point of departure, one might say, is consciousness of its own compromised position—but at the same time as admitting its deep involvement in the market, such a gesture also attempts to counter it. Ideally, the market-reflexive gesture displays an awareness that at certain times and in certain markets—the knowledge market, the market of institutions, the commercial art market—it may actually be in demand. After all, market reflexivity is not produced by the artist alone; it is generated

67 See Pat Hackett (ed.), *The Andy Warhol Diaries* (op. cit.), 136: "Everyone was talking all afternoon about the big auction coming that night, with the paintings of mine in it that Peter Brant put up for sale." (May 1978).

68 Ibid., 411.

in part by the specific markets in question. Every market therefore brings forth its own brand of market reflexivity.

One thing not meant by market reflexivity is direct intrusion of the market into artistic production. Even picture format may be determined by market practices, as Georg Baselitz recently revealed in an interview, stating that his choice of large canvases for his recent "Remix" paintings was based in part on the fact that they are easier to sell.[69] This admission of explicit market orientation is interesting insofar as it proves the presence of the market even in such a (supposedly) purely formal matter. But it stands less for market reflexivity than for the procedure of translating external requirement into aesthetic principle—a tried and tested approach since the beginning of modernism, if not before, whereby a necessity resulting from market conditions becomes an artistic parameter. By contrast, market-reflexive gestures address market conditions in terms of their potential to change.

It is one thing to expose the gesture's immanent link to society. It is another to claim for artistic gestures a form of self-consciously intervening market reflexivity. Can gestures act?

Such personalizing talk of the market-reflexive gesture seems to suggest they can. But in fact, it is not gestures or artworks themselves that act in a market-critical manner. Instead, it is the viewer who interprets certain gestures as market-reflexive, even anti-market. Market reflexivity is always a matter of attribution and interpretation. And every interpretation includes an element of projection and wishful thinking. But this doesn't mean that the assessment of a given work as "market-reflexive" is pure invention, derived solely from the viewer's subjective fantasy. Ideally, it is linked to some given artistic feature that makes it appear fitting and justified. An artwork certainly can send out signals of market reflexivity, but it requires a viewer who is receptive to its message.

Here, when specific artworks are said to exemplify market reflexivity, or, to be more precise, that they possess market-reflexive potential, the aim is not to draw up a personal or exclusive canon. The selection makes no claim to completeness, and the practices chosen function as examples only. It was not possible to take all artistic procedures fulfilling the criteria into consideration. And it is also not about awarding the label "market-reflexive" in the sense of a normative aesthetics. Market reflexivity is not obligatory, and works lacking it may also be of interest. Moreover, signs of market reflexivity are not effective in every case—just because a painting's surface is wallpapered with checks doesn't automatically make it market-reflexive.

The Artist as Market Strategist?

In *Dialectic of Enlightenment*, Adorno and Horkheimer cite an anecdote of the mortally sick Beethoven, who cast aside a novel by Sir Walter Scott, decrying, "The fellow writes for money!" though he himself acted as a businessman to market his quartets. One might consider this a case of double standards, but to Adorno and Horkheimer it is the "most grandiose" example of the "unity of the opposites of market and autonomy."[70] They demand that the artist's production include an awareness of this unity. The questionable nature of any such aesthetic prescription notwithstanding, this description comes close to my concept of market reflexivity. Market reflexivity, too, calls for relinquishment of what Warhol once termed "deep-rooted, long-standing art fantasies."[71] But this abandonment of an idealistic belief system does not imply that market and aesthetic autonomy are identical. Rather than canceling each other out, their opposition is in fact the precondition for their constituting a unity.

69 See Georg Baselitz on "Remix Paintings," interview by Heinz Norbert Jacks, "Weit im Abseits von allem." in *Georg Baselitz: Zero für den Maler*, ed. Karola Grässlin (Cologne: Buchhandlung Walther König, 2006), 23.
70 Theodor Adorno and Max Horkheimer, "The Culture Industry As Mass Deception," in *Dialectic of Enlightenment* (op. cit.), 127.
71 Andy Warhol, *The Philosophy of Andy Warhol* (op. cit.), 178.

For Adorno and Horkheimer, it is the artist who brings an awareness of the connection between autonomy and commercialization to bear on his work. The artwork is furnished with an awareness borrowed from the artist, so to speak. There seems to be no avoiding the premise of the "thinking artwork," a scenario in which the viewer renders this thinking concrete, putting it into words.

Studies that view the market as a condition for possible artistic autonomy are the exception in art history. And while in Adorno's production aesthetic the onus for thinking is on the art object, artist monographs focusing on the market tend to expect the artist-subject to do all the thinking and acting. In this vision the artist is painted as a sovereign market strategist.[72] It is to the credit of such studies, including Svetlana Alpers's pioneering *Rembrandt's Enterprise: The Studio and the Market* (1988), that they do away once and for all with the romantic notion of the genius detached from market conditions. The market is described as a factor facilitating artistic production. But despite the author's intuition for the importance of the market, it remains a problem of such approaches that they tend to style the individual artist as a rational market strategist. Alpers brands Rembrandt a "pictor economicus," insinuating that he was guided mainly by economic necessities in his painterly production.[73] In his study of Rembrandt's bankruptcy in 1654, Paul Crenshaw goes so far as to read this bankruptcy as a deliberate ploy by the painter to win back artistic freedom.[74] And a recent study on Courbet presents him primarily as a clever strategist who switched his focus to the production of landscapes solely due to increased demand for the genre.[75] The artist appears here as a tactical operator who uses his artwork as an instrument, creating the exaggerated image of a single-minded player who views his work as a mere means to an end. The problem with such a view is that it presupposes a rational subject capable of successfully realizing plans as conceived—and ignores the coincidences and unpredictability of the artistic material that make a crucial contribution to the peculiarity of a visual language.

The image of the market-savvy artist as strategist also ignores the vagaries and contingency of a life that cannot be brought fully under control. It misses the abyss of a subject, which is not transparent unto itself, but which may act irrationally, and certainly does not always pursue a reasoned objective. This, in any case, is the key insight of psychoanalysis, which has no place in the topos of "the artist as businessman." However methodical and entrepreneurial an artist's approach may be, the power of the irrational will thwart his plans. It is one of the lessons of poststructural and psychoanalytic theories that the subject must be understood as fundamentally restricted in its autonomy. Such a subject, who is not master in his own house, must be assumed in market reflexivity. In this view, the market-reflexive artist may well act strategically, but without always knowing what he's doing or why he's doing it.

Market Reflexivity Demands Hubris: Courbet and Klein

Where market-reflexive gestures are found, hubris is never far away. In pronouncements made by artists whose work refers to market conditions, demonstrative displays of hubris are the norm. Gustave Courbet and, a century later, Yves Klein regularly issued statements as to their greatness. In 1959, Klein tried to obtain funding for a one-page advertisement in the tabloid magazine *Paris Match* with the following text: "The greatest painter in the world, Yves Klein, is a

72 One laudable exception that avoids such a stylization is Alexander Alberro's book *Conceptual Art and the Politics of Publicity* (Cambridge: MIT Press, 2003).

73 See Svetlana Alpers, *Rembrandt's Enterprise: The Studio and the Market* (Chicago: University of Chicago Press, 1988), 118.

74 See Paul Crenshaw, *Rembrandt's Bankruptcy: The Artist, His Patrons and the Art World in Seventeenth-Century Netherlands* (op. cit.), 157.

75 See Jörg Zutter, Petra ten-Doesschate Chu, *Courbet: Artiste et promoteur de son oeuvre* (op. cit.), 7: "In France and abroad, in official and private exhibitions, he presents works of very diverse types: hunting scenes, still lifes, portraits, nudes, genre scenes, and a large majority of landscapes, all genres that answer to the demand of collectors and dealers." (trans. NG)

Frenchman."[76] Leaving aside the grotesquely overdrawn arrogance, the seemingly desperate nationalism, and the comical presumptuousness of this claim, Klein's statement does reproduce a mode of thinking in superlatives (the best, the greatest) which continues to dominate parts of the art market and art history to this day. Another remarkable aspect here is his readiness to cooperate with a tabloid magazine, which he apparently considered a suitable medium in which to announce his global fame. Klein clearly wanted to get to the heart of the tabloid press, once again running the risk of cementing his reputation as a frivolous prankster.[77] In postwar Paris, celebrity status was only permitted in exceptional cases—Picasso, for example, or Bernard Buffet. The latter soon learned the downside of popularity in the form of abuse from art critics, who called him the "Rembrandt of the stock market speculators."[78] At the same time, however, Buffet was an art star showered with official honors—a role taken as a model by Klein when he claimed to strive for "total success" comparable to that achieved by Buffet.[79]

In the case of Courbet, hubris is used as part of a struggle with the authorities. When he organized his own exhibitions in the immediate vicinity of the official Salons, he was certainly speculating on the crowds and the publicity. But his exaggerated self-confidence and self-praise were aimed more at denying the legitimacy of the official organs of recognition, his way of facing them down.

In a letter written in 1846, for example, Courbet informed his parents that he and all his artist friends considered the self-portrait he had submitted to the Salon to be one of the three best works in the whole exhibition.[80] He writes himself a glowing report, but unlike Klein, he cites members of his own peer group as guarantors for the correctness of his assessment. It is this approval from friends and fellow artists—rather than media popularity or official recognition—that he declares the true sign of quality. With this rhetoric, Courbet proves himself a defender of the principle of the artist's artist, a status he also claims for himself. Peer recognition, he affirms, is synonymous with artistic relevance.

In an 1853 letter to his patron Alfred Bruyas, Courbet lauds himself for turning down an offer of cooperation from a government representative (Le Comte de Nieuwerkerke) explaining that he, Courbet, was his own government.[81] In so doing, he refused to recognize the legitimacy of the existing government of Napoleon III, who came to power by a coup d'état. Metaphorically, he claims the status of an executive for himself, which is proof of wit and humor, especially when he tries to underpin the exaggerated claim with a reference to his own special status as the "proudest and most arrogant man in France."[82] Instead of waiting for art history to declare him an exceptional being, Courbet insisted during his lifetime that he was unmatched where pride and arrogance are concerned.

This mix of self-stigmatization with a positive twist and styling oneself an exceptional being, however, is also a legitimate response to asymmetrical power relations. Faced with the officially legitimated power of his opponent, it was essential to compensate for the illegitimate nature of his own position by an exaggerated and impertinent claim to legitimate power. Artistic hubris is always also a strategy for survival. The assumed power of the powerful can only be countered by claiming power for oneself. Legend has always cast both Courbet and Klein as "naïve" artists— naïve and impetuous. Perhaps the market-reflexive artist must retain a measure of naïveté, or rather faux naïvité, since only a naïve view allows him to rise above the situation. A certain degree of naïveté—that is, childish underestimation of real conditions—is clearly necessary if one is

76 Thomas McEvilley, "Yves Klein: Conquistador of the Void," in *Yves Klein 1928–1962: A Retrospective* (Houston: Institute for the Arts, Rice University, 1982), 55.
77 On the tendency to look down on him in artistic circles, see Pierre Descargues, "Yves Klein by Pierre Descargues," in *Yves Klein* (exh. cat., The Jewish Museum, New York, New York, 1967), 26.
78 Quoted from Clemens Krümmel, "Der Maler Bernard Buffet – zwischen Verriss und Rehabilitation," *Texte zur Kunst*, issue 45 (March 2002): 85.
79 See Sidra Stich, *Yves Klein* (Stuttgart: Cantz Verlag, 1994), 139.
80 Petra ten-Doesschate Chu (ed.), *Letters of Gustave Courbet* (op. cit.), 62.
81 Ibid., 114–117.
82 Ibid.

to symbolically reject these conditions. To elevate himself above the seemingly given and supposedly unassailable, the market-reflexive artist strikes the pose of someone who is more than a match for such conditions.

The Power of Public Image

Traditionally, fine artists have had recourse to their public image as a suitable arena for demonstrations of greatness and uniqueness. As a rule of thumb, the greater the hubris, the more self-promotion. In the case of Yves Klein, the artist's second identity as a judoka offered ample opportunity for such theatrics; he loved to pose barefoot wearing a judo jacket, as if to symbolize victory in inter-artist rivalries. After several test runs, he executed his famous *Leap Into The Void* (1960) again in the presence of a photographer.[83] Klein needed photographic documentation of his dangerous experiment to stake his claim of overcoming even the laws of gravity, as a man equal to any test of courage. Such acts of self-dramatization always transport the claim to absolute validity of an artist-subject, thereby also proclaiming his artistic program.

But Klein's poses also do justice to the fact that the site where meaning is produced has shifted in media society from the art object to the person of the artist. Today, the artist must represent the idea of his art personally, taking it on and living it. Klein harnessed even the most personal events to his art, such as his marriage to Rotraut Uecker in 1962.[84] As well as being spectacular and sensational, the wedding also served as a mouthpiece for Klein's art. Knights of the Order of Saint Sebastian, of which he was a member, formed a guard of honor, and the bride wore a crown in Yves Klein Blue. It seems fair to name Klein a precursor to today's much-maligned "event culture." His legendary exhibition "Le Vide" (1958) at Galerie Iris Clert is the best example of this transformation from artist to impresario, since it became a total event. *Le tout Paris* is said to have attended the opening of this show of "naked walls."[85] There were no artworks on display in the conventional sense.[86] All furnishings and fittings had been removed from the gallery space, so that the "emptiness" evoked in the title was guaranteed, an emptiness Klein claimed was the prerequisite for an experience of "immaterial pictorial sensibility."[87] "Immateriality" was Klein's magic formula and the name of his dubious (because restorative) attempt to give art back its transcendental dimension.

As if to emphasize the official character of the event, Klein had two uniformed republican guards posted in front of the gallery entrance (that was hung with a programmatic blue curtain) as if it were a state occasion, giving himself a reception appropriate for a government leader. His triumphal procession was planned to the last detail, and the original concept even included bathing the obelisk on Place de la Concorde in blue light, although this didn't make it past bureaucratic hurdles. Like only Courbet before him, Klein seemed to be making the claim that he was his own government. Except that, unlike Courbet, he was serious. Klein set new standards, and not only in terms of megalomania. "Le Vide" was a pioneering work because it declared an empty room to be the content of art, thereby shifting attention to the institutional framework. But during the evening, blue cocktails were served, ensuring that visitors absorbed his trademark—his specially patented "International Klein Blue"—in liquid form, forcing upon them the kind of "impregnation" that featured so prominently in his evocations of "immateriality." This open-

83 See Thomas McEvilley, "Yves Klein: Conquistador of the Void," in *Yves Klein 1928–1962: A Retrospective* (op. cit.), 67.
84 See Sidra Stich, *Yves Klein* (op. cit.), 243–244.
85 See Pierre Restany, "Yves Klein: Latest Prophet of Europe," in *Yves Klein* (exh. cat. The Jewish Museum, New York, op. cit.), 12.
86 See Sidra Stich, *Yves Klein* (op. cit.), 131–156.
87 He did, however, paint the walls with lithopone, so that the room literally breathed. And a few elements of his programmatic blue, which, as the businessman he was, he had patented as "International Klein Blue," were positioned outside the gallery and in various rooms. The window onto the street was painted blue and a blue curtain masked the gateway to the courtyard beside the gallery. In this way, "Yves Le Monochrome," as he called himself, ensured the strategic presence of his trademark. See ibid.

ing, then, was planned specifically with a programmatic objective in mind—that of publicizing his artistic position to maximum effect.

Admittedly, carefully planned after-opening dinners and parties by the artist and/or gallerist have been an unwritten convention in the art milieu since Dada and Surrealism, if not before. Today, there is renewed emphasis on the right location, chosen to transport the desired meaning. After the opening of Raymond Pettibon's show at Contemporary Fine Art in Berlin (2008), for example, the assembled company convened at a punk bar in Kreuzberg, as if to relive Pettibon's former association with the post-punk and hardcore scene—an attempt to steep his work in a rebellious, subcultural aura, which functions as one of the ingredients for its marketing.

With "Le Vide," too, Klein focused attention on the social event, demonstrating his awareness of the blurring between art and party. Today, the after-opening party is indeed to be considered integral to the production of meaning. In many cases, an analysis of the party setup sheds light upon the problems of a given artistic proposition.

The Self-Portrait as Propaganda Zone

Further proof that the work of art and its marketing cannot be strictly separated is provided by the genre of the self-portrait, since every self-portrait, as Petra ten-Doesschate Chu rightly points out, includes an element of self-marketing.[88] But it also goes beyond this, since its primary function is to communicate an artistic self-image. The many self-portraits painted by Courbet, for example, are not exclusively vehicles for identity formation or self-stylization. They also tell us something about the artist's attitude to the genre and to art in general. They make his position known and give us a key to interpretation. According to Chu, when choosing his poses for these pictures, Courbet looked to the literary world for clues as to what it means when a field of cultural production becomes an industry.[89] In the late nineteenth century, writers mutated into commodity producers, selling their texts for a line price to mass-circulation periodicals. They also set new standards in terms of self-dramatization, achieving celebrity status via theatrical public appearances, which, Chu says, Courbet used as models for his many self-portraits.[90] Courbet's work in this genre certainly created a highly theatrical image of him as a bohemian, as in *Self-Portrait (Man With Pipe)* (1848–49), where he presented himself as a sensitive and effusive "poseur," as T. J. Clark puts it so fittingly.[91] But his drooping lids and bedroom eyes are a warning against interpreting this pose too narrowly. As well as identification, it also signals distance. Courbet continually reinvented himself in a succession of self-portraits. When he portrays himself lying on the ground injured (*Self-Portrait As A Wounded Man*, 1844-1854) and as a bug-eyed lunatic (*The Desperate Man,* circa 1843), this corresponded to the pathos-laden, overdrawn image of the Romantic artist, which his portrait both lays claim to and distances itself from. A pose is struck and simultaneously exposed to ridicule, as Courbet always seems to be slightly mocking it. In other words, his self-portraits reveal an artistic position that takes art seriously as a realm of possibility, but without believing in it unconditionally. Any pose is dubious—while it aims for credibility, it should never be fully trusted.

That the self-portrait is the perfect place to proclaim an artistic self-image had already been proven by Rembrandt. In this context, Svetlana Alpers makes the revelatory observation that most of Rembrandt's early self-portraits show him decorated.[92] In *Self-Portrait with Velvet Beret* (1634), he painted himself with a golden chain, which, Alpers writes, was a token of honor that indicated royal favor. Does this mean that Rembrandt tried to transform his desire for official recognition into an artistic fait accompli? Are they to be

88 See Petra ten-Doesschate Chu, "Courbet and the Press," in *The Most Arrogant Man in France: Gustave Courbet and the Nineteenth-Century Media Culture* (op. cit.), 5–16.

89 Ibid.

90 Ibid., 17–28.

91 T. J. Clark, *Image of the People: Gustave Courbet and the 1848 Revolution* (London: Thames and Hudson, 1973), 44.

92 See Svetlana Alpers, *Rembrandt's Enterprise: The Studio and the Market* (op. cit.), 67–68.

read as signs of his worldly ambition? Only in part. Alpers recalls that for Rembrandt, the golden chain offered the kind of "effect of substance" which he so valued in his painting. In other words, the reason for the motif was an immanently painterly one. But Alpers also persuasively argues that these chains amount to staging a mark of favor in the studio, which becomes the self-imposed framework within which honors are awarded. By painting these honors himself, Rembrandt illustrates the shift from court to studio and thus to the market, which played a key role in his production. Like Courbet after him, Rembrandt, too, seems to have been reluctant to acknowledge official authorities—beyond his own mastery in the studio.

Such hostility to authority was also characteristic of *the* market-reflexive artist par excellence: Marcel Duchamp. Despite the historical distance separating him from Courbet and even more so from Rembrandt, Duchamp shared their dismissal of official approval. After *Nude Descending a Staircase* was rejected by the Salon des Indépendents in 1912, he withdrew from the art world, as he explained to Pierre Cabanne, to work as a librarian "free of any material obligation."[93] The artist used this interview to stage his oft-evoked withdrawal, which remains part of his myth to this day. In truth, however, his cannot be called a marginal existence at the fringes of the art world.

Duchamp mastered the use of perfectly styled self-dramatization as a vehicle for his artistic program. One need only think of his famous alter ego Rrose Sélavy, devised in the 1920s and used as the signature on the few works he made during this period.[94] As well as expressing doubt in the principle of authorship, the use of a pseudonym also stands for the realization that any artistic work requires a signature. Like a writer, Duchamp created his own nom de plume, as if to protect himself from the consequences of his "provocations." His apparent claim to female identity was reinforced by the official artist's portrait as Rrose Sélavy, made by Man Ray in 1921, in which Duchamp appears styled in drag as a refined lady with all the insignia of female elegance: from fur collar and decorative hat to delicately extended fingers. In this way, Duchamp claimed to represent both sexes, undermining the norm of the artist heretofore conceived of as a heterosexual male. But beyond the resulting destabilization of gender stereotypes, the male artist's "becoming a woman" is also to be understood as an incorporation of the Other, assuming qualities associated with "femininity." It is an expansion of power, which in Duchamp's case makes a striking contrast to his much-evoked and mythologized withdrawal.

Between Art Trade and Auction House: Marcel Duchamp and Damien Hirst

It is true that between 1925 and 1934, Duchamp hardly appeared in public as a fine artist.[95] But during this period, while refusing the traditional definition of artistic production he did act as an art dealer, acquiring, among others, a group of twenty-two works by Brâncuşi which he sold as the need arose. In his conversations with Pierre Cabanne, he explained these supposedly effortless and casual activities: "Whenever I needed money I'd go to Roché and say, 'I have a small Brâncuşi for sale, how much will you give me." And: "One must live. It was simply because I didn't have enough money. One must do something to eat."[96] This suggests that a certain degree of commercial activity is necessary to survive as an artist. The irony of Duchamp's position, however, is that he funded his refusal to participate in any form of exhibition by selling artworks, of all things. Negation and abstinence, then, can only be had at the price of engaging with the market at some other point. This also applies to those artists who followed Duchamp's refusal of production, whether in reference to Melville's *Bartleby*, or via the examination of a "non-

93 Pierre Cabanne, *Dialogues with Marcel Duchamp* (London: Thames and Hudson, 1971), 41.
94 See Dieter Daniels, *Duchamp und die anderen. Der Modellfall einer künstlerischen Wirkungsgeschichte in der Moderne* (Cologne: DuMont, 1992), 89.
95 See Dieter Daniels, "Der Rückzug aus der Kunst," in ibid., 82–97.
96 Pierre Cabanne, *Dialogues with Marcel Duchamp* (op. cit.), 74.

productive attitude" (Josef Strau). Notwithstanding the fact that even a non-productive attitude also has market potential in the sense of immaterial labor, an artist who refuses to produce must make a living somehow. In most cases, this comes down to the need to come to an arrangement with the art market in some other way.

In this context, it is significant that Duchamp seems to have been entirely comfortable with the idea of auctions. In 1926, he organized the sale by auction of eighty paintings by Picabia at the Hôtel Drouot.[97] In other words, he initiated an auction of works by a fellow artist, which puts Damien Hirst's latest auction project into historical perspective.[98] According to historian Filippo Baldinucci, Rembrandt, too, attended auctions to bid up pictures on the grounds that it benefited the standing of his profession.[99] Artists acting as dealers and speculators, then, is nothing new. (Although it does of course make a difference whether one joins in the bidding, like Rembrandt; organizes an auction of a friend's work, like Duchamp; or delivers one's own work directly to Sotheby's in London, as Hirst did in September 2008.)

Hirst's initiative is further evidence of his serene market realism. If his works are going to end up in an auction house anyway, it seems only logical to produce them directly for the secondary market and to cut out the primary market—especially at a time when primary and secondary markets overlap to an ever-increasing degree. As the seller of his works, Hirst also stood to gain a share of the speculative profit from which artists are typically excluded. In Hirst's case, the risk of his dealers abandoning him in outrage over his direct cooperation with the secondary market was negligible, on account of his status as one of the world's most commercially successful artists. In fact, his dealers were quick to announce their intention to join in the bidding, and it was Hirst's gallerist, Jay Jopling, who bought the first lot of the evening.[100] Everyone gains when Hirst channels his artistic production into the auction sector, especially as the art market took it as a last opportunity to flaunt its image as a crisis-proof sector, unaffected by the worsening bank crisis and the collapse of the global financial system. Coincidentally, the bankruptcy of Lehman Brothers was announced at the same time as the auction. However much the art world was at pains to ignore these events by practicing business as usual, deep down people had long been bracing themselves for the end of the boom. Under these conditions, Hirst's personal quest to equate artistic relevance and speculative value already resembled an analysis of what had become history. For the various sectors of the art market had long begun looking for some way to symbolically underwrite now less-than credible market values. In this context, symbolic capital was writ large. What Hirst's gesture tells us, however, is that it is ultimately pointless trying to produce anything other than an object of speculation. Understood as a break with a belief system called "Art," it was an accomplished provocation. But it also amounted to an artistic declaration of bankruptcy. Hirst's auction squandered the potential of artistic praxis, which consists in its being something other than an object for speculation. Whereas Rembrandt and Duchamp situated their auction activities outside of their own production, for Hirst there no longer seems to be any difference between the two. Market reflexivity exists here only in the sense that Hirst succeeded in staging the one-dimensional equation of art and market as a dead end. Pointing to this dead end was indeed the conceptual achievement of his auction project.

Seminal Moments of Market Reflexivity

The example of Hirst shows that shrewd reaction to structural changes in the art market can only be considered "market-reflexive"

97 Ibid., 73.
98 See Holger Liebs, "Das goldene Kalb. Der Künstler als Unternehmer: Keiner vermarktet sich schlauer als Damien Hirst," *Süddeutsche Zeitung*, July 25, 2008.
99 Quoted from Michael C. Fitzgerald, "Introduction," in *Making Modernism: Picasso and the Creation of the Market for Twentieth-Century Art* (New York: Farrar, Straus & Giroux, 1995), 5.
100 See Rose-Maria Gropp, "Der Hirst-Block oder das goldene Kalb lebt," *FAZ*, September 20, 2008.

in a very limited sense. So far, our definition of market reflexivity required an artist's practice to make reference to the activities of a specific market from which the artist does not exclude himself. But it also included the possibility of refusing that market's demands. And there is no trace of such a refusal in Hirst's case, which instead demonstrates the fact that every segment of the art market—including the increasingly influential auction market—brings forth its own type of market-sensitive art.

Market reflexivity can also be found, although in a more investigative form, in the knowledge market, and to a lesser extent in the market of institutions. In the 1990s, some art institutions specialized in this form of market reflexivity, like the Generali Foundation in Vienna, which commissioned a critical examination of the history of its collection. Artists working in the tradition of Institutional Critique, such as Andrea Fraser, were invited with the expectation that their work would critically appraise the institution's history.[101] For historical Institutional Critique, the situation was different. Haacke's piece on the *Shapolsky Group* (1971) for his show at the Guggenheim Museum fell victim to censorship not least because it exposed the corrupt machinations of a real-estate investor.[102] Here, as so often, it was a diagrammatic aesthetic that performed the inclusion of economic data into the art world. By suggesting a link between the art and real-estate markets, Haacke risked literally everything—his exhibition was cancelled before it ever opened. Thanks to this work, proof was furnished that the real-estate market casts a long shadow reaching into the supposedly economy-free zone of the public museum. The conventional wisdom that the public museum is free of the business world's dirty deals was shattered for good. In its insistence on a fundamental connection between the market and aesthetic autonomy, historical Institutional Critique is certainly market-reflexive. What it usually lacks, however—unlike the approaches it inspired in the 1990s—is the self-reflexivity that is crucial to the market reflexivity under discussion here. The investigations of some one like Hans Haacke seem to claim an absolute distance to the incriminated goings-on, which are exposed from a position of moral superiority. But in the face of the deeply pervasive nature of the neoliberal regime, it no longer seems possible to claim this kind of absolute distance. Rather, critical distance must be constantly reassessed, and always on the basis of recognition of the artist's own involvement. Consequently, the artist is not only part of the solution, but also part of the problem. This is not to detract in any way from the historical achievements of Institutional Critique, which in fact paved the way for the current form of market reflexivity insofar as it viewed art as a form of social critique that could reflect on economic aspects usually kept hidden from view.

Against this backdrop, I would suggest a reading of Courbet's famous picture *The Meeting, or Bonjour, Monsieur Courbet* (1854) as Institutional Critique avant la lettre and as the market-reflexive gesture par excellence. Not only does it capture the transition from feudal system to private collector, but in it Courbet also declares himself—the artist—an active market player. This reading of his work as a precursor to Institutional Critique may be at odds with the orthodoxy of Institutional Critique itself, according to which painting as a medium is fundamentally incapable of such critique.[103] In my view, however, painting is not problematic or obsolete per se. What must be questioned is the manner in which it is deployed. Courbet's picture depicts an encounter between himself and his patron, Alfred Bruyas, accompanied by his servant, in a complex relationship of dependency, but one in which Courbet—as one might expect—ultimately proves the more independent. It is thus an allegory of his specific market situation that provides the artistic motif. The painting was supposedly nicknamed "Wealth Greeting Genius," which indicates his contemporaries' grasp of its thrust.[104] For it is wealth, represented by

101 See Andrea Fraser, *Report* (Vienna: EA-Generali Foundation, 1994).

102 See Hans Haacke, *Obra Social* (Barcelona: Fundació Antoni Tàpies, 1995), 70–72.

103 See Isabelle Graw, "On Conceptual Gestures in Allegedly Expressive Painting, Traces of Expression in Proto-Conceptual works, and the Significance of Artistic Procedures," in *Art After Conceptual Art* (op. cit.), 123.

104 See Petra ten-Doesschate Chu, *The Most Arrogant Man in France: Gustave Courbet and the Nineteenth-Century Media Culture* (op. cit.), 101.

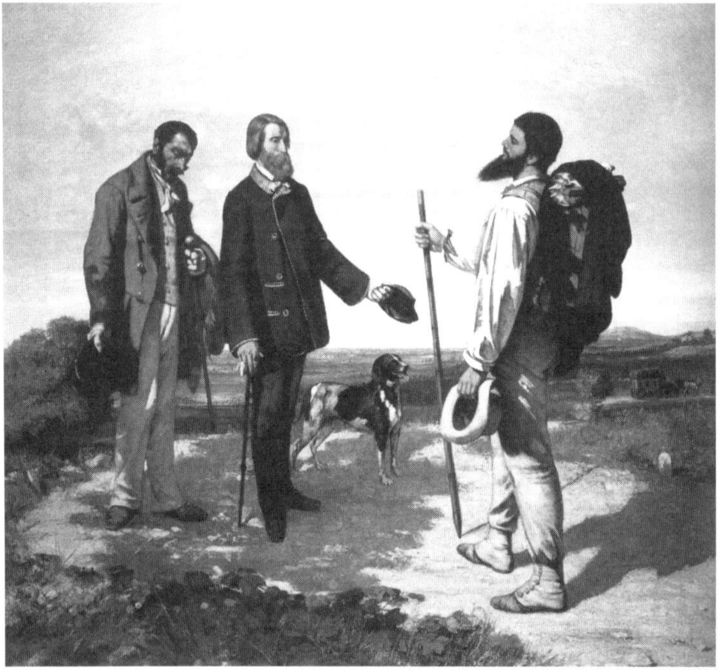

Gustave Courbet, The Meeting, or Bonjour, Monsieur Courbet, *1854*

Bruyas and his servant with head bowed in deference to Courbet, which greets genius here, and not the other way round. Bruyas has quite clearly been the first to remove his hat in greeting, whereas Courbet, styled as a rambler, was already carrying his in his hand.[105] As if to illustrate the superiority claimed by Courbet, his figure claims more space in the picture. This figure was based on the topos of the vagrant who goes entirely without belongings and entourage. His possessions, including painting equipment, are wrapped up in a backpack. Compared to this representation of Courbet, in which he spiritedly swings his staff and radiates vitality, Alfred Bruyas is depicted in a way that makes him look decidedly frail. Here, Courbet shapes the balance of power in his own favor, and this despite the fact that, according to T. J. Clark, he never stopped looking for financial backers throughout his life.[106] His existential dependence on Bruyas is readily apparent in the picture's origin as a commissioned work. But in the spirit of market reflexivity, Courbet not only used this commission to demonstrate his own involvement in the market, but also staged himself as an itinerant free-sprit who could be stopped by no one. A relationship of economic dependence is affirmed, then, but also rephrased, as if the patron should consider himself lucky that the vital artist allows him to take some part in his artistic freedom. Dependency is reformatted such that the artist seems finally to triumph over capital—the same capital on which he nevertheless continues to depend.

Conceptual Market-Reflexive Gestures

While Courbet's reflection on the market provides a taste of the private collector's power in today's "collector culture," conceptual market-reflexive gestures deal with the structural affinity between the art and financial markets that was already becoming apparent in the early twentieth century. The heyday of conceptual market reflexivity, however, can be situated in the 1960s and 70s when the commodification of art was targeted and the art market was felt by progressive artists to be both overly powerful and alienating.[107] Via conceptual market-reflexive gestures, artists tried to engage actively with a market that seemed to condemn them to powerlessness. Instead of delivering an artwork in the conventional sense, the artist transformed himself into a market agent who declared the act of exchange an artistic object. In many cases, the artist himself took on the role of a businessman drawing up contracts, playing an active role in shaping business rather than keeping out of it. This was an unfamiliar image of the artist, but one which today, after Jeff Koons's self-stylization as a former stockbroker, is normal rather than unusual.

105 Ibid., 102.
106 See T. J. Clark, *Image of the People: Gustave Courbet and the 1848 Revolution* (op. cit.), 77.
107 See Ian Burn, "The Art Market: Affluence and Degradation," in *Conceptual Art: A Critical Anthology*, eds. Alexander Alberro and Blake Stimson (Cambridge / London: MIT Press, 1999), 320–333.

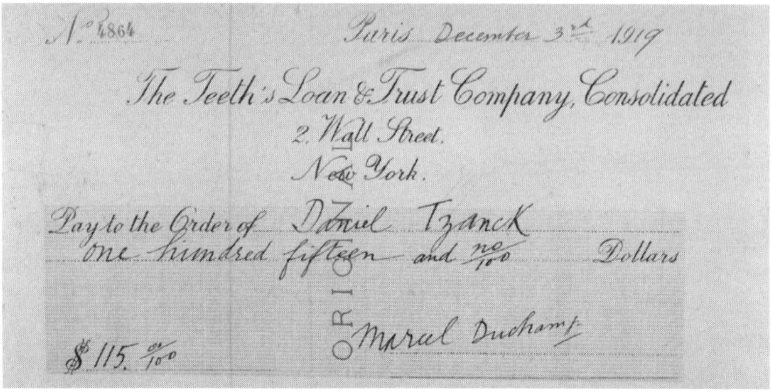

Marcel Duchamp, Tzanck Check, *1919*

In lieu of art products, it was most often checks, vouchers, and certificates that were fed into the market. One might think that the market-reflexive conceptual gesture steals away the last small difference between artwork and means of payment. But just as it pushes forward the equation of money and art, it also uses the privileges associated with "Art."

Marcel Duchamp's *Tzanck Check* (1919)—the prototype of the market-reflexive conceptual gesture—is a good example of this. In 1911, shortly before emigrating to New York, he used this check to pay his dentist, Dr. Daniel Tzanck, for some treatment. It is the enlarged facsimile of a check.[108] Art and money are equated with each other, but at the same time the difference between them is emphasized by the artistic treatment of the subject. Check and artwork are comparable with respect to their role as proxies: just as the value of an artwork cannot be defined in terms of the object itself, the value of a check is redeemed elsewhere. But both can be used as currency, since artworks, too, are accepted as payment. However no bank would ever pay out the sum of $115 marked on this fake check. This work is a reminder of the fact that the asking price for an artwork is not identical to its value. Just as the check will bounce, there are works that fetch high prices but whose value is deeply dubious.

With his check, Duchamp also presents the art market as an archaic barter society in which payment in kind for services rendered is nothing unusual. From Duchamp to Picasso to Kippenberger, artists have paid hotel, restaurant, and dentist's bills with their work. But the real point in Duchamp's case is that he gave his dentist a non-redeemable check, which, according to the criteria of the time, also hardly qualified as an artwork.

Although Duchamp created the check by hand, he did try to give it the appearance of something printed. He gave his own handwriting an anonymous quality so that the check looked as if it had been officially issued. By mimetically adopting the pose of a bank clerk, he created a precedent for the kind of "administrative aesthetic" (Benjamin Buchloh) used by early Conceptual artists to mimic the logic of a managed world.[109] The check was to be redeemed from the imaginary "Teeth's Loan & Trust Company Consolidated." Duchamp poses as creditworthy and appeals for the kind of trust that is one of the main driving forces behind an art market, which one could describe, to quote Bourdieu, as a "good-faith economy." Every art transaction does indeed presuppose a high degree of trust, especially since the value of an artwork is ultimately a matter of faith. Duchamp's imaginary company also sheds light on the present, in which many artists—including Jeff Koons and Sarah Morris—present themselves as "corporations." At first glance, the market-reflexive potential of such "artist corporations" seems to consist of the way in which they expose the artist's interest in earnings. After all, every corporation aims exclusively for turnover and profit. But this market-reflexive admission of a personal profit motive is made at the price of harmonizing the art/market relationship. The artist who demonstrates professionalism by starting a business is acting entirely in the spirit of the corporate art market.

As the seat of his company, Duchamp chose Wall Street, the center of financial capital, as if anticipating the subsequent popularity of

108 See Bernard Marcadé, *Marcel Duchamp: La vie à credit* (Paris: Flammarion, 2007), 207.
109 Cf. Benjamin H.D. Buchloh, "From the Aesthetic of Administration to Institutional Critique," in *L'art Conceptuel: Une perspective* (Paris: Musée d'Art Moderne de la Ville de Paris, 1989), 41–53.

art among financial investors and hedge fund managers.[110] His check seems to have predicted the shift in the art market from Paris to New York, which was already taking place in the movement of exiles at the time. It is also significant that he filed his check in English, the language of mercantilism. In this way, Duchamp framed himself as someone versed in the language of business.

Duchamp's check refers to an immaterial value, despite its concrete materiality. But the dentist must have considered it potentially valuable, as he conserved it with great care. Twenty years later, Duchamp offered to buy it back, for an unknown price.[111] He was clearly eager to integrate this prototypically market-reflexive gesture into his oeuvre.

Duchamp's preliminary work on market reflexivity has been built upon in various ways. Klein's ritual transfer of immateriality (1962) is one notable example, as well as Robert Morris's *Statement of Aesthetic Withdrawal* (1963) and *Money* (1969). Having declared empty zones in exhibitions as zones of pictorial immaterial sensitivity, Klein proceeded to sell these zones.[112] He had special receipts printed, as if to take the bureaucratic flair of *Tzanck Check* one step further. But whereas Duchamp's check was a method of payment, Klein's receipts were proof of a transaction: they were meant to confirm sales of his "immateriality." By endorsing their value, he anticipated the increased importance of the immaterial—this invocation of "immateriality" might indeed be said to prefigure the "immaterial labor" of post-Fordism, which seeks to mobilize the individual's entire personality. Although Klein's notion of immateriality had more to do with the mystic qualities of "pure presence," he did try to activate the sensory, emotional, and cognitive skills, which the "capitalist command" (Maurizio Lazzarato) now tries to incorporate.[113]

Klein didn't give immateriality away for free, which illustrates its increased value. For each of the zones, identical in formal terms, he asked a different price. Whereas Duchamp confronted his dentist with the factual worthlessness of his check, Klein declared immateriality as something beyond economic calculability. Finally, no price for it is a fair price. His pricing policy seems both to demonstrate the arbitrariness of any price for art and to lay claim to its pricelessness. During his show at Galleria Apollinaire (1957), Klein had already asked different prices for eleven monochrome panels of the same format.[114] The message was that the price of their symbolic relevance could not be calculated by the usual parameters (size). But Klein expected even more from those who purchased his immaterial zones. Buyers not only had to pay for the zone in pure gold—the epitome of substantial value—but were also obliged to throw half of the gold into the river as part of a handing-over ritual. The above-mentioned receipt was also to be burned, as if the immateriality acquired by the buyer was above any equivalent. Following the ritual transfer, the buyer literally went away empty-handed, while Klein reserved the right to keep the other half of the gold himself. In this model, the artist is rewarded for his sensitivity, whereas the collector experiences immateriality without any possession whatsoever. Klein's ritual actions may have been guided more by spiritual ideas than by a critique of the economy, but they did reflect on the market insofar as they revolved tirelessly around the problem of value.

Robert Morris, on the other hand, was far from dissolving existing power relations between collector and artist in such a mythical promise of immateriality. His *Statement of Aesthetic Withdrawal* arose from an allegedly angry reaction to a buyer's failure to pay for *Litanies*—a lead-covered box with a key ring and keys engraved with quotations from Duchamp.[115] The buyer in question was no less than Philip Johnson who had purportedly—as usual in the art

110 See Melanie Gilligan, "Derivative Days: Notes on Art, Fince, and the Unproductive Forces," *Texte zur Kunst*, issue 69 (March 2008): 146–153.

111 Ibid.

112 See Sidra Stich, *Yves Klein* (op. cit.), 155–156.

113 See Maurizio Lazzarato, "Immaterial Labor," in *Radical Thought in Italy: A Potential Politics* (op. cit.), 133–147.

114 See Sidra Stich, *Yves Klein* (op. cit.), 86.

115 See Robert Morris, *Continuous Project Altered Daily: The Writings of Robert Morris* (Cambridge: MIT Press, 1995), 113.

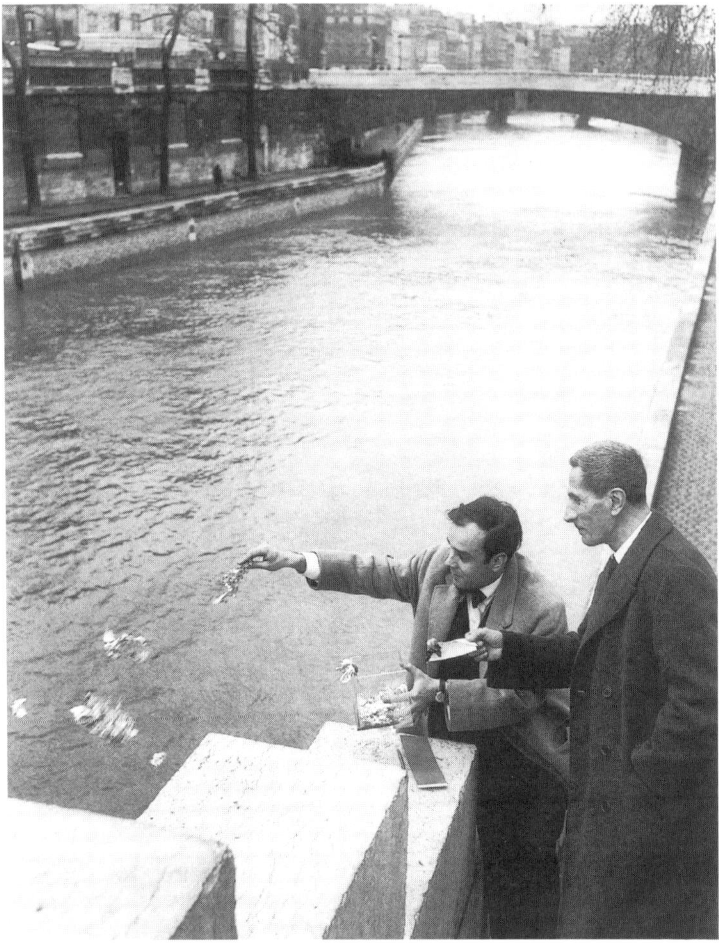

Yves Klein and Dino Buzzati during the ritual transmission of immateriality, January 26, 1962

world—not honored his obligation to pay. Morris produced a written declaration with which he attempted to withdraw all aesthetic quality and content from the object. But when the artist himself performed this withdrawal in *Statement of Aesthetic Withdrawal*, the gesture actually enhanced the symbolic value of *Litanies*. The work itself poses as a performative contradiction—it presents itself as art that does not want to be art. Although it still bears shadowy traces of the original work, its aesthetic relevance is negated by the integrated statement. The power to determine whether something is art here lies within the artwork, and with the artist—the market is stripped of its defining judgment of aesthetic accomplishment. Because the artwork itself now resolves the art/non-art tension, those who don't pay are punished with non-art. But the work also profits from the Johnson anecdote, which becomes lucrative and intrinsic to it, generating additional significance and symbolic value. Like Courbet, Duchamp, and Klein before him, Morris, too, intervenes in an existing power relation to reshape it *on his own terms*, as well as making an important contribution on the theme of value.

With *Money*, Morris himself played the role of museum trustee and speculator, as if to demonstrate the fluid borders between public museum and speculative interest via firsthand experience. As his contribution to the legendary "Anti-Illusion: Procedures/Materials" show at the Whitney Museum (1969), Morris proposed the following: the trustees of the museum were to put a certain sum at his disposal, with which he would purchase "blue chip art"—that is, works by commercially successful colleagues—in New York and sell it at a profit in Europe. Three things are striking here: Morris refers to the purchasing power of European collectors at the time, he is prepared to sell his insider knowledge, and he slips into the role of the art agent, exposing himself to attack and entering a zone of compromise. The profit made on his deals was to go solely to the museum. A fantastic offer, one might think, but the trustees declined on the grounds that the project was too risky. Morris had to content himself with smaller sums invested on Wall Street, under trustee supervision. But his project qualifies as market-reflexive insofar as Morris does not exclude himself from the activities of the market. As an art agent, he embodies a hybrid of artist, speculative collector, and agent acting on behalf of the museum. In retrospect, it is astonishing that his insider knowledge, which he wanted to convert into cash, so to speak, was viewed with such suspicion. At the time, the value of the "information capital" possessed by Morris as an informed artist had yet to be widely acknowledged. It is significant that his role as art

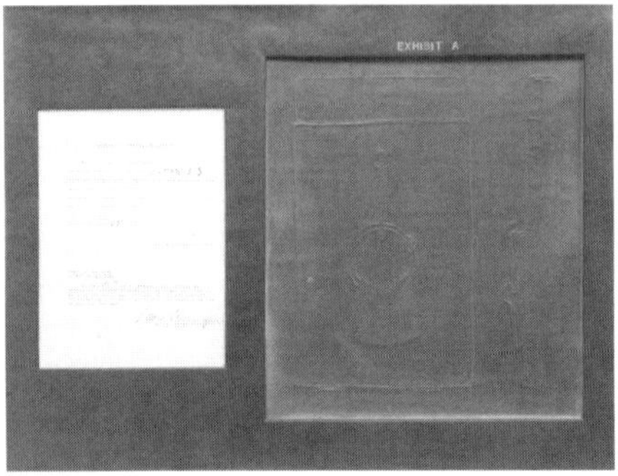

Robert Morris, Statement of Aesthetic Withdrawal, *1963*

agent would have emphasized the proximity between the artist and this still-suspect figure. Unlike Klein, who secured half of the profit (in gold) for himself, Morris intended to cede financial profit to the museum. As a sign of selflessness? Not at all. Unlike Klein, the nonprofit character of Morris's project must have been important insofar as anything else would have damaged its investigative, progressive orientation and its critique of the economy. If Morris had kept any of the profit for himself, the project's credibility would have been endangered.

Market Reflexivity After the Bioeconomic Turn: Andrea Fraser and Merlin Carpenter

Whereas today's art world has become a global culture industry, the market faced by artists like Duchamp, Klein, Morris, and Warhol was relatively manageable in scale. According to Ivan Karp, the circle interested in Pop art in the early 1960s numbered around fifty to one hundred people.[116] Today's art world, as an "industry producing visuality and meaning," is far removed from such modest proportions. It has gone global and its events—blockbuster shows and ever-increasing numbers of biennials—attract large audiences. Artists practicing market reflexivity today also face an intensification of the celebrity principle observed by Warhol, as manifested by the heightened interest in the artist as a person. One tangible sign of this personalization of the artwork is the way visitors to art fairs commonly talk about having spotted "a good Koons" or "a fantastic Kippenberger:" The art and the person become identical. The other side of this subjectivization is the reification of the artist (already discussed in the case of Courbet), who, under the conditions of celebrity culture, takes on even more object-like characteristics and is expected to stage himself accordingly. These are the conditions that the market-reflexive contemporary artist is facing today. He may refuse to make products, but this will only fuel the fetishization of his person. Or he may allow his artwork to precede him, hiding behind it, so to speak—but this will not prevent his work from being mythologized, nor impede the mystification of his person.

In the performances of Andrea Fraser and the interventions of Merlin Carpenter, this double bind is not resolved but posited as something that cannot be circumvented. If the biopolitical turn that also occurred in the art market results in an increased demand for the personality and life of the artist, then both Fraser's performative lectures, which put her very much on show as the speaker, and Carpenter's painting actions, which give public exposure to an other wise hidden working method, fulfill and disappoint this demand at the same time.

The key to their market-reflexive potential, however, is that Fraser and Carpenter wholeheartedly take up the conditions they analyze, putting themselves entirely at their mercy, as if to prove that the figure of the artist in a celebrity-oriented society is the actual problem. Art criticism's openness to Fraser's and Carpenter's knowledge-producing practices is also due to an expanded profile that allows artists to act as critics. By regularly publishing texts, Fraser and Carpenter have, in their own ways, shown themselves to be critics and analysts of the present who examine limitations and possibilities in an art world governed by economic constraints, which is, more-

116 See interview with Ivan Karp in John Wilcock, *The Autobiography and Sex Life of Andy Warhol by John Wilcock with a Cast of Thousands* (op. cit.), unpaginated.

over, growing increasingly conservative in political terms.[117] In other words, their texts are part of an ongoing discussion to which they make a contribution. Implicitly, however, they also call for the significance of artistic practice not to be sought in objects alone: If criticism is a key site for the production of meaning, then artistic and critical production are shown to be structurally related activities.

Such forms of art as criticism are welcome in certain sectors of the art market, where they find approval and buyers (although standards of remuneration in the "knowledge market" cannot be compared with those of the "commercial art market"). The reason critics in particular are so notoriously underpaid lies in the intangible nature of the surplus value they produce. The expenditure of their labor contributes to an artwork's symbolic relevance; they create symbolic value, which could be said to correspond to Marx's notion of surplus value insofar as its value is also far greater than what the critic costs the market.[118] Moreover, on the level of the primary art market, and more so on that of the secondary market, this "surplus value" generated by the critic resembles "something created out of nothing" (Marx). What is completely forgotten here is how this impression of relevance was generated in the first place. When artists like Fraser and Carpenter emphasize the role of criticism by declaring text an important site for the production of meaning, this acknowledges and renders visible the criticism that often goes unacknowledged within the commercial process.

The capitalist system clearly has the ability to render processes of value creation invisible and to bring forth new interpretations. This is the only way to explain how the original intention of an artistic project with a socio-critical orientation so often flips into its opposite in the course of its passage to market conditions. Any attempt by Fraser to demystify the supposedly unified and authentic artist-subject doesn't ultimately prevent the mystification of her own person; any voiding of the categories of "painter" and "picture" carried out by Carpenter will intensify the fetishization and symbolic charge of his pictures in the long term. But this does not mean that such attempts are in vain—on the contrary. What is decisive for their market-reflexive potential, however, is that they have absorbed the knowledge of this logic of exploitation. In her lecture performance *Official Welcome* (2001), Fraser presented herself in a Gucci bikini, demonstratively highlighting the inevitable objectification of the artist under the conditions of celebrity culture. And during his appearance for "The Opening" at the Mercedes headquarters in Berlin, Carpenter got into his own vintage Mercedes, as if to accuse himself of a neo-bourgeois sense of style and dubious embracing of event culture. The examples of Fraser and Carpenter are also at odds with the idea that market-reflexive gestures are generated solely by the will and assertiveness of the artist-subject. It is the specific market situation in any given case that gives rise to the syntax and aesthetic form of their works. Be it a gallery, a museum, or a boutique—in the work of Fraser and Carpenter, all of these places must be understood as *coproducers* of market reflexivity. At his show "A Roaring RAMPAGE of Revenge" (2005) at Reena Spaulings Fine Arts, for example, Carpenter left the more creative part of his exhibition to the gallerists (John Kelsey and Emily Sundblad), who were asked via a kind of instruction piece to paint the canvases with motifs of the collapsing World Trade Center, on which the artist later continued to work.[119] Fraser, too, always includes in her lecture manuscripts official announcements and interview statements from the specific institutional context under study, such that market reflexivity proves to be fundamentally rooted in the institutions themselves.

117 See Andrea Fraser, "A 'Sensation' Chronicle (2001)," in *Museum Highlights: The Writings of Andrea Fraser*, ed. Alexander Alberro (Cambridge / London: MIT Press, 2005), 179–211; see also Merlin Carpenter, "The Tail that Wags the Dog," in *Canvases and Careers Today: Criticism and its Markets*, eds. Daniel Birnbaum and Isabelle Graw (Berlin/New York: Sternberg Press, 2008), 75–88.

118 See Karl Marx, "The Rate of Surplus Value," in *Capital: Critique of Political Economy, Vol. 1* (op. cit.), 320–339.

119 They were asked to paint the canvases with quick "pseudo-abstractions" of motifs of the Twin Towers collapsing in the style of Josh Smith, a very commercially successful artist represented by the gallery at the time.

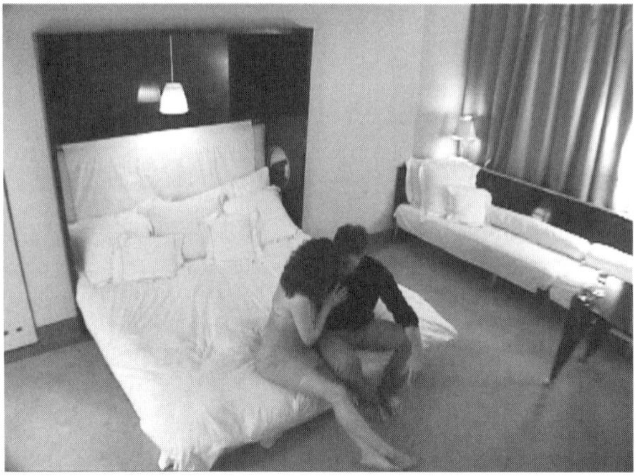

Andrea Fraser, Untitled, *2003*

Sell Yourself! (Andrea Fraser)

Working in the tradition of post-studio practice, Andrea Fraser has often refused the conventional production of "objects that can be appropriated materially."[120] Instead, her performances continue the insights of historical Institutional Critique and aim to render visible the mental, social, and economic power relations that are embedded in all artistic production, but which usually remain hidden. The key to the market-reflexive potential of Fraser's work, however, lies in the fact that—unlike classic practitioners of Institutional Critique like Haacke and Asher—she always puts herself on the line in her performances. She takes on the role of the museum guide (*Welcome to the Wadsworth,* 1991) or the drunken Kippenberger (*Kunst muß hängen,* 2001), putting herself at their mercy, so to speak. In *Official Welcome*, she switched back and forth between several roles, as if to present "Art" as a system of social relations. Fraser sometimes embodied the curator, making "meaningful" but essentially empty speeches, then the monosyllabic artist, then the critic full of pretentious phrases, then the female bad-girl artist who gets personal straight away. The fact that she slipped into each of these roles herself also signals the impossibility of adopting an absolute distance from them. Fraser makes no secret of the fact that she also identifies with the different institutions she subjects to in-depth analysis, be it the male art star or museum culture. At the start of her Documenta performance, for example, she confessed to wishing she had been invited to this event.[121]

At first glance, Fraser's performances seem to accommodate the market's desire for the "personality" of the artist. They are, after all, based on her "presence" and on her much noted talent as an actress. But at second glance, it becomes clear that they demolish any belief in an authentic and unified artist-subject, as her lectures always consist of a blend of different institutional voices.[122] She is all of these people, whose rhetorical mannerisms she so convincingly performs, and at the same time she is also Andrea Fraser, the artist. The distinction between authenticity and contrivance remains suspended even when she suddenly bursts into tears, as in *Official Welcome.* The dividing line between real and fake crying, between authentic and constructed subject, proves once again to be a fluid one.

Fraser's *Untitled* (2003) is the ultimate market-reflexive work, as it seems to fulfill all of the criteria for market reflexivity to excess. Not only does the work point to a specific state of the art market as a collector culture, where private collectors dictate their terms to public institutions, but it also gives the collector exactly what he essentially aims for—the whole person of the artist, who takes herself to market, body and soul. Listed as a "commissioned piece for a collector," the work is a video that shows Fraser having sex with this collector.[123] In return for a fee, the artist offered him her sexual services. Not only was he allowed to have sex with her, but he also received a copy of the video, as proof of this sexual encounter organized by art-market players, in which artist and collector expose

120 Andrea Fraser, "An Artist's Statement," in *Place Position Presentation Public* (Maastricht: Jan van Eyck Academie, 1993), 62.
121 Andrea Fraser, "A Speech On Documenta," in *Museum Highlights: The Writing of Andrea Fraser* (op. cit.), 149–151.
122 See Georges Baker, "Fraser's Form" in *Andrea Fraser: Works 1984–2003,* ed. Yilmaz Dziewior (Cologne, DuMont, 2004), 26.
123 See *Andrea Fraser. Works 1984–2003* (op. cit.), 233.

themselves in equal measure. Unlike the collector in Klein's ritual actions, Fraser's collector does not go away empty-handed. Instead, he possesses a sexual experience whose value, according to a romantic concept of love, cannot be expressed in terms of money. The romantic concept of love and the idealist concept of art agree in considering their object removed from the zone of the economic. Nevertheless, Fraser's collector holds the documentation of his sexual performance in his hands, which identifies him as a player, as a participant in art. But he is also exposed.

If this piece were aimed solely at taking Baudelaire's comparison of the artist with a whore literally, and pushing it to absurd lengths, then it would only be market-reflexive in a limited sense since the equation of art and money or art and prostitution fails to recognize the differences between them. But the work is market-reflexive insofar as it draws the consequences from bioeconomic encroachment into even the most intimate areas, such as emotions, the body, and private life. Sex, too, is now subject to bioeconomic principles of optimization—it is expected to be "good." Whereas Fraser's previous performances brought her emotional, cognitive, and acting skills to bear, she now also offered up her sexual skills. She had already used her body in earlier works, for example in the striptease as part of *Official Welcome*, thus further intensifying the objectification of the actress inherent in any performance.[124] But offering herself to the collector in the most intimate way, by engaging in sex with him, raises the stakes of this experimental setup to the extreme. The fact that Fraser was interested in more than just equating the female artist with a prostitute and the collector with her customer is also made clear by the video. The sex engaged in by the couple seems more oppressive than exciting—the relationship between art and market, or between their respective representatives, is fraught with tension. Although they have sex, there is no real coming together, as if to illustrate the structure of the art / market relationship as a unity based on opposition.

Emptying and Non-Performance: Merlin Carpenter

Whereas Fraser literally sells herself in *Untitled*, Carpenter has always approached the art market's lust for personality with a mixture of refusal and seeming accommodation. Like Courbet before him, Carpenter's praxis could be used to show that Institutional Critique and painting are not mutually exclusive. "A Roaring RAMPAGE of Revenge" (2005) is a good example of such Institutional Critique by painterly means, especially as the pictures referred to the exhibition space in a number of ways. First, the gallerists were called on as assistants to do the creative work, which was an almost simplistic illustration of the trend toward expanded professional profiles: When gallerists like those of Reena Spaulings see themselves as cooperative projects, as hybrids of the artist-dealer and critic, then they may as well go ahead and paint their artists' exhibitions themselves. In a second step, we were reminded that various segments of the New York art market are especially keen on precisely this kind of depoliticized cooperation. Onto the canvases prepared by the creative work of his gallerists, Carpenter painted the exclusively positive press reports about the gallery that had accumulated in the course of one year. In this way, the pictures themselves testified to the effusive enthusiasm for the Reena Spaulings project on which critics seemed to be pinning such high hopes. Precisely because it had the reputation of being such a progressive downtown gallery, the enthusiasm knew no bounds. Whereas Carpenter deploys the vocabulary of Institutional Critique site-specifically, and practices an almost clichéd version of it in his painted reviews, Fraser explicitly situates her praxis in the tradition of Institutional Critique, with its focus on epistemological gain. Unlike Fraser, Carpenter's works seem to warn the viewer not to take them too seriously.In his contribution to the

124 See Anke Kempkes, "The Art of Talking Art. Die Kunst von der Sprache der Kunst," in ibid., 11.

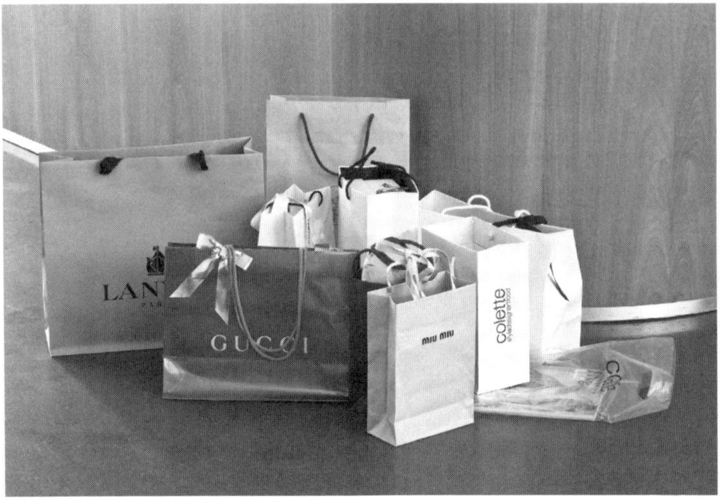

Sylvie Fleury, Insolence*, 2007*

"Make Your Own Life: Artists In & Out of Cologne" show in 2006, the emphasis was on refusal, although he did deliver work—empty shopping bags including receipts. They can be read as an allegory of attempts to empty art, the inverse of which is the mystification of the artist as personality. The title of this group show referred to a statement by Kippenberger, who once said artists should start with their own lives, using them as the basis for their work.[125] The curator projected this idea of a self-determined life, not always kept in check by the art market, onto the Cologne art scene of the late 1980s and early 90s. It is true that for a brief period, the city played host to a circulation of ideas and views that were not immediately noticed by the main market players. But certain segments of the U.S. art market at the beginning of the twenty-first century were especially interested in these ideas because they promised intellectual gain and an element of rebelliousness. Under the conditions of bioeconomic encroachment, the very idea of a "self-determined" life as suggested by "Make Your Own Life" seems at least as dubious as the retroactively glorified view of a Cologne art scene now associated only with those figures most prominent today. From an American point of view, an artist like Carpenter belonged to this scene, and was therefore invited to participate (as was Andrea Fraser). His work

Make Your Own Life (2006), consisting of these empty shopping bags, delivered the curator's imperative straight back to him. Prior to the show, Carpenter requested a sum of four thousand dollars in cash for production costs, without giving details of what it would be used for. After arriving in Philadelphia, he splurged the money as fast as he could: on designer clothes, drinks, records, restaurants. This was a display of pure wastefulness, especially as the value of clothing, not to mention drinks, diminishes with use. What visitors to the exhibition saw were the empty bags—Yves Saint Laurent, Gucci, Kiehl's—as if taking Sylvie Fleury's sculptures closer still to a literal emptying. Just as the artist refused any representation of his life in Cologne, he used the show's conditions of production for his own personal consumption while withholding the evidence. Just as Klein kept half the gold, Carpenter kept the amassed consumer goods, especially the clothes, for himself, as if pointing to the importance of a prominent public persona for which the shopping bags act as traces.

This relationship between objectified artist-subject and subjectified art object is also dealt with in Carpenter's exhibition series "The Opening," which began in 2007 and ended in 2009. Whereas his contribution to "Make Your Own Life" aimed to withhold the "life" of the artist desired by the curator, the focus in these openings, during which the works are produced, is on personality and "liveliness." The artist has left his studio, as if to tear down the final barrier separating him from direct contact with the market. Criticized by artists like Daniel Buren for mystifying art, the studio is a thoroughly ideological location. It can serve as a protective zone, but it also preserves the belief in art as Other to the market. Carpenter leaves the studio behind, declaring the exhibition the site that facilitates painting, and the opening an opportunity for producing pictures. If, as an "entrepreneurial self," the artist is increasingly occupied with business, bureaucratic matters, and social activities

125 See Isabelle Graw, "Seen from Here: On Myths of Cologne, Heteronomy, and Scenarios of Withdrawing and Dropping Out in the Face of the Increased Significance of 'Life'" *Texte zur Kunst*, issue 63 (September 2006): 124–132.

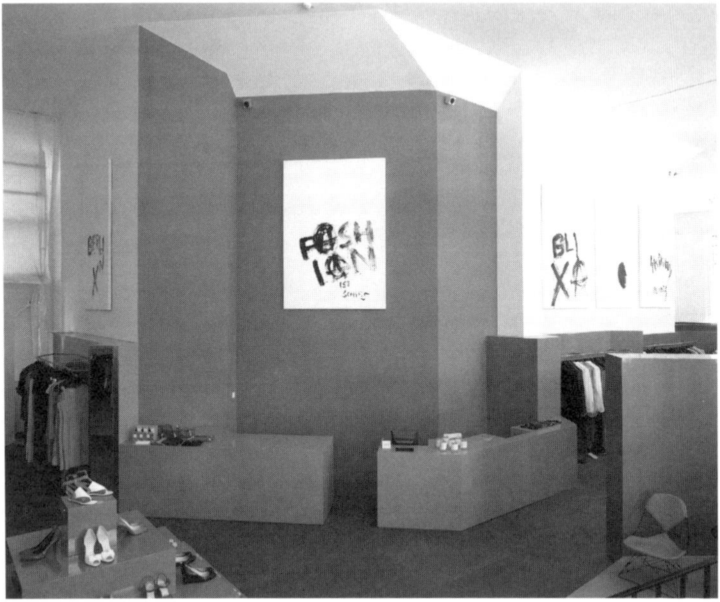

Merlin Carpenter, installation view of "The Opening," 2008, at The Corner Berlin, organized by Galerie Christian Nagel

(networking), then there is no time left for "real" artistic work. Complaints that all the interacting, communicating, and managing leave no time for one's own work are already commonplace among cultural producers. From this notorious lack of time, Carpenter seems to draw the conclusion that he should perform his artistic work in public—during the vernissage. Each of the "Openings" is carefully designed and adapted to the specific location. In New York (2007), a pianist was hired and the gallery decorated with elaborate flower arrangements. In Zurich (2008), tables were laid for a festive nouveau riche dinner, and in Los Angeles (2008), a DJ played classical music. At every location, however, "The Opening" also featured specially prepared canvases hung on the walls, apparently awaiting further work.

Carpenter's painting performance seemed to disappoint with intent, however, not least because it forewent any sense of theatricality. Anyone hoping for the sight of an artist getting physical in front of the canvas à la Georges Mathieu had to make do with a brief appearance during which the task was dealt with in almost no time.

The impression of non-performance was reinforced by aloof body language signaling "back off." Despite this, Carpenter uses the rhetoric of painting: splashes, smearing, graffiti-like symbols and lettering. Although studio practice seems to have been demystified once and for all, these pictures reduced to a gestural minimum carry within them a potential for fetishization, the more so because they testify to a fleeting but unforgettable moment. Some pictures function as speech acts with insulting messages, such as "Die Collector Scum" (*The Opening: The Black Paintings #8,* 2007). But this death wish for the collector is also aimed at his traditional receptiveness to imposition and insult, making him all the more likely to acquire this very work as proof of a relaxed attitude and self-irony.

Carpenter's "The Opening" series is also market-reflexive not only in the way it takes into account the transformation of the art world into a culture industry modeled on the fashion industry, but also because it demonstrates the structural relationship between luxury goods and art-as-commodity—doing so in the most blatant way possible. After all, the comparison between art and luxury goods is now unexceptional. Instead of taking place in a gallery, the Berlin exhibition (2008) was held both on the premises of Mercedes' main dealership and in a well-known luxury fashion boutique (The Corner). At Mercedes, he painted canvases while driving by in his own Mercedes. For the performance at The Corner, which took place immediately after this, he climbed a ladder—which was more performative in the sense of using the body more, although this impression was counteracted by body language signaling withdrawal.

But this cultivation of a kind of "minimal presence" can also be read as the ultimate means to generate personal aura. The person who does *not* perform on the stage ends up having the most stage presence.

Whereas in *Untitled*, Fraser seemed to have relinquished all self-protection in order to quite literally surrender herself to the collector—at least for a certain period of time—Carpenter exposed himself briefly in "The Opening" series, but in such a way as to fall short of all expectations of performance. Where Carpenter's non-performances disappoint and present everything as a big joke, Fraser's fulfilling of a wide range of roles aims for insight and analysis. Their approaches also draw different conclusions with regard to the art market as a bioeconomic value-enhancement machine: Fraser proceeds to sell her body, while Carpenter withholds his "life" from the curator. But with regard to the importance of criticism, their practices are very similar, declaring text as the site where meaning is actually produced by an artwork that explains everything other than itself.

Final Remarks: The Value of Criticism

The concept of a "knowledge society" refers to a situation in which knowledge is highly valued and has become a marketable commodity, where the capacity for intellectual and affective labor is exploited. "Knowledge society" is thus another way of describing the dynamic of a capitalist system that includes knowledge and other kinds of unpaid labor (from idle talk to the production of meaning) in its profit logic. Signs of the particularly high value of knowledge can be found not only in the art world, which has traditionally been open to knowledge, but also in the lifestyle press and fashion magazines. As one of "Germany's most successful gallerists," during the art boom Harry Lybke of Galerie Eigen+Art was asked by a Sunday broadsheet to comment on the relationship between art and commerce.[126] Straight away, he emphasized the importance of art history and of "being part of the discourse." His artists were not aiming for commercial success, he said, but for success in the history of art. Playing down economic ambitions is of course de rigueur in a business that thrives, as we have seen, on belief in the pricelessness of its product. But it is significant how vehemently Lybke emphasizes the function of art history as a creator of value. In its role as a producer of "knowledge" and "meaning," it is becoming a decisive factor.

German women's magazine *Gala* also recently showed signs of a new cult of knowledge in an article praising the "nerd look" achieved by wearing nerdy men's glasses from Dior, cultivating a bookish air, and making frequent visits to library.[127] Here, knowledge is elevated to the status of the ultimate "must-have." After years of pursuing only good looks, a perfect body, and loads of money,

126 See "'Investieren in Kunst ist vollkommener Unsinn'. Der Galerist Harry Lybke über den Irrtum der Spekulanten, die Langmut der Sammler und warum deutsche Malerei so teuer ist," *Frankfurter Allgemeine Sonntagszeitung,* August 29, 2006.

127 See *Gala*, March 13, 2008: 104.

now it's time to get to work on the intellect as the final frontier of optimization. But this does not mean that the lifestyle press has stopped presuming wealth or recommending stays at expensive spas, exorbitant beauty treatments, and a personal trainer. The different and potentially opposing ideals appealed to here complement one another: sometimes beauty and wealth are emphasized, at others, inner values or extensive reading. While *Gala* declared nerdiness the new hip attitude, *Die Bunte,* another German gossip magazine, claimed in all seriousness that the latest trend was to have "one's own museum," as if this were an option for ordinary mortals.[128] While the prohibitive cost makes this trend impossible to follow, all that is required for the nerd look is enough money for a pair of designer frames and a library membership card.

The art world is a knowledge-based economy in which both privileges—the privilege of knowing more and the privilege of having more money—traditionally coincide and compete with one another. Just as the representatives of knowledge (artists, critics, art historians) insist on their own criteria for judgment, art-market players try to define the value of knowledge with regard to its commercial potential. The complementariness of these two reference systems can be studied particularly well in the art world. Until recently, the market model seemed to be triumphing, as the value of knowledge was measured more and more in terms of commercial success. At the same time, in a knowledge society, knowledge, information, and criticism are considered desirable commodities. But it doesn't follow that criticism can be wholly absorbed or even totally neutralized. After all, it is still possible to keep certain insights for oneself instead of channeling them into the market. But for its part, the market knows how to put this technique of insider knowledge to its own use, making its strategic potential seem rather limited. Although the various markets are becoming increasingly similar and overlapping more and more, differences do still exist between them. The knowledge market, for example, judges on the basis of its own criteria, allowing approaches that would be unthinkable in the commercial sphere. Conversely, not every form of criticism is welcomed by the commercial market, which also suggests that different markets are governed by different laws. Critics have often formulated justified objections to commercially successful practices that only made an impact indirectly or in the long term.

Art criticism in particular seems to be currently undergoing a change of function. On the one hand, it is coveted beyond all else as a key creator of all-important symbolic value. In certain segments of the market, on the other hand, it is granted only an apologetic form of court reporting fatally reminiscent of the genre of the press release. A negative review may also have a favorable impact on the value-creation process—"all press is good press"—but due to the cooperation imperative discussed in detail above, well-argued negative reviews have become a rarity. If you criticize someone in network capitalism you risk social death. But it is also understandable that no one wishes to waste their life analyzing things of which he essentially disapproves.

This book was written during the art boom, but it is not tied to a specific economic climate. It uses its findings based on an analysis of the present in order to clarify the relationship between art and market in a fundamental fashion, independent of economic trends or cycles. The special quality of this relationship consists in the way it is characterized equally by conflict and a form of inner cohesion. Symbolic and market value are linked like communicating vessels, but they also contest each other's validity. Even if the art market were to totally collapse, as it threatened to do in the course of the recent global banking crisis, this complex interrelation between art and market would remain in force.

128 See *Die Bunte*, 32/2007: 88.

Acknowledgments

Countless people have contributed to this book, often in casual exchanges too numerous to list here. The many invitations I received to symposia allowed me to describe the belief system of the art world with greater precision. I am also grateful to all those who invited me to their events, discussions, after-opening dinners, and parties.

First, I must thank Jörg-Uwe Albig, who played a crucial role in selecting the book's original title. Tom Holert read the manuscript of the first two chapters very closely and provided indispensable critical remarks. Diedrich Diederichsen made important suggestions on the problem of value. Helmut Draxler encouraged me to tighten my account of the trend toward a naturalized market and to write not only from the viewpoint of the boom. My always-stimulating dialogue with Sabeth Buchmann, for example, on the merits of Rancière's aesthetic philosophy, also supplied a basis for ideas in this book. My energy would eventually have run out without regular exchanges with Benjamin Buchloh, who never ceased to inspire me. Encouragement and support also came from Merlin Carpenter, who read the English version with a critical eye and had the idea for the cover image. My correspondence with Jutta Koether, especially her reports on the New York art scene, provided material for my analysis. Her critical comments on the German version of the book were also very useful, as were those made by Albert Oehlen. David Lieske shared his insider's view of the gallery world with me, and Josephine Pryde regularly sent useful material from the world of celebrities and fashion. Stephanie Tasch provided me with material and brightened my days at the library. If André Rottmann, Stefanie Kleefeld, Anke Ulrich, and Sabine Ofenbach had not continuously produced issues for *Texte zur Kunst*, this book would probably never have been written. I am also grateful to André Rottmann for asking me to publish my thoughts on symbolic and market value before this book appeared, as it led to a shift in emphasis. Beatrice von Bismarck and Ulf Wuggenig graciously invited me to their Bourdieu conference

(Berlin 2007), prompting me to re-engage with his central theoretical concepts. Anselm Haverkamp has always supported my academic vision with great openness. I am grateful to Daniel Birnbaum, with whom I founded the Institute for Art Criticism in Frankfurt; the results of the conferences we organized there benefited this study. Special thanks are due to the students of the Städelschule Academy of Fine Arts in Frankfurt. They accompanied the development of this book in the form of a series of lectures over several semesters, and their questions and critical commentary had a significant influence on the shape it took.

I would like to thank my publisher Caroline Schneider for her enthusiasm, Nicholas Grindell for his outstanding translation and careful preparation of this new English edition, Kari Rittenbach and Matthew Evans for their thorough proofreading of the manuscript, and Markus Weisbeck for the inspired graphic design.

Lastly, I would like to thank my parents Annette Eisenberg-Graw and Winfried Graw, who have always given me their generous support. And finally, the gratitude I feel toward my husband Markus Müller and my daughter Margaux Albertine can hardly be put into words. The former was a source of invaluable input, especially for the sections on Warhol, and the latter always reacted to her mother's lack of time with cheerful calm. Without their presence, my mostly desk-bound life during this project would have felt meaningless and dreary. They not only rendered my work feasible, but also constantly sweetened it.

Berlin, September 2009

Index of Names

Subject Index

Image Credits

Page 32
Gustave Courbet
The Wave, circa 1870
Standort: Eigentum Städelscher Museums-verein e.V.
Städel Museum, Frankfurt am Main
Photograph © Städel Museum—Artothek

Page 38
Damien Hirst
For the Love of God, 2007
© Damien Hirst. All rights reserved/ VG Bild-Kunst, Bonn 2009

Page 50
Richard Prince
Untitled (Woman with Compact), 1983
© Richard Prince

Page 52
John Currin
Jaunty and Mame, 1997
© John Currin. Courtesy Gagosian Gallery, New York

Page 54
Jeff Koons
Amore, 1988
© Jeff Koons

Page 70
Michael Asher
Installation view at Claire Copley Gallery, 1974
© Michael Asher

Page 82
André Cadere in front of the Palais des Beaux-Arts, Brussels, September 1974
Courtesy André Cadere Archives, Brussels

Page 84
Lee Lozano
Dialogue Piece, 1969
© The Estate of Lee Lozano.
Hauser & Wirth

Page 88
Hans Haacke
Der Pralinenmeister (The chocolate master), 1981
© VG Bild-Kunst, Bonn 2009

Page 90
A.R. Penck
Weltbild 1 (World picture 1), 1961
© VG Bild-Kunst, Bonn 2009

Page 96
Julian Schnabel
I Went to Tangiers and Had Dinner with Paul Bowles, 1990
Private Collection
© Julian Schnabel

Page 98
Julian Schnabel in Amagansett, N.Y., 1981
Photograph © Rita K. Katz

Page 128
Jorge Pardo
4166 Sea View Lane, 1998
Courtesy neugerriemschneider, Berlin

Page 134
Jörg Immendorff
"Den Eisbären mal reinhalten," 1968
From the artist's book *Hier und Jetzt: Das tun, was zu tun ist*
(Cologne/New York: Gebr. König, 1973)

Page 136
YSL Raspail Canvas Tote, Cruise 2008 collection
© Yves Saint Laurent

Page 184
Andy Warhol
192 One-Dollar Bills, 1962
Collection Marx, Berlin
© 2010 The Andy Warhol Foundation for the Visual Arts, Inc./Artists Rights Society (ARS), New York

Page 206
Gustave Courbet
The Meeting, or Bonjour, Monsieur Courbet, 1854
© Musée Fabre, France/Giraudon/ The Bridgeman Art Library

Page 208
Marcel Duchamp
Tzanck Check, 1919
© Succession Marcel Duchamp /
VG Bild-Kunst, Bonn 2009

Page 212
Yves Klein and Dino Buzzati during the ritual transmission of immateriality, January 26, 1962
© VG Bild-Kunst, Bonn 2009

Page 214
Robert Morris
Statement of Aesthetic Withdrawal, 1963
© VG Bild-Kunst, Bonn 2009

Page 218
Andrea Fraser
Untitled, 2003
DVD, 60 min.
Courtesy Friedrich Petzel Gallery, New York

Page 222
Sylvie Fleury
Insolence, 2007
Courtesy Sprüth Magers Berlin London
© Sylvie Fleury

Page 224
Merlin Carpenter
Installation view of "The Opening," 2008, at The Corner Berlin, organized by Galerie Christian Nagel
© Merlin Carpenter

Page 246
Photograph © Heji Shin

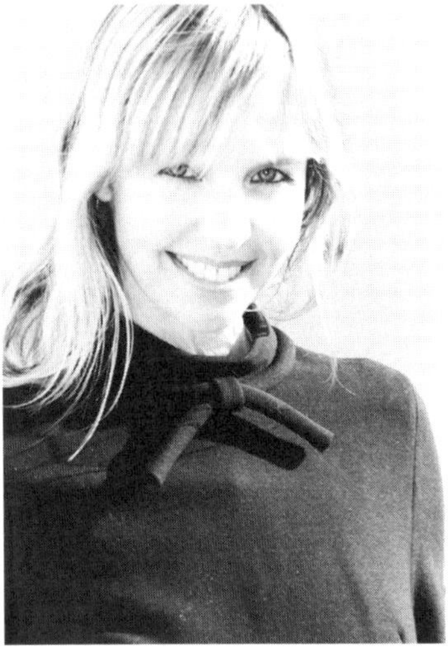

Isabelle Graw is Professor for Art Theory and Art History at Staatliche Hochschule für Bildende Künste (Städelschule), where she co-founded the Institute of Art Criticism. She is an art critic and co-founder of *Texte zur Kunst* in Berlin.

Isabelle Graw
High Price
Art Between the Market and Celebrity Culture

Publisher: Sternberg Press

First published as *Der große Preis: Kunst zwischen Markt und Celebrity Kultur*
© 2008 DuMont Buchverlag, Köln

Cover image: Photomontage by Markus Weisbeck including
Candy Darling, Andy Warhol, and Sylvia Miles, 1971
© Bettmann / Corbis © 2010 The Andy Warhol Foundation for the Visual Arts,
Inc. / Artists Rights Society (ARS), New York
American Singer Madonna, 1991
© Christophe d'Yvoire / Sygma / Corbis

Translation: Nicholas Grindell
Editorial Work: Tatjana Günthner
Copy Editing: Matthew Evans
Proofreading: Kari Rittenbach
Design: Isabelle Brombach, Markus Weisbeck, Surface, Berlin / Frankfurt am Main
Printing and binding: GGP Media GmbH, Pößneck
ISBN 978-1-933128-79-5

Sternberg Press
Caroline Schneider
Karl-Marx-Allee 78, D-10243 Berlin
1182 Broadway #1602, New York, NY 10001
www.sternberg-press.com